At a Century's Ending

At a Century's Ending:

REFLECTIONS, 1982–1995

George F. Kennan

W.W. NORTON & COMPANY
New York * London

Library of Congress Cataloging-in-Publication Data

Kennan, George Frost, 1904–
    At a century's ending : reflections 1982–1995 / George F. Kennan.
        p.   cm.
    Includes index.
    1. United States—Foreign relations—Soviet Union.   2. Soviet
Union—Foreign relations—United States.   3. United States—Foreign
relations—20th century.   4. Kennan, George Frost, 1904–
I Title.
E185.8.S65K44   1996
327.73047—dc20   95-21278

ISBN 0-393-03882-3
ISBN 0-393-31609-2 pbk.
W.W. Norton & Company, Inc.
500 Fifth Avenue, New York, N.Y. 10110
W.W. Norton & Company Ltd.
10 Coptic Street, London WC1A 1PU
1 2 3 4 5 6 7 8 9 0

Contents

⋯⋖∽⋗⋯

Foreword

M y friend John Lukacs recently wrote that while each of the last
few centuries of European history seemed to have a certain specific character of its own, in no instance was a century neatly bounded
by the years that formally defined it.[1] And he noted that the century
now ending was one that really began in 1914 and ended in 1989. If
this was a valid perception, then my own life, as a person old enough
to have some awareness of what was happening on the larger scale
around him, has embraced very neatly the dimensions of this twentieth century. (I was ten years old in 1914, and eighty-five in 1989.) It
was out of my experience with this particular span of time, supported
by whatever reading I was able to do about other periods and loci of
history, that my own view of the modern age was shaped.

I view the twentieth century as a tragic one in the history of European (including American) civilization. The two world wars were,
as Lukacs pointed out, the two great "mountain ranges" of the century. And the first of these two mountain ranges was not only in itself
a tragedy of immeasurable dimensions, but one that lay at the heart of
a great part of the subsequent misfortunes of the century. One has only
to recall that it was out of this First World War, arising in fact in the
midst of it, that the Bolshevik seizure of power occurred in Russia in
1917. This was a development destined to estrange Russia from the
West and to place her outside the boundaries of any positive collabo-

---

[1]John Lukacs, *The End of the 2oth Century: And the End of the Modern Age* (New
York: Tichnor and Fields, 1993), pp. 1–3.

ration with any of the major Western powers for the remainder of the century. The Russian Revolution had a tragically paralyzing effect, sometimes dramatically visible, sometimes unfortunately obscured, on the efforts of the other great powers to cope successfully with most of the remaining unhappy legacies the 1914–18 war left in its train.

And legacies of this description there were—in abundance. The most dangerous of them had to do with the interwar years in Germany. It is easy, of course, and often useless to speculate on what might have been. Yet it is hard to imagine that Hitler's rise to power in Germany could have proceeded as it did if the Germany in question had not been marked by a number of the consequences of the First World War: by the punitive peace so foolishly imposed by the French and British on a struggling Weimar Republic whose leaders bore no responsibility for the origins of the war; by an economic depression flowing so largely from the strains of the recent armed conflict; and by the irresponsibility and extremism of the Moscow-dominated world-Communist movement, playing as it did, and particularly in Germany, directly into the hands of Hitler.

The Second World War was thus a consequence and in some respects a continuation of the First. And this second great orgy of wastage of human and material resources (for what else could major war between industrially and technologically advanced countries now be?) had its own consequences, quite different from but scarcely less tragic than those of its predecessor. One of these was the Cold War, destined to dominate much of international life over the remainder of the century. Another was the development, and introduction into national arsenals, of the nuclear weapon. A third was the sudden disintegration of the old European colonial empires without any institutional framework into which the pieces could be fitted.

The Cold War involved relatively few human sacrifices; and these fortunately, occurred rather at its edges. It did involve the political division of the European continent for some forty years; and it involved a further great wastage of material substance in the frantic competition in armaments by which it was accompanied. A great deal of this reflected exaggerated and unnecessary military fears on both sides—unnecessary because neither side wanted another major war, although each suspected the other of doing so. One of its worst effects, however, was to saddle both sides, once it was over, with enormously bloated military and military-industrial establishments—establishments that had become in themselves vested interests and in a sense addictions, and the curtailment of which presented burdens no one on either side was prepared to assume in their entirety.

Closely connected with this last condition was the invention and production of the nuclear weapon. One of the first effects of this development was to throw great confusion into all established strategic thinking; for none of the previous theories of the relationship of war to political purpose had taken account of the possibility that the sheer destructiveness of weaponry might advance to a point where war could easily become suicidal, and the very concept of "victory" thus become devoid of meaning. The realization of these implications came slowly, however, to military minds taught to believe, as they had been over most of the twentieth century, that success in war depended precisely on the degree of destruction you could bring not only to the armed forces of an enemy country but to the civilian infrastructure as well. And the result of all this confusion was the accumulation in the hands of the two superpowers of fantastically redundant quantities of nuclear weaponry—a situation that had the ironic effect of first driving both of them to the very edge of unutterable disaster, but then of causing them both to pause at that brink. When the Cold War ended, the superpowers and others who were trying to play the nuclear game were thus left with huge stockpiles of poisonous nuclear wastes that they did not then know, and still do not know, how to dispose of safely. This situation is to be dumped upon our descendants, who will curse us for saddling them with so dangerous and almost insoluble a problem.

The sudden collapse of the great European colonial systems was also a development extensively influenced and expedited by the two world wars. The ways in which this occurred varied, of course, with the mother country in question, with the nature of its relationship to its colonies, and with the compulsions leading to this change. And it is not my intention to comment at this point on the general desirability or undesirability of this development as a whole. It did have the effect, however, of casting out onto the surface of international life a host of new and, for the most part, small communities that had had no previous experience with national independence. Practically all of these appear to have been accepted almost automatically, certainly without much further inquiry, into membership into the United Nations. The number of participants in international organizations has increased from the twenty-nine initial members of the League of Nations to the nearly 200 members of the U.N. This has had a profound effect on the formal structure of the international community—an effect illustrated by the fact that the United Nations Assembly now includes a majority of members that had no separate identity at all at the outset of this century, and which, accordingly, are relatively new to both the experiences and the responsibilities of sovereign independence.

To understand the significance of this change, account must be taken of two further developments of the past century, very recent ones in fact, that impose strains on international organizations. Both are of global rather than national or even regional importance, in the sense that they demand of all mankind that it step outside the tribal, national, imperial, and religious conflicts that have traditionally divided it, and recognize that problems are now emerging that affect all branches of the human family alike. These are the problems of global environmental deterioration and overpopulation, of the fact, in short, that mankind is overstraining and exhausting those very natural resources that have made the planet so friendly and hospitable—so uniquely hospitable, in fact—a home to civilized life.

To confront these problems successfully is going to require decisions and actions of a global nature; and these, in turn, can be provided only by a structure of an international community sufficient to the task at hand. But neither of the two major international entities set up in the course of this past century, neither the League of Nations nor the United Nations Organization, was designed by people who had environmental decay or overpopulation in mind. Both were established primarily in the hope that they could promote the peace and stability of international life—that they could moderate, that is, the conflicts *among* human collectivities. They were not set up to mobilize and organize all these collectivities for the collaborative confrontation with problems that were common to all of them yet not in essence of the usual political kind.

The one of these two organizations that has survived into our time, the United Nations, ought to be, and could conceivably be, developed into something more suitable for the confronting of these global problems were it not for the fact that it suffers, as did its predecessor, from one serious flaw of design. There was a fatal deficiency in the Wilsonian concept that underlay both these efforts of international organization: namely, the failure to recognize the essential difference between the *nation* and the *state* and the assumption, for purposes of international organization, that the two are identical. What constitutes a nation is a subjective sense of identity—a condition that can mark the small and weak collectivity as well as the great and powerful one, but says nothing about the capacity of a collectivity to bear the burdens of an unrestricted sovereignty and to contribute usefully, in the capacity of a state, to international life. The theory of *one nation = one state*, taking as it does no account of such differences, has led (as mentioned earlier) to the establishment within the U.N. Assembly of a majority of members in which the capacity for useful contribution is either entirely lacking or seriously limited. Full membership in the U.N., now regarded as the sole recognized status for independent participation in international life, leaves no place for the small national entity or the tiny insular community that recognizes its inability to meet the full requirements of an independent sovereignty but is reluctant to retain the status of a helpless minority within the confines of a greater country. And this situation prevails in an age when the theoretical status of unlimited sovereignty, even as an attribute of the larger and better-qualified state, is becoming more and more unreal and absurd. In the face of such deficiencies, the existing structure of the international community—a structure barely sufficient, if sufficient at all, for the purposes for which it was originally established—can hardly be expected to provide the formal framework for a successful confrontation with the global problems now threatening the intactness of our natural environment.

So here we are all stand—we of the Western world—at the end of this sad century: still partially crippled, genetically and morally, by the injuries we brought to ourselves in the two internecine wars of the earlier decades, and confronted now with emerging global problems for the solutions to which neither our ingrained habits nor our international institutions have prepared us.

The papers included in this book were all written in the final declining decades of the twentieth century. Slender as these contributions were, and constituting no more than responses to particular circumstances of the moment, they could not be expected to deal in depth with the century's broader issues. But the implications of these broader problems for those of the passing scene were never far from my mind at the time of writing.

The papers that dealt with Russian matters served, however (or so I thought), to bring out and to emphasize something of no small importance for the understanding of the great totalitarian tyrannies of the century. There was during the Cold War a fairly widespread belief in military and hard-line circles that the great dictatorships, supported as they were by modern, highly armed police establishments and by a total monopolization of the media of communication, had reduced entire peoples to a state of abject and cowering subordination, the endurance of which was effectively unlimited. Such a system, it was thought, was subject to no seriously disruptive *internal* forces. Barring overpowering hostile outside influences, it could be maintained indefinitely. It could be put to an end, in fact, only by massive military attack.

The strong premonitions of impending change in Russia that found expression in certain of the papers in this book served, in my view, as evidences of the incorrectness of that belief. What these premonitions bring to the fore is a perception of no small importance for the theory of politics and government: namely, that political systems supporting great personal tyrannies, such as those of Hitler, Stalin, and Mao, share in the mortality of the tyrant himself. They become the victims of—in effect, the participants in—his illnesses, his aging, and his death. They cannot long survive his passing. The fact is that the aging dictator and his closest minions, concerned to stave off their own demise, often tend themselves to neglect or to destroy, in the interests of their own immediate safety, those tendencies or elements within the system that might, had they been encouraged, have given it greater chances for useful change and further survival.

These insights are not spelled out in the body of the papers; but they underlie some of the intimations, or premonitions, brought forward in them; and they suggest that a greater knowledge of the historical background of events, and a greater sensitivity to the actual conditions of Soviet society, might have served us better than did the essentially military preoccupations of the Cold War enthusiasts.

The papers not primarily concerned with Russia treat a variety of wider subjects. Here, one's views and reactions could only flit like fireflies around the edges of the great happenings and movements of the times. But each of them was designed to have its own small incandescence; and it was my hope (how many other authors have not had similar ones?) that they would leave a bit better illuminated than before each of the small niches and corners of reality into which they intruded. If, then, something like a broader view of this present disturbing age—of its dangers, its enigmas, and its possibilities—were to make its way, if only inadvertently, through the variety of smaller vistas, so much the better. But this is something of which the reader will be a better judge than the author.

G. F. K.
Princeton, N.J.
January 1995

Part One

BACKGROUND

The War to End War
(1984)

———⚬———

Sixty-six years ago, on the 11th of November 1918, there ended that four-year orgy of carnage known as the First World War. When the shooting ceased, some 8.5 million young men lay dead and buried either in Flanders Fields or near the other great battlefields of the war. Over 20 million more had been injured—many of them maimed for life. Nearly 8 million were listed as missing or as having been taken prisoner. Of those who survived, countless thousands were to return to their homelands shattered ("shell-shocked" was then the word), confused, and desperate, to face the problems of daily life in a society impoverished morally and materially by the enormous wastage the war had involved. And for every one of those who had died, there were now others, loved and loving, including outstandingly the parents, for whom a large part of the meaning of life had evaporated with the news of the particular death in question. Europe, in short (and with it, in far smaller degree, the United States), had perpetrated a vast injury on its own substance: the sacrifice of the greatest capital it possessed, a flesh-and-blood capital—the cream of its young male manpower of the day, beside which the tremendous economic wastage of the struggle pales to insignificance.

No human mind will ever be capable of apprehending the magnitude of this tragedy. The numbers exceed the individual capacity for imagination. The computer would not know what to make of them.

Originally published (in a different form) in the *New York Times,* November 11, 1984.

The tragedy of each individual young soldier, cut off in the flower of his years, deprived of the privilege of leading a life through, carrying away with him into the agony and squalor of his battlefield death all that he thought he had been living for and all the hopes and love invested in him by others, was in itself immeasurable—infinite in its way. And then—8 million of them?

The only hope that could have given solace to these men in their final moments and in the hardships endured before those moments (for service at the front, even where survived, was seldom fun) was that there was some sense in this great effort of destruction—that it would be, as people then depicted it, the war to end war, that the triumph of one's particular cause would assure the emergence of a more hopeful, more promising civilization.

Were these comforting assumptions vindicated? Not a bit of it. The war merely shattered what little unity Western civilization had to that point achieved. The Russian Revolution—a direct product of the war (although not without other causes as well)—estranged one great portion of the Western heritage from the remainder of it for more than half a century to come, and probably much longer. The vindictiveness of the British and French peace terms; the exclusion of Germany and Russia from the peace conferences; the economic miseries of the postwar years; the foolish attempts to draw the blood of reparations and war debts from the veins of the exhausted peoples of the continent—these phenomena, all direct consequences of the war, assured that only twenty years after its ending, Europe would stand confronted with the nightmare of Adolf Hitler at the peak of his power, and with the imminence of the Nazi-Soviet pact, which would usher in a second vast military conflagration, comparable in its tragic dimensions to the one that had just occurred. Where, in all this sordid and tragic story, was the meaning of victory? Millions lost. Civilization itself the loser. Where were the victors?

What is one to make, in retrospect, of this self-destructive madness? One searches through the dusty archives of the prewar years for its reasons—for the failures of understanding and of foresight that made it possible. One finds that, as is usual in the causality of great events, the reasons were multiple and complex. There was, as has been often pointed out, the failure of the statesmen of the time to realize that another war might be long and unduly exhausting. Many were still bemused by the misleading example of the Franco-Prussian War of 1870–71: the mirage of the glamorous little war, quickly and dramatically won by "our brave boys" and followed by triumphant victory parades in the capital city of the deservedly defeated opponent. But there were, of course, deeper failures of understanding than this. There was the extreme romantic nationalism of the time (and not, alas, of that time alone): this mass escapism through which people unsure of their personal identity seek reassurance by identification with an idealized national collectivity. But equally serious, and equally unnoted at the time, were developments in the military field: the professionalization of the military career; the rise of great military bureaucracies; the growing separation of military and political thought; the abandonment of the concept of limited military operations conducted in pursuit of limited war aims and the embracing in its place of the vainglorious dreams of total war, unconditional surrender, and the total victory that was supposed to make all things possible.

And we of this age? How about us? We are now at a distance of sixty-six years from Armistice Day 1918. We have before us the example not just of that war but of a second one no less destructive and even more unfortunate in its consequences. How fine it would be if it could be said of us that we had pondered these ominous lessons and had set about, in all humility and seriousness, to base our national conduct on a resolve to avoid the bewilderments that drove our fathers and grandfathers to these follies. How nice if we could say that we had all recognized the silliness of entire peoples seeing themselves as more virtuous, deserving, and generally glorious than others, and waging self-destructive wars in the service of this fatuous illusion. How encouraging if we had developed an awareness of the unwithstandable momentum of vast military preparations, and if we had recognized the unreality of the very idea of victory in armed encounters between great industrial powers in this age of advanced technology.

If civilization is to survive, these perceptions must come, ultimately, to the governments of all great nations. The question is only: will they come soon enough? The time given to us to make this change is not unlimited. It may be smaller than many of us suppose.

Historical Inevitability and World War (1890–1914)

(1985)

I suppose anything is possible, but I think that regardless of what the statesmen of the time did in the period after 1890, it was doubtful that there would not have been a First World War. I was struck reading a document written by Jacques Bainville, a French historian, who spoke prophetically in 1919 about what was coming. He said that a perceptive person can often see what is bound to happen in the future, but he can never see *when* it is going to happen. And I think that is probably true. In other words, I don't think the continued buildup of European armies, not to mention the spirit in which they were being built up, could have continued without there being a catastrophe at some point. This is one of the things that I've singled out in my second volume on the Franco-Russian alliance.

The two chiefs of the general staffs who drew up the Franco-Russian Military Convention of 1894 insisted to their governments that from that time on, mobilization had to be considered the first act of war. In fact, the Russian general said—and this was in a private secret report that he wrote—"This time, when it comes to fighting, when it gets near to it, we want all the diplomats to shut up; they mustn't interfere in any way when we get anywhere near to mobilization; they mustn't try to stop it; because that would put us at a military disadvantage." This meant that Europe was in great danger that the Austrians would mobilize against a Balkan country. Then the Russians would mobilize against the Austrians; and that would mean that the

Talk given at the Kennan Institute, Washington, D.C., April 2, 1985.

20

Germans would start in, and then the French. This is precisely what actually happened. Europe was living under this danger, just as today the sophistication of nuclear weapons decreases the time necessary to detect an approaching attack. Today, we are entering a situation in which the explosiveness of international life is heightened to a point where it becomes very difficult to believe that someday something will not set it off. This was rather the situation in 1914.

On the Peace Settlements of World Wars I and II

I think it's being increasingly recognized that the Second World War was an almost unavoidable prolongation of the first one, resulting from the very silly humiliating and punitive peace imposed on Germany after World War I. The treatment of Germany in the 1920s and early 1930s by the French and the British (here, we Americans were not involved because we had concluded a separate peace and didn't sign the Versailles Treaty) was bound to favor the emergence of precisely those extreme forces that arose in Germany in the 1930s. I've often been struck at the total illogic of the Western democratic governments in both wars, but particularly in the first one. We said at the time that the kaiser's regime was responsible for this war. This is the way that peoples look at things during a war. We said that Germany had to have a democratic government. And thus a fully unprepared people were expected to run a republican government, beginning practically from the very day of defeat. Poor Friedrich Ebert, the first president of the Weimar Republic, and his men—were decent people, and they did the best they could. But the punitive peace undermined Ebert's government time after time. The French were still trying to collect reparations down to a late date. Then concessions were made to Hitler that had been denied to his relatively moderate and decent predecessors. Now what sense did this make? And you had something of the same after the Second World War, although the peace was not as punitive.

On Russian, French, and Soviet Negotiating Techniques
(1890–95)

It is very interesting to compare Russian and French diplomacy, and Russian negotiating styles with Soviet styles today. The Russians, of course, were themselves highly secretive; and they insisted that the French should be secretive as well. They kept telling the French: "If you leak a word of these negotiations, we will stop them instantly and refuse to be bound by anything that we've said." There were actually only five people in Russia who were permitted to know that these negotiations were even taking place. There was the tsar, the minister of foreign affairs and an aide who kept the papers for him, the chief of the general staff, and the minister of war. The negotiations were so secret that when immediately after the conclusion of the Military Convention both the tsar and the foreign minister died, practically no one in Russia knew it had taken place, and it had very little influence on Franco-Russian affairs for some years.

French diplomacy during this period—as always—was marked by a high degree of sensitivity, suspicion, intense emotional involvement with the negotiations, and worries about what the Parliament would think—worries that the Russians didn't share at all. The French needed to have one eye trained back over their shoulder to see how this was going to wash with what they called in Gabriel Hanotaux's time *l'opinion,* that of both Parliament and the press. Also, the French were more ably represented at their posts abroad than the Russians. They kept very good men at their embassies—beautifully trained diplomats who knew what they were doing.

Russian diplomacy was quite good at its conspiratorial secret center, but its envoys were not always of high caliber. The Russians had a very inferior man in Paris throughout this period. One of the great worries of the Russians was how much he would learn about the negotiations; they didn't want their own ambassador to know too much about what was going on. You get a reflection of this today in recent arms negotiations, where the Russians sometimes request of the Americans, "Please don't tell the other people on our negotiating team what you know about Russian armaments, because they are not supposed to know about these things." It was the same way in the 1890s.

Russian diplomacy was somewhat like Soviet diplomacy today. The Russians were hesitant to speak openly and freely. You had to guess what they were talking about from time to time. The same complaints that the French registered against the Russians in the nineteenth century are registered by Westerners against the Soviets today. The French prime minister and foreign minister were often beside themselves with fury at the way the Russians did things, and it was always up to the wise old hands—the French diplomats in Petersburg—to say to their government, "Now hold your horses; just be patient; don't think that it's all ruined; just hold on a while, and we'll produce the result."

This makes me think of the style of my late colleague Tommy Thompson, ambassador to Russia in Khrushchev's Time, who was the best man we've ever had in dealing with the Soviet regime. So many times when other people would say, "This negotiation is quite hopeless, we might just as well go home," Tommy would say, "Now listen, just take it easy; wait a little while; you'll see there'll be a change, and we'll get somewhere." And indeed he was always right. You find just the same responses coming from French diplomats in the late nineteenth century.

On the Formation of the Franco-Russian Alliance (1875–1895)

I referred earlier to an excellent work by James Joll on the origins of World War I. This book gives a great deal of attention to what Joll believes to be the aggressive tendencies of Hohenzollern Germany and advances the idea that the Russians had no choice but to ally themselves with the French. I find that difficult to accept. Perhaps I'm missing something, but up to the death of Bismarck in 1890, the story is quite clear. Bismarck did not at all want war with Russia. He had to argue with the more belligerent of his generals and say to them, "Look here, why are you all talking and planning about this war with Russia? We don't want a square kilometer of Russian territory; they don't want any of ours. Why in the world should we be planning to fight a war with them?" And he said, very perceptively, "Don't you people realize that if you were to get into a war with Russia and you should be in any way successful and should advance into that country, you would never find a place to stop? The farther you went in, the weaker you would become, and nobody would surrender to you." He had recognized the Napoleonic experience. Hitler didn't. So in Bismarck's time, there would have been no question of an invasion of Russia. After Bismarck, of course, there was a kaiser who had the unfortunate habit of speaking sharply and acting weakly. He was a man whose bark was much worse than his bite, but he did do a lot of damage to Germany with his fiery and boasting speeches and so forth. There were people among the Russians who thought that sooner or later they would have to fight Germany, but I don't see any evidence that the kaiser's government itself wanted a war with Russia. Some of the Russians did want it.

After the Russian-Turkish war of 1877 and 1878, in which the Russians felt themselves humiliated by Bismarck at the Congress of Berlin, Russian army leaders and chauvinists were not happy about the division of Poland. The Austrian part of the divided Poland stuck out like a great salient north of the Carpathian Mountains into territory that the Russian general staff wanted to dominate. They were determined to get rid of this salient if they possibly could, and many of them wanted to go to war with Austria for this purpose. The Russian Orthodox Church and its leaders, particularly its "Oberprokuror," Konstantin Petrovich Pobedonostev, the famous reactionary, wanted war as well. They also had great grievances against the Austrians, over Catholic control of this portion of Poland. They wanted to eliminate that control because they felt that it was a Catholic infection threatening their orthodox community. So there were strong feelings in Russia about the necessity of someday fighting another war with Austria.

But when the military people thought about this, they wondered how such a war could be fought. "If we fight a war with Austria, the Germans will sit there as they did during the Russian-Turkish war, and when we and the Austrians have exhausted ourselves, they will come in again as they did in 1878 and dictate the peace." This is the way they saw it. Actually, Bismarck did not dictate the Treaty of Berlin, but he was perceived as having done so. The Russian generals said, "We don't want to suffer that a second time. This means that we can't really have a successful war with Austria unless we first tend to Germany in some way, and the only way that we can handle Germany is to have the French fighting them on the other side."

The Russians and French formed an alliance because each wanted the other to fight Germany. As to what would have happened had they chosen not to ally, this, of course, is the sort of hindsight that one is not granted. The Russian foreign minister, Nikolai Karlovich Giers, whom I admire very much—a moderate man, a man of peace and a seasoned diplomat—wanted a balanced relationship between Germany and France. He wanted an alliance with neither, but he wanted acceptable and reasonable relations with Germany, and had he been able to succeed—without the Franco-Russian alliance, and without the splitting of the continent that the alliance meant—I think that perhaps Europe could have muddled along for a long time without war. Then perhaps other things—commercial developments, technological developments, the breakdown of colonialism—might have produced a different world that none of us can picture. Giers himself continually pointed to this and said, "Look, if you conclude this exclusive alliance with the French, you're going to divide the European community, and no good will come out of it. You want to retain flexibility; you want to be able to face uncertain, unpredictable situations; nobody can tell what's going to happen twenty years from now; you shouldn't be pinned down to a treaty like this." There was a lot of good sense in that.

When I think of his warning against splitting the continent, I think also of the unsuccessful and no doubt misguided efforts that I and a few other people made twenty or twenty-five years ago to prevent the division of the European continent—to have some sort of a German disengagement and a withdrawal of Soviet and American forces before the split of the continent could become frozen for decades. So I have a certain sympathy with Giers for trying to avoid the type of commitment the Franco-Russian alliance called for.

On Romantic Nationalism

Of course, a certain amount of weight must be given to the opinions of Alexander III and Nicholas II and the ways they saw things. Their personalities and personal attitudes had a great deal to do with the origins of World War I, more so than single individuals anywhere else. Alexander III was anti-German and particularly anti-Hohenzollern. Incidentally, he challenged the right of the kaiser to call himself an emperor. There is a marvelous passage in my second book on the alliance that I dug out from some curious Russian records. When Giers once had occasion to talk to Alexander about what the French wanted them to do, Giers asked the tsar why Russia should want to fight the Germans. His question was the equivalent of what Bismarck had said to his generals: "What would our objectives be? What would we want to do with the Germans if we fought them?" Alexander III said that the goal would be to break Germany up, the way it used to be. When Giers told his senior assistant, Count Vladimir Nikolave-vich Lamsdorf, about this conversation, Lamsdorf—a highly intelligent man who was later foreign minister himself—said that the emperor was crazy. He said, what would happen in case of a German defeat was that Germany would not be broken up, but that Russia would be taken over by the socialists, and then there'd be trouble.

Such prejudices on the part of Alexander III were inherited by his son, but the people who were really responsible for these attitudes were the chauvinists in the press, the army, and some of the political parties that began after 1905. They had the weirdest ideas. Even men such as Dmitri Aleksandrovich Milyutin, the minister of war under Alexan-der II, still wanted to conquer Constantinople. Why did they feel they had to do this? The Suez Canal had removed the dangers their pre-occupation with the Turkish straits was originally aroused by. Never-theless, this was part of the romantic nationalism of the time. The chau-vinists saw their future in a great victory over the Austrians and in the acquisition of the Dardanelles. These were the sorts of follies that peo-ple got into because of the prevailing nationalistic mood. In my first volume on this period, I went into detail about the story of the tremen-dous failure of the Russian attempt to make a puppet state out of Bul-garia in the 1880s. The Russians put a great deal of emotion into this effort. Here was where their glories were going to be exhibited. All I can tell you is that the people behind these follies somehow carried the day against more moderate people.

If you look more deeply into the question of romantic national-ism, I think you'll find that this was a fever that occurred primarily in people who had been displaced by the Industrial Revolution and the changes of the early nineteenth century—people whose origins were in a rural environment, but who had moved to the city. In addition, the new intelligentsia in Russia was particularly affected. Intellectuals were vulnerable to these chauvinistic feelings, and you couldn't rea-son with them very much. I think there were extraordinary prophetic voices in Russia going back to the early nineteenth century—not only about the war but about the revolution. I always think of Do-brolyubov's remark that it would not be to a constitution that a liberated Russian people would go; they would go to the pub to break windows and hang the gentry. And that is what happened.

Russia, the Soviet Union, and Constantinople

The Soviet interest in Constantinople goes back to the Turkish acquisition of that city in 1453. There are religious overtones here, which the Soviet government cannot acknowledge but which still affect the Russian people. Of course, one must remember that the consolidation of Russian power on the European land mass took place at the expense of the Turkish Empire. Fighting the Turks became something of a habit up until the building of the Suez Canal. This was of great importance because so many of the East-West lifelines from Asia to Europe passed through Constantinople. But when the Suez Canal was opened, all this was greatly modified. The British no longer had the same interest in the straits. For the Soviets to command Constantinople would have required a great extension of the Soviet Empire, because such an endeavor would involve control of a lot of the Balkans as well. The Russians would have to consolidate their hold over Bulgaria, Romania, and probably Hungary. One can say they've already done that; but I think there are still questions about the future of these nations. They would also have had to control Asia Minor.

On the Nature of Modern Weaponry and the Future of Europe

I don't think that today's nationalism, while present here and there, plays anywhere near the role that it did before 1914. But I think that the misunderstandings about modern weaponry and the bewilderment about the utility of warfare for some strange reason have not been cured at all. Even the fact that we now have weapons that so obviously cannot be used without disaster does not seem to prevent people from playing around with speculations about who could win a nuclear war. This terrifies me, because it carries to an extreme the realities that I've been addressing in the period before 1914 concerning these same misunderstandings about the growth of technological capabilities and modern warfare.

I don't think it's too late. I still think such attitudes can be reversed, but only when people have come to realize that modern weapons—and it's not only the nuclear ones—are no longer serviceable instruments of national policy. Conventional weapons might be retained for purely defensive purposes—for example, for border defense—but beyond that, even they cannot be used by anybody without disastrous results. I want to avoid saying that if we could get rid of the nuclear weapons, everything would be all right. I don't feel this at all. I feel very strongly that Europe in particular could not stand another suicidal bloodletting comparable to the two world wars it has been through. It could not stand such a war and have enough left for anybody to care about. I think that that would be the final end of European civilization. So even if there were no nuclear weapons, I would say that Europe cannot fight a third world war. Too much has already been destroyed. The genetic damages of the two world wars must be taken into account. I think that time is growing short and that people must begin to realize the futility of modern warfare very soon or the final catastrophe can be upon us. But I do think that things can be turned around.

On U.S.–Soviet Arms Control Negotiations

My own feeling is that the present U.S.–Soviet arms talks in Geneva were poorly prepared. The Soviets are entering into these talks with a suspicion much more profound than they show on the surface, and it will take quite a lot to change things around. I don't mean to say that their position is correct and ours is all wrong. I'm merely saying that the way things have been done hasn't improved the chances for success. I think if we had wanted success, we would not have continually alleged that the Soviets were returning to the bargaining table only because we frightened them into doing so. That wasn't a very good way to start off. I also think that we would not have chosen this period to militarize the shuttle and announce that it's being taken over by the military in order to place reconnaissance devices over the Soviet Union. This was announced at the time when the talks were being arranged, and the first shuttle flight was then scheduled for the day after the President Reagan took office for his second term, as though this were the beginning of his new military program in space. And I must say that all the talk about the Strategic Defense Initiative and the M–X missile on the eve of the negotiations was not helpful. I don't see that the Soviets can regard the M–X as a bargaining chip; and I think they are confused and rendered uncertain by the Strategic Defense Initiative. They don't know what the initiative will mean for the efficacy of their strategic weapons, and therefore they don't know how many of these weapons they are going to need in the future.

All this is going to interfere with the negotiations, and for this reason I'm not very optimistic about them. I think it will take some time to straighten things out and to reach an atmosphere in which we can make much progress. I'm sorry to say this. I don't want to underestimate the problems with which the administration has to deal. I don't doubt for a moment the president's sincerity when he says he wants to reduce the nuclear arsenals of both sides. Perhaps it can be done someday, but it's going to take longer than anybody has anticipated.

I think there is a lesson in the resumption of U.S.–Soviet arms control talks, because the Soviets in part were inspired by budgetary difficulties in connection with the maintenance of their armed forces. It seems that the Soviets found their military expenditures so much of a burden at an awkward time that they wanted to obtain a general reduction of armaments that would reduce their budgetary problems and save face as well. Perhaps we can learn from this, but only if we are not going to exploit Soviet motivations as a way of damaging their prestige. If one says, "We can't get along with the Russians, and we're going to build until you cry uncle," this is self-defeating because you get their backs up, and they feel they can't yield without losing their prestige. Russian diplomacy in the nineteenth century was also extensively influenced by such considerations.

Flashbacks
(1985)

———··⦅∞⦆··———

The passage of the fifty-year interval since the establishment of Soviet-American diplomatic relations at the turn of the year 1933–34
led to an intensive search by a large number of people—publishers, editors, television interviewers, arrangers of academic-lecture series, you
name them—for someone who was involved in that particular episode
and whose memories could instruct or divert those today whose impressions of what it all amounted to might be dim or nonexistent.
There was a search, in particular, for someone who could relate that
event to the previous state of Soviet-American relations and to the immediately following years of the Stalin era. This search soon revealed,
to my surprise no less than to that of its authors, that of all those thus
directly involved in the episode itself I appeared to be the sole survivor
(on either side), and of those who served in the Soviet Union off and
on through the remainder of the Stalin period I alone seemed to have
the dubious double distinction of being an eyewitness and trying to
be a historian. The pressures, therefore, centered on me.

Others who have studied, thought about, and written about as well
as experienced much of a given phase of history will understand the
distaste with which at an advanced stage of life one receives the suggestion that one should undertake an analytical effort to put the whole
subject once again in historical perspective. Historical perceptions,
like *affaires de cœur,* are a matter of a particular stage in one's life; attempts at repetition are unlikely to be successful. When my mind re-

Originally published in *The New Yorker,* February 25, 1985.

turns to the events in question, what comes to it are primarily the memories of individual experiences along the way. Some of them, it seems to me, speak for themselves; and I would rather recall them as they were, and let them tell their own story, than try to embroider them analytically.

With apologies to my own memoirs, in which most of the recollections had some sort of place, I offer a few of these recollections here to any who might like to know what it was like or (to borrow the common query of the TV interviewer) "how it felt" to be involved with Soviet-American relations at the moment of their establishment and in the ensuing years of Stalinist horror. To stress the responsibility of these memories in speaking for themselves and to distance the young man who received the experiences from the elderly one who now recalls them, I take the liberty of putting them in the narrative present.

I must begin at a point a bit more than fifty years ago—in 1932, to be exact—just before the establishment of diplomatic relations that we have lately been recalling. My wife and I are living, at this point, in Riga, Latvia. Latvia is a country that has until recently been part of the Russian Empire and will soon become part of the Soviet one but is now, during a twenty-year interval, independent. The atmosphere of the old, prerevolutionary Russia still hangs over it. The city of Riga is itself a smaller edition of the prerevolutionary St. Petersburg, but without the palaces. The sleigh in which I am sometimes driven to the office in winter—a one-passenger open-air affair, in which the fur-coated passenger sits behind and below the massive figure of the bundled coachman on the box—is right out of Tolstoy. In summer, because we are poor, we live in a little wooden cottage out at the seashore. I commute on the suburban trains. The trains and the passengers, I among them, seem to be right out of Chekhov's stories. And if one goes farther into the countryside, all that one sees—the cobbled roads, the swamps and fields, the birch trees and evergreen forests—is the purest Russia. I drink it all in, love it intensely, and feel myself for a time an inhabitant of that older Russia, which I shall never see again in the flesh.

In the office, here in Riga, my work is the study of the Soviet Union. I have already been established as a Russian expert. I know the Russian language, and I, with two or three others, go thoroughly and systematically through the Soviet newspapers and magazines, reporting to our government on what they reveal of life in the Soviet Union. It is through these thousands of pages of small-type, poor-quality newsprint that I am obliged to form my first picture of the great Communist country that lies so near at hand and extends so far away to the east. I, like my colleagues, am appalled at the propaganda that pervades every page of this official Soviet literature—at the unabashed use of obvious falsehood, at the hypocrisy, and, above all, at the savage intolerance shown toward everything that is not Soviet. I am seized, as are my colleagues, with the desire to strip away this brazen facade and to reveal, in the reports to Washington, the reality that lies beneath it. And I am surprised to find how easy it is, if one looks carefully and thoughtfully, to perceive what does lie beneath these gray and brittle pages, and to realize that the meaning of the propaganda is not in the literal text but in the subtle changes that occur in it from day to day— changes that every sophisticated Russian knows how to decipher and to interpret, as we ourselves, in time, learn to do. And this is my introduction to the Soviet Russia.

Let us jump ahead now to the days, fifty-one years ago this past November, when diplomatic relations were being established between the United States and the Soviet Union. I happen at this time to be at home on leave of absence, and I am chosen to accompany, as interpreter and diplomatic secretary, our first ambassador to the Soviet Union, Mr. William C. Bullitt, on his journey to Moscow, where he is to present his diplomatic credentials.

Bullitt is a striking man: young, handsome, urbane, full of charm and enthusiasm, a product of Philadelphia society and Yale but with considerable European residence, and with a flamboyance of personality that is right out of F. Scott Fitzgerald—a man of the world, well educated, fluent in French and German, confident in himself, confident of the president's support, confident that he will have no difficulty in cracking the nut of Communist suspicion and hostility that awaits him in Moscow. He is not a radical, but he is not afraid of radicals. He was once a friend of John Reed, and he was later married, for a time, to Reed's widow.

From Le Havre, where the ship lands, we travel by train, via Paris and Berlin, to Moscow. The train takes two nights and two days. Also on the train is Maxim Litvinov, the Soviet commissar for foreign affairs. He, too, has just been in Washington, negotiating the establishment of relations, and he is now returning to Moscow.

On the second day of that long railway journey, on a brutally cold afternoon, when the train has been rolling for hours over the frozen fields of western Poland, we stop for a while at the Polish town of Bialystok, and Litvinov gets out and paces gloomily up and down the station platform, coat collar up against the wind. Bullitt goes out and joins him, and Litvinov then tells Bullitt (as Bullitt later reports to me) that this place, Bialystok, is actually the place where he was born and brought up; and he observes how strange it is for him to find himself there again after all this time, and confesses to Bullitt that he never wanted to be Soviet foreign minister in the first place—that his real ambition had always been to be a librarian. And from this very human confession I begin to realize what I am never to be allowed to forget: that these Soviet Communists with whom we will now have to deal are flesh-and-blood people, like us—misguided, if you will, but no more guilty than are we of the circumstances into which we all were born—and that they, like us, are simply trying to make the best of it.

Well, then, a few immensely exciting days later, Bullitt and I are standing with three or four other people in the middle of the vast parquet floor of one of the great empty ballrooms in the Kremlin palace, and Bullitt is giving his little speech and presenting his credentials to the titular head of the Soviet state—old Daddy Kalinin, as we used to call him—who is the only man of peasant origin in the Soviet leadership, and looks the part, with his venerable gray beard. And a few moments later, Kalinin is speaking kindly to me, and telling me with what excitement and enthusiasm he and his friends, when they were young radical students, had read the books about Siberia written by my grandfather's cousin the elder George Kennan. The books were, Kalinin says to my astonishment, the bible of the early Bolsheviks.

Such was the Russia of that day—and this. It could whipsaw you at times between its great extremes: the cold and the hot, the cruel and the tender, the callous and the humane.

Another change of scene. It is now my first winter in Moscow—the winter of 1933–34. Bullitt has gone home to organize an embassy staff and has left me here for two or three months as our first regular diplomatic representative in Communist Moscow. The Stalinist terror has not yet begun, though it is not far off. The political atmosphere is still relatively relaxed.

My wife has joined me. We are the first American diplomatic couple to appear in the Moscow diplomatic corps. We are sometimes invited to parties: marvelous Russian-American parties in shabby Moscow apartments, at which nobody cares whether the apartments are shabby or not, or where you are to put your coats, or what there is to eat and drink—parties that are full of good talk, endless talk, in the Russian manner. And later in the evening, we all go out to the great Park of Culture and Rest along the Moscow River and skate down the broad ice-covered paths from rink to rink, under the frozen Russian stars, to the strains of the "Skater's Waltz" rendered by scratchy loudspeakers somewhere up in the trees.

Let us jump ahead again. It is now 1937. I am still in Moscow. But times have changed. Difficulties have arisen. The terrible Stalinist purges have begun. Bullitt, disappointed and embittered (because he was too impatient and wanted everything at once), has left Russia, never to return. His place has just been taken by a new ambassador, a shallow and politically ambitious man who knows nothing about Russia—has no serious interest in it. His only real interest is in the publicity he can get at home. We are ashamed for him before our diplomatic colleagues, not because of his personal qualities or imperfections (I have no idea what those were) but because of his obvious unfitness for the job. To us, the Foreign Service officers stationed here, his having been sent out as our chief seems like a gesture of contempt on the president's part for us and our efforts—a revelation of how little the American political establishment knows or cares about the Foreign Service. And it brings home to me for the first time that, however much a Foreign Service officer may learn about the government to which he is accredited, he learns at least as much (and it is sometimes a harsh lesson) about the government he represents.

But to get back to my story: the purges are now at their height. The new ambassador is invited to attend the second of the three great public purge trials—the visible tip of the immense iceberg of terror and cruelty that is now crushing Soviet society. He takes me with him as his interpreter, and I, sitting next to him, whisper into his ear what I can of the proceedings. He understands nothing of what is really going on. He even thinks the accused are genuinely guilty of the preposterous charges to which they are confessing, and he sententiously pronounces this opinion, during the intermission, to the assembled American journalists. But I do know what is going on; and the sight of these ashen, doomed men, several of them only recently prominent figures of the regime but now less than twenty-four hours away from their executions—the sight of these men standing there mumbling their preposterous confessions in the vain hope of saving themselves, or perhaps members of their families, from disaster, the sight of their twitching lips, their prison pallor, their evasive, downcast eyes—is never to leave my memory. Nor is the impression mitigated by the fact that they would happily have seen the same thing done to others. Revolution is indeed, as someone has said, a beast that devours its own children.

Let us now move ahead again—some years ahead this time. Many things have happened in those intervening years. I have served in a number of other places: Washington, Prague, Berlin, Lisbon, and London. But I am now once more in Russia. It is wartime—the final months of the Second World War. Averell Harriman is the ambassador in Moscow—and an excellent ambassador he is. I am his No. 2. The Russians are now our allies, and the Soviet Union is now winning victories. The building we live and work in faces the Kremlin across a great sea of asphalt pavement; and night after night, we hear the booming of the gun salutes in celebration of the victories and see the fireworks rising triumphantly from Red Square.

I look on the war with mixed feelings. I have recollections of nearly two and a half wartime years spent in Germany, most of that time in the early period of the war, before our country entered the contest. I have no love for Hitler. I have never questioned the necessity of defeating him. But I also have no hatred for the German people.

One July Sunday, I stand among the curbside spectators on one of the great circular boulevards of Moscow and watch fifty thousand German prisoners forced to march through the city at double time, as a spectacle for the Moscow populace. I have told about the episode in my memoirs.

It is a hot day. The sun beats down. The men, obviously just removed from the freight cars in which they have been transported, are weak, tired, and thirsty. But they are hounded along. Those who fall are pulled aside to be picked up later. Mounted guards ride their horses into those who show signs of lagging behind. It is a cruel spectacle. I don't doubt that the German Nazis are doing worse than this to many innocent people, in Russia and elsewhere. But I am sickened. These young men are presumably draftees, most of them nineteen or twenty years old. They are no more responsible for the accident of birth that brought them to this place than are the young Russians who fight against them. They, like the rest of us, didn't choose their parents, or the time or the country of their birth. The crowds of Russian spectators, mostly women, look on impassively at this spectacle, but insofar as I can divine their real reactions from their eyes and their expressions, these people are not devoid of sympathy for the prisoners. Russians—especially these Russians—have experienced too much of suffering not to feel for it when they see it before them.

It occurs to me, standing there at the curb, that in a great war like this the populations are all victims alike. Their fate and their sufferings bear no relation, as a rule, to the propaganda slogans and pretensions and professions of the governments that drive them to this slaughter. There are times and instances, I have no doubt, when a people has no choice but to stand up and fight. But such cases are rare, and I come away with the conviction that one should beware of all the collective hysterias of modern nationalism—the artificially fanned hatreds, the chauvinistic self-idealization, the professions of noble principle. The tragedies of war are a thousand times as deep as these hysterias, and put them all to shame.

We come now to the year 1945 and the month of May. It is victory day—the day of the ending of the war in Europe. The city of Moscow goes wild with joy and relief. People pour out onto the streets by the million. This is their day. They cannot be controlled; nor does anyone seriously try to control them.

The Party leaders, true to their ingrained habits, try to channel the street demonstrations to places where the cheers and wavings will appear to be tributes to the regime's own wise war leadership. It does no good. To everyone's consternation and amazement, even to ours, the only place in Moscow where crowds of this order choose to gather and to demonstrate seems to be the enormous square before the American Embassy. They crowd up against our walls in thousands, waving and cheering—they cannot be induced to go anywhere else. After some hours of this, I, being in charge of the embassy at that moment, feel it necessary to acknowledge in some way this great demonstration of good will; and I go out onto one of the pedestals of the high pilasters on the front of the building and say a few simple words to the crowd in Russian, congratulating them on the common day of victory. They love it and roar their approval. But Stalin, learning of it, resents it intensely. It is the first time a bourgeois representative has been publicly cheered by a Soviet crowd. This is taken by Stalin as a humiliation, and I should know that someday I shall be made to pay for it if there is any way he can cause me to do so.

A few more months pass. It is the winter of 1946. The war has ended. The problems of policy are now those of the postwar future. In mid-February, Averell Harriman is away for a time, and again I am left in charge of the embassy. I am ill in bed, as I recall it, with a severe sinus infection. Among the incoming telegrams brought to me one morning for my consideration is one from the Department of State informing me that the Russians are declining to join the World Bank and the International Monetary Fund. The department's telegram reflects bewilderment over the reasons for this attitude. Why, it asks me, should the Russians decline to take part? How do I explain it?

I am filled with impatience and disgust at this naïveté. For two years, I have been trying to persuade people in Washington that the Stalin regime is the same regime we knew in the prewar period, the same one that conducted the purges, the same one that concluded the Non-Aggression Pact with the Nazis—that its leaders are no friends of ours. I have tried to persuade Washington that dreams of a happy postwar collaboration with this regime are quite unreal; that our problem is deeper than that; that Stalin and his associates are now elated with their recent military and political successes and think they see favorable prospects for extending their political influence over all of Europe through the devices of infiltration and subversion. Until they are weaned from these rosy hopes, I argue, it is useless for us to suppose that they will participate in idealistic schemes for worldwide collaboration under our leadership—particularly in such areas as economics and finance, where their ideological commitments are wholly different from our own.

To explain all this, I sit down and draft a preposterously long telegram—some eight thousand words, if I remember correctly—going right back to the beginning and describing, as though in a primer for schoolchildren, the nature, the ambitions, the calculations of these men. It is a grim and uncompromising picture. I wonder uneasily what the reaction will be at home. To my amazement, it is instantaneous and enthusiastic. The telegram goes the rounds in official Washington—to the other departments and to the White House. It is even made required reading for hundreds of senior military officers. For the first time in my life (and the last, incidentally), I seem to be on the same wavelength as official Washington. But, more important and more significant than that, I seem to have aroused a strain of emotional and self-righteous anti-Sovietism that in later years I will wish I had not aroused.

The scene shifts to Washington in the years from 1947 to 1949. I have been given a high position with policymaking responsibilities in the Department of State. It is still primarily Soviet-American relations that I am concerned with, but the problem now is with my own government, not with the Soviet one. I have my own concept of what American policy should be in this immediate postwar period. It is a simple concept: first, of course, to pursue "containment"—in the sense of restoring economic health and political self-confidence to the peoples of Western Europe and Japan in order that they may be resistant to local Communist pressures—and prove to the men in the Kremlin in this way that they are not going to succeed in extending their rule to further areas by political intrigue and intimidation, that they cannot serve their own interests without dealing with us; and then, when a political balance has been created, to go on to the negotiation with Moscow of a general political settlement.

Well, the first part of this concept proceeds without difficulty. The Marshall Plan, which is an integral part of it, is marvelously successful. And something very similar is accomplished, primarily on my initiative, for Japan. The time for negotiations, as I see it, is approaching. Here the difficulties begin. The subject of any real negotiations with the Russians would have to be the removal of the unfortunate division of Germany and Europe to which the final operations of the recent war have led. But our European allies do not want that, nor does the emerging German leader, Konrad Adenauer; and the secretary of state agrees with them. They all mistake the Soviet threat for a military one, and feel that there must be a military response, in the form of the NATO alliance. I am not enthusiastic. I feel that this will cause us to take our eye off the ball of economic recovery. I particularly deplore the idea of bringing West Germany in as a partner. This, I maintain, will freeze the division of Europe and make it impossible to remove, and will create bitter problems for the future. But I am overruled. Military thinking, here and in Europe, has taken over from political thinking. People are reverting to nineteenth-century patterns of thought—and this in the nuclear age, to which, it seems to me, these patterns are not relevant. But I can do nothing to stop it. I also disagree with our government's intention of developing the hydrogen bomb. Robert Oppenheimer and I would both prefer to have another try at negotiation with the Russians before we take this fatal step. Again, I am overridden. So at the end of 1949, I give up my job as head of the Planning Staff, am soon granted, at my request, a long leave of absence without pay (for at this point they are glad to get rid of me), and go off to Princeton to try to become a scholar.

But the respite is not long. Only a year and a half passes before I am called to Washington again and appointed ambassador to Moscow. The assignment has nothing to do with Soviet-American relations. The present ambassador, it seems, is leaving. It is the election year of 1952. For purely domestic-political reasons, the administration is afraid to leave the post vacant. Foreign policy—policy toward the Soviet Union plays no part in the decision. It never occurs to people in the administration that the position of American ambassador to Moscow has anything to do with policy toward the Soviet Union. They don't really know, to tell the truth, what an ambassador is for. But it suits their book that someone should be out there, at this politically delicate moment, to keep the chair warm. So now I am again in Moscow, but this time in the lofty and lonely position of ambassador.

Gone now is the familiarity with one's Foreign Service colleagues that marked the earlier years in that city. I reside in the solitary splendor of Spaso House. But it is a gilded cage. The political atmosphere could not be worse. The Korean War is still on. People on both sides expect it soon to develop into a real Soviet-American war. The embassy is isolated from the population as never before. I, as ambassador, am the Soviet Union's Enemy No. 1. The walls of the embassy compound are floodlit from the outside and patrolled by armed guards, like a prison's. Five burly gentlemen—all carefully picked colonels of the internal and border guards—are stationed at the gate day and night. Wherever I go, whether on foot or by car, they accompany me. Never did anyone have more constant companions. We politely salute each time I come out; but we never speak. Yet as the months go by—the months of this constant silent companionship—I see that they are doing their duty faithfully, as I am trying to do mine. And I sense growing up between us a certain tacit, helpless sympathy; for, once again, what are we all if not the products of the accidents of birth?

On some of the warm summer nights, we walk—this odd little cortege—among the crowds in the Park of Culture and Rest, where once, in happier times, I skated. We are anonymous here. We merge with the crowds, for my guardians are in civilian clothes, and I am informally dressed and look much like anyone else. If the other people knew who I was, they would be interested but frightened, as would my guardians; for it would be dangerous for anyone to have even the most casual conversation with me. So I walk among these crowds of people, observing them, hearing their conversation, near to them in one way but endlessly far from them in another; seeing, but myself unseen; hearing, but myself unheard. I console myself by fancying that I am an invisible disembodied spirit from another time or another planet, privileged to move about amid the life here below but never to participate in it, never to communicate with it—to be always near it but never part of it.

Next picture. It is still 1952, but a few more weeks have passed. I am now in Western Europe for a few days—in Geneva, where I have a young daughter in boarding school. I suddenly receive a phone call from the American consulate general in that city. A telegram has been received from the embassy in Moscow. The embassy has just received a note from the Soviet Foreign Office saying that I am declared persona non grata, which means that they will no longer recognize me as ambassador and I shall not be permitted to return to Moscow. The news has not yet been announced to the world press but will be shortly. Within six months, now, of his own death, Stalin is apparently in a strange state of anxiety and suspicion; and presumably he suspects me of God knows what.

I am thunderstruck. I cannot know, of course, that this will be the end of my Foreign Service career, but I know that it will mean a great change in my life. In one way or another, an epoch is ending for me. I also know that at any moment the world press will be tracking me down, demanding statements, interviews, photographs. I am not prepared for all this. It is too sudden. To give myself a little protection and a few moments to think about what has happened, I escape to a nearby movie house and sit there in the dark, trying to figure out what has happened to me and how I should respond to it. And shortly, to my intense disgust, I find myself watching with interest the silly movie, and I have to pinch myself to turn my eyes away from the screen and take account once again of my altered situation. In such absurdity, such human weakness, such childish helplessness, there approaches the rather ignominious end of some twenty years of official service in the Soviet Union.

I return home, of course, with my family. The presidential election of 1952 has just taken place. A new administration—in some respects like the one we have today—has installed itself in the seats of power in Washington. No one having said anything to me about what I am now to do, I live quietly through the winter at our farm in the country. The weeks go by. Finally, I come to Washington to see the new secretary of state. He receives me civilly, and casually tells me that he knows of no niche for me in the department or in the Foreign Service. I am, in other words, fired. No reason is offered. But, says he, before you go, I would like you to give me your impressions of the situation in Russia today. I pull myself together and do this. "Well, well," he says. "You know, when you talk about these things, you interest me. Very few people do. I hope you will come down here from time to time and let me have your views on what is happening in Russia." I ask him how it is proposed to announce my dismissal to the press and the public. The secretary says I should go to see his press secretary—he will work it out.

I go to see the press secretary. He professes helplessness. "Honestly, I wouldn't know what to say," he says. "Would you have any suggestions?" I tell him I would like to have a few moments to think about it. So I go out to a restaurant for lunch, take out a piece of paper, and draft, so to speak, my own death warrant—the terms of my dismissal from the Foreign Service. I take it back to the press secretary, who reads it and says to me, "Geez, Mr. Ambassador, that's elegant—I couldn't have written that."

With these expressive words, twenty-six years of foreign service, and twenty years of official involvement with Soviet-American relations, years always full of irony, come to an ironic end.

Well, thirty-odd years have now gone by since I left the government service. I have continued to be involved with Russia, both tsarist and Soviet, but this time as a historian—no longer as a participant. Some of the books I write deal with the final years of the prerevolutionary Russia and the first years of the Soviet one. The work is not unrewarding. I come to know my principal historical characters—the heroes or antiheroes of my books—as though I had known them in the flesh. I relive, together with them, their times, their struggles, their disappointments. I know, as they could not know, that they are all actors in what will ultimately be seen as a tragic drama; but I try to judge them for what they were, and for what they knew. And I find it striking that here, again, as in all my years of official service in Russia, I am myself remote from the people I am observing. I see them again, as I once saw the Soviet Union in Riga, through the record of the printed word; but I must myself remain unseen, as I was on the paths of the Park of Culture and Rest—must always be *near* to what interests me but never be *of* it.

I would like, of course, to be able to communicate to those now in power something of what I see through these historical lenses; for I fancy myself to perceive, in these records of the past, lessons that, if they were closely looked at, could help us all to identify the hopeful roads into the future and to refrain from entering, and from pulling others along with us, on those paths at the end of which there is no hope, and from which no one ever returns. The efforts I make in this direction are not crowned, as a rule, by any conspicuous success; but there are certain professions, such as medicine, teaching, and the priesthood, in which one does not inquire anxiously into the results of one's efforts, and the writing of history is one of them. The effort, here, is its own reward. The results are the concern of a Higher Authority.

Communism in Russian History
(1991)

———··◄∞►··———

1

Russia was for many centuries separated, geographically and politically, from the development of Western civilization and culture, and
thus came late into what, for most of Europe, would be called the modern age.[1] But the eighteenth and nineteenth centuries, witnessing as
they did an extensive overcoming of these earlier barriers, permitted
a very considerable progress in the modernization of Russian society.
By the time the country was overtaken by the First World War, its situation was not entirely discouraging. Industrialization was proceeding
at a level only two or three decades behind that of the United States.
There was under implementation a program of education reform that,
if allowed to continue unimpeded, would have assured total literacy
within another two decades. And the first really promising program
for the modernization of Russian agriculture (the so-called Stolypin
reforms), while by no means yet completed, was proceeding steadily
and with good chances for ultimate success.

Originally published in *Foreign Affairs* (Winter 1990–91).

[1] My reflections have been stimulated by Professor Robert C. Tucker's new study
of the crucial and formative years of the Stalin dictatorship (*Stalin in Power: The Revolution from Above, 1928–1941* [New York: W. W. Norton, 1990]). For anyone who,
like me, lived in Moscow through parts of the period he describes, Tucker's account
was bound to stir many reflections about the place of those terrible years, and indeed
of the entire Communist epoch now coming to an end, in the historical development
of the Russian state. Some of these reflections find expression in the present article.

These achievements, of course, had not been reached without conflicts and setbacks. Nor were they, alone, all that was needed. Still to be overcome as the war interceded were many archaic features in the system of government, among them the absolutism of the crown, the absence of any proper parliamentary institutions, and the inordinate powers of the secret police. Still to be overcome, too, was the problem of the non-Russian nationalities within the Russian Empire. This empire, like other multinational and multilingual political constellations, was rapidly becoming an anachronism; the maintenance of it was beginning to come under considerable pressure.

But none of these problems required a bloody revolution for their solution. The removal of the autocracy was, after all, destined to be achieved relatively bloodlessly, and the foundations of a proper parliamentary system laid, in the first months of 1917. And there was no reason to despair of the possibility that Russia, if allowed to develop without war or violent revolution, might still encompass a successful and reasonably peaceful advance into the modern age. It was, however, just this situation, and just these expectations, that were to be shattered by the events of the final months in that fateful year of 1917.

2

The Russian oppositional movement of the last half of the nineteenth century and the first years of the twentieth had always included extreme radical factions that did not want reform to proceed gradually, peacefully, and successfully. They wanted nothing less than the immediate and total destruction of tsarist power and of the social order in which it operated. The fact that their own ideas of what might follow upon that destruction were vague, unformed, and largely utopian was not allowed to moderate the violence of their intentions. Participating, though in quite different ways, in both of the major revolutionary parties, the Socialist Revolutionaries and the Social Democrats (out of whom the Communists emerged), these factions found themselves, in their bitter opposition to gradual reform, in a state of limited and involuntary alliance with the most radical reactionary circles at the conservative end of the political spectrum. After all, these latter also did not want to see change proceed gradually and peacefully, for they did not want it to occur at all. So it was not by accident that the ideas and aims of both extremist elements were to find a common expression, as Robert C. Tucker has so persuasively pointed out in his recent work, in the Stalin of the future.

Up to the outbreak of war, to 1917 in fact, the leftist extremists had met with very limited success. In the final prewar years, they had actually been losing political position and support. What changed all this, and gave them opportunities few of them had ever expected, was Russia's involvement in the war, and particularly the ill-considered attempt by the provisional government to continue the war effort into the summer of 1917, in the face of the epochal internal political crisis already brought about by the recent fall of the monarchy.

It had been a folly, of course, for Russia to involve itself a decade earlier in 1904–5 in the war against Japan. This alone had brought the country to the very brink of revolution. It was a greater folly (and this might have been clear, one would think, to Russian statesmen at the time) to involve Russia in the far larger strains of participation in a great European war. The war was, of course, not the only cause of the breakdown of the tsarist system in 1917; it may be fairly said, however, that without Russia's involvement in the war that breakdown would not have come when it did or taken the forms that it did, and that anything like a seizure of power by the Bolshevist faction would have been improbable in the extreme. Seen in this way, the establishment of Communist power in Russia in November 1917 has to be regarded as only one part of the immense tragedy that World War I spelled for most of European civilization. But the consequences of the Russian Revolution were destined long to outlive the other immediate effects of the war and to complicate the world situation over most of the remainder of the century.

By mid-1917 in any case, the die was cast for Russia. The stresses of the first two and a half years of war, together with those of the earlier months of that year—the exhaustion of army and society, the sudden collapse of the tsarist police force, and the program of land reform that lent itself so easily to demagogic exploitation—made possible the successful seizure of power, first in the major cities, then throughout the country, by Lenin and his associates. Thus the straitjacket of Communist dictatorship—the restraint under which it was destined to writhe throughout the life span not only of the generation then alive but of its children and grandchildren as well—was fastened upon an unprepared and bewildered Russian society.

One hesitates to summarize what this development was to mean for Russia. No summary could be other than inadequate. But the effort must be made, for without it the Communist epoch now coming to an end cannot be seen in historical perspective.

Let us start with what happened to most of the educated and culturally important elements of the Russian society of that time. The Leninist regime, in the initial years of Soviet power, succeeded in physically destroying or driving out of the country the greater part—most of an entire generation, in fact—of what would have been called, in the Marxist vocabulary of that day, the "bourgeois" intelligentsia. Stalin later completed the process by doing the same to most of the Marxist intelligentsia that remained. Thus Lenin and Stalin contrived, between the two of them, to eliminate a large portion of the rather formidable cultural community that had come into being in the final decades of tsardom. And with this loss there went, more important still, the loss of much of the very cultural continuity of which this generation was an indispensable part. It would never thereafter be possible to reunite fully the two frayed ends of this great chain of national development, now so brutally severed.

Not content with these heavy blows to the country's intellectual and cultural substance, Stalin, as soon as his power was consolidated in 1928, turned to the peasantry and proceeded to inflict upon this great portion of the population (some 80 percent at that time) an even more terrible injury. In the Stolypin reforms, emphasis had wisely been placed on the support and encouragement of the most competent and successful segment of the farming population. Stalin, in his sweeping campaign of collectivization launched in 1929, did exactly the opposite. He set out to eliminate precisely this element (now referred to by the pejorative Russian term of "kulaks"), to eliminate it by ruthless confiscation of what little property most of its members possessed, by deportation of a high proportion of those and other peasant families, and by the punishment—in many cases the execution—of those who resisted.

The results were simply calamitous. They included a major famine in certain key agricultural regions of the country and the loss, within a short time, of some two-thirds of the country's livestock. Through these cruel and ill-considered measures, a blow was dealt to Russian agriculture that set it back by decades, and from which it has not fully recovered to the present day.

The collectivization campaign roughly coincided in time with the First Five-Year Plan, the announcement of which in 1928–29 made so deep and so favorable an impression upon many well-meaning people in the West. Actually, the plan as announced, and later the claimed statistics on its completion, masked a ruthless and reckless program of military industrialization. This program did indeed provide certain basic components of a great military industry, but did so in an extremely hasty and wasteful manner, at vast expense in human deprivation and suffering, and with reckless abuse of the natural environment. Despite limited improvements in later years, these same features were destined to mark much of Soviet industrialization down through the ensuing decades.

It was on the heels of these early Stalinist efforts at revolutionizing the Soviet economy that there was then unleashed upon Soviet society that terrible and almost incomprehensible series of events known historically as "the purges." Beginning with an obvious effort on Stalin's part to remove from office and destroy all those remnants from the Lenin leadership in whom he suspected even the slightest traces of resistance to his personal rule, these initial efforts, savage enough in themselves, soon grew into a massive wave of reprisals against a great portion of those who at that time were taking any part in the governing of the country or who enjoyed any prominence as members of the cultural intelligentsia.

So terrible were these measures, so arbitrary, indiscriminate, and unpredictable was their application, that they culminated, in the years 1937 and 1938, in a deliberately induced mass frenzy of denunciation— a frenzy overcoming millions of innocent but frightened people who had been encouraged to see in the reckless denunciation of others, even others they knew to be as guiltless as themselves, the only possible assurance of their own immunity to arrest and punishment. In the course of this hysteria, friend was set against friend, neighbor against neighbor, colleague against colleague, brother against brother, and child against parent, until most of Soviet society was reduced to a quivering mass of terror and panic. In this way, a considerable proportion of the administrative and cultural elite of the Soviet Union—tens of thousands upon tens of thousands of them—were induced to destroy each other for the edification, perhaps even the enjoyment, of a single leader, and this while lending themselves to the most extravagant demonstrations of admiration for and devotion to this same man. One searches the annals of modern civilization in vain for anything approaching, in cynicism if not in heartlessness, this appalling spectacle.

So preposterous, so bizarre, so monstrously destructive, and so lacking in any conceivable necessity or advantage to anyone at all were these measures that it is impossible to imagine any rational explanation for them, even from the standpoint of the most fearful, jealous, and suspicious of tyrants. What, in these circumstances, explained Stalin's motives in launching and directing them? And how was it possible that an entire society could submit passively to so dreadful an abuse of its social intactness and moral integrity? These are crucial questions.[2]

Suffice it to say that when Stalin finally perceived that things had gone too far, when he realized that even his own interests were being endangered and finally began to take measures to dampen the terror and the slaughter, several million people were already either languishing or dying in the labor camps, and a further number, sometimes estimated in the neighborhood of a million, had been executed or had died of mistreatment. To which tragic count must be added those further millions who had themselves escaped persecution but who cared about the immediate victims—their parents, lovers, children, or friends, and for whom much of the meaning of life went out with the knowledge, or the suspicion, of the sufferings of the latter. Bereavement, in short, had taken its toll on enthusiasm for life. Fear and uncertainty had shattered nerves, hopes, and inner security.

3

It was, then, on a shaken, badly depleted, socially and spiritually weakened Russian people that there fell, in the first years of the 1940s, the even greater strains of the Second World War. Russia, to be sure, did not become formally involved in that war as such until June 1941.

---

[2]Insofar as the historical evidences provide answers, Tucker has given them in his book, and they richly deserve reading. But they are extraneous to this bare listing of the misfortunes endured by the Soviet peoples under Communist rule.

But the interval had been in part taken up with the war with Finland, which alone had caused some hundreds of thousands of Russian casualties. And what was then to follow, after the German attack, was horror on a scale that put into shade all the sufferings of the previous decades: the sweeping destruction of physical installations—dwellings, other buildings, railways, everything—in great parts of European Russia, and a loss of life the exact amount of which is not easy to determine but which must have run to close to 30 million souls. It is virtually impossible to envisage, behind these bare words and figures, the enormity of the suffering involved.

It will, of course, be observed that if the tragedies of the 1920s and 1930s were brought to Russia by its own Communist regime, the same cannot be said of those of the 1940s. These were the doing of Hitler. Stalin had actually gone to great lengths to appease Hitler with a view to diverting the attack; it was not his fault that he did not succeed.

There is much truth in this statement. Nothing can diminish Hitler's responsibility for bringing on what the Soviets have subsequently referred to (ignoring most of the other theaters of operation in World War II) as the Great Patriotic War. But it was not the whole truth. Stalin himself heightened in many ways the horrors of the struggle: by the cynicism of his deal with Hitler in 1939; by the subsequent treatment of Russians who had become prisoners of war in Germany; by his similar treatment of those civilians who had found themselves on territory that fell under German control; by the brutal deportation of entire subordinate nationalities suspected of harboring sympathies for the German invader; by the excesses of his own police in the occupied areas, of which even the appalling Katyn massacre of Polish officers was only a small part; and by the liberties allowed to his own soldiery as they made their entry into Europe. More important still, one will never know what might have been the collaboration in the prewar years between Russia and the Western powers in the confrontation with Hitler, had the regime with which those powers were faced on the Russian side been a normal, friendly, and open one. Instead, to many in Europe, the Soviet state looked little if any more reliable and reassuring as a partner than did the Nazi regime.

Let us, however, leave such speculations aside and proceed with our recitation of the miseries that overtook the Russian people in these seven decades of Communist power.

It was an even more weary, even more decimated and ravaged Russian people that survived the trials and sacrifices of the war. And their miseries, as it turned out, were not yet at an end. War against a hated enemy had aroused elementary nationalistic feelings among the Russian people. So long as hostilities were in progress, Stalin had wisely (if presumably cynically) associated himself with those feelings. The people and regime had thus, as it seemed, been brought together in the common effort of resistance to the Nazi invasion. And this had produced new expectations. Not unnaturally, there was hope in all quarters, as the war neared its end, that victory would be followed by a change in the habits and methods of the regime—a change that would make possible something resembling a normal relationship between ruler and ruled, and would open up new possibilities for self-expression, cultural and political, on the part of a people long deprived of any at all.

But Stalin soon made it clear that this was not to be. Government would continue as it had before. There would be no concessions to the Soviet consumer; there would only be more of the same ruthless effort of military industrialization, the same suppression of living standards, the same familiar yoke of secret police control. Seldom, surely, has a more bitter disillusionment been brought to an entire people than this callous indifference on Stalin's part to the needs of a sorely tried population just emerging from the sufferings of a great and terrible war.

This, however, was the way things were to be. And the final years of Stalin's life, from 1945 to 1953, wore their way much as the final prewar years had done: the same tired litanies of the propaganda machine; the same secrecy and mystification about the doings of the Kremlin; the same material discomforts; and the same exactions of a police regime the ferocity of which seemed, if anything, to be heightened as an aging Stalin became increasingly aware of his dependence upon it for his personal security and for the preservation of his own power.

Even Stalin's death brought about no sudden or drastic change in the situation. Stalinism, as a governing system, was by now far too deeply planted in Russian life to be removed or basically changed in any short space of time. There was no organized alternative to it, and no organized opposition. It took four more years before Khrushchev and his associates succeeded in removing from power even those in the leadership who had been most closely associated with Stalin in the worst excesses of his rule and who would have preferred to carry on in much the same manner.

But Khrushchev himself did not last very long thereafter, and in the ensuing years, down to the mid-1980s, the country was ruled by a number of mediocre men (Yuri Andropov, Mikhail Gorbachev's patron, was an exception). While they had no taste for the pathological excesses of Stalinist rule (which, as they correctly saw, had endangered everyone, themselves included), these men were heirs to the system that had made these excesses possible, and they saw no reason to change it. It represented, in their eyes, the only conceivable legitimation of their power and the only apparent assurance of its continuation. It was all they had and all they knew. The sort of systemic changes Gorbachev would eventually endeavor to bring about would have surpassed the reaches of their imagination. And after all, from their standpoint, the system appeared to work.

But it did not, of course, work very well. The Soviet system involved the continuing necessity of suppressing a restless younger intelligentsia, increasingly open to the influences of the outside world in an age of electronic communication, and increasingly resentful of the remaining limitations on its ability to travel and to express itself. Beyond that, it rested upon an economy that, just at the time when the remainder of the industrialized world was recovering from the war and moving into the economic revolution of the computer age, was continuing to live in many respects in the conceptual and technological world of the nineteenth century, and was consequently becoming, on the international scene, increasingly uncompetitive.

Finally, the ideology as inherited from Lenin was no longer really there to support this system. It remained as a lifeless orthodoxy, and Soviet leaders would continue on all ceremonial occasions to take recourse to its rituals and vocabulary. But it had been killed in the hearts of the people: killed by the great abuses of earlier decades, killed by the circumstances of the great war for which Marxist doctrine offered no explanations, killed by the great disillusionment that followed that war.

It began to become evident, in short, in those years of the 1970s and early 1980s that time was running out on all that was left of the great structure of power Lenin and Stalin had created. Still able to command a feigned and reluctant obedience, it had lost all capacity to inspire and was no longer able to confront creatively the challenge of its own future. The first leader to perceive this, to read its implications and to give a dying system the coup de grâce it deserved, was Gorbachev.

One cannot end this review of the blows suffered by Russian society at the hands of its own rulers over the decades of Communist power without being aware of the danger of a certain Manichaean extremism in the judging of those rulers and of those who tried faithfully to follow them. Not all that went by the name of communism in Russia was bad; nor were all of those who believed in it. And to recognize the tragic consequences of its exercise of power is not to question the intellectual seriousness or the legitimacy or the idealism of the world socialist movement out of which, initially, Communism arose. One's heart can go out, in fact, to those many well-meaning people in Russia and elsewhere who placed their faith and their enthusiasm in what they viewed as socialism and who saw in it a way of bringing Russia into the modern age without incurring what they had been taught to see as the dark side of Western capitalism. It is important to recognize that Russian Communism was a tragedy not just in its relations to others, but also a tragedy within itself, on its own terms.

But it is impossible, in my view, to review the history of Communism-in-power in Russia without recognizing that the left-extremist wing of the Russian revolutionary movement, as it seized power in 1917 and exercised it for so many years, was the captive of certain profound and dangerous misconceptions of a political-philosophical nature, revolving around the relationships between means and ends, between personal and collective morality, between moderation and unrestrained extremism in the exercise of political power—misconceptions that were destined to have the most dire effects on the nature of the authority it was assuming to itself. It was the Russian people who had to pay the price for these misconceptions, in the form of some of the most terrible passages in their nation's long and tortured history. Seen in this way, the October Revolution of 1917 cannot be viewed otherwise than as a calamity of epochal dimensions for the peoples upon whom it was imposed.

4

And what of the future?

It is not easy, in any discussion of Russia's future, to avoid preoccupation with the distressing and dangerous state of disarray that pre-vails in that country today, and to distinguish the short-term aspects of this situation from those causal features that may be expected to have determining significance in the longer future.

The post-Communist Russia we now have before us finds itself not only confronted with, but heavily involved in, the Herculean ef-fort to carry out three fundamental changes in the national life of the country.

The first of these changes is the shift of the vital center of political power from the Communist Party, which has had a monopoly on power for so many years, to an elected and basically democratic gov-ernmental structure. The second is the shift of the economy from the highly centralized and authoritarian administrative basis that has gov-erned it since the 1920s to a decentralized free-enterprise system. The third is the decentralization of the structure of interrelationships among the various national components, originally of the tsarist empire and more recently of the Soviet Union, that has generally prevailed over the last three centuries.

These three changes, if successfully implemented, would represent in many respects an alteration of the life of the Russian state more fun-damental than that which the Communists endeavored to introduce into Russian life in 1917—more fundamental, because whereas the Communists' changes purported, rather vaingloriously, to deny, ig-nore, and consign to oblivion the Russian past, the present efforts at change are linked, consciously or otherwise, to that past, and reflect an inclination not only to respect but in part to resume the struggles for modernization that marked the final decades of tsardom. If suc-cessfully carried through, these changes would constitute the greatest watershed in Russian life since the Petrine reforms of the early eigh-teenth century.

What are the chances for success in this momentous effort? Many factors would have to enter into any adequate answer to that question; they cannot all be treated here. But certain outstanding ones may well deserve attention in this context.

First, in estimating the chances for success of the first two of these efforts at change—the basic reforms of the political and economic sys-tems—one has to take account of the enduring effects of seven decades of Communist power. One is obliged to note that when it comes to the bulk of the population, the state of preparedness to meet these challenges is smaller than it probably would have been in 1917. It is sad to reflect that among the many other disservices that the Soviet regime did to traditional Russia, not the least was the fact that it left, as it departed, a people so poorly qualified to displace it with anything better.

It would be easy to regard the Communist decades as a tragic seventy-year interruption in the normal progress of a great country and to assume that, the interruption now being over, the country could pick up where things left off in 1917 and proceed as though the interruption had never occurred. The temptation to view things that way is heightened by the evidence that many of the problems the country now faces, as the heavy Communist hand withdraws, represent the unfinished business of 1917, existing much as it then did because so little of it was, in the interval, sensibly and effectively addressed.

But things are not quite like that. The people we now have before us in Russia are not those who experienced the events of 1917; they are the children and grandchildren of the people of that time—of those of them, at least, who survived enough of the horrors of the ensuing years to leave progeny at all. And these children and grandchildren are divided from their parents and grandparents by something more than just the normal generational change. The intervening events, primarily Stalinism and the carnage of the wartime battlefields, were decisive, each in its own way, in their legacy for future generations. Certain people were more likely than others to survive them; it is to these latter that the next generation was born. We have already noted the decimation of much of the prerevolutionary Russian intelligentsia in the early years of Communist power. This has had its effects; of those who saw something of Russia before that decimation was completed, I am surely not alone in noting a certain comparative brutalization in the faces one now encounters on the Moscow streets—a result, no doubt, of long exposure to not only the exactions of a pitiless dictatorship but also the ferocious petty frictions of daily life in a shortage economy.

Nor may we ignore the social effects of all these upheavals. Political persecution and war left tragic gaps in the male parental population, particularly in the villages. Family structure was deeply destabilized, and with its stability there were forfeited those sources of inner personal security that only the family can provide. As so often before in the more violent passages of Russian history, it has been on the broad and long-suffering back of the Russian woman, capable of bearing a great deal but also not without its limits, that an inordinate share of the burdens of the maintenance of civilization has come to rest. The effects are painfully visible in a whole series of phenomena of that woman's life: the weariness, the cynicism, the multitudinous abortions, the fatherless families.

Particularly distressing is the fact that so many of the present younger generation have very little idea of what has happened to Russia in these past decades, of why it happened, or of its effects. With the lives of the tens of millions who perished in the earlier vicissitudes went also their memories and the lessons learned from the events of those times. This younger generation has been thrust with little parental guidance and almost no historical memory into a world whose origins it does not know or comprehend.

It was inevitable that this state of affairs should have had its effects on intellectual outlooks. It is true that a larger part of the population than was the case at the time of the revolution has now received at least a grade school education and some technological training. But on the philosophical, intellectual, and economic sides, the picture is a disturbing one.

The governmental structure to which the center of gravity of political power is now being transferred from what was formerly the party's political monopoly may adequately serve as the outward framework for a new and democratic form of political life, but only that. It will have to be filled in at many points with an entirely new body of methods, habits, and—eventually—traditions of self-rule. For this, the minds of the younger generation are poorly prepared. It is not too much to say that there was much more real understanding for the principles and necessities of democratic rule—for the compromises, the restraints, the patience, and the tolerance it demands—in the Russia of 1910 than is the case today.

And the same applies when it comes to an understanding of economic realities. Seven decades of relentless suppression of every form of private initiative or spontaneity have left a people trained to regard themselves as the helpless and passive wards of the state. Seven decades of economic hardship and low living standards have largely destroyed good-neighborly relations, and have produced an atmosphere in which a great many people peer spitefully and jealously every day over the backyard fence to assure themselves that their neighbors have not contrived to get something they themselves do not possess, and if the neighbors have done so, to denounce them. All this has encouraged the prevalence of a sweeping and exaggerated egalitarianism, under the influence of which it is sometimes held to be better that all should continue to live in a state of semi-poverty and abject dependence upon centralized power than that any should be permitted to take the lead, by their own effort and initiative, in elevating themselves even temporarily over the living standards of others.

Faced with such attitudes, it will not be easy to make quick progress in the systemic changes Gorbachev and others are trying to bring about. These are not the only handicaps of this sort, but they will perhaps prove the most recalcitrant and long-lasting. For what will be required for their correction will be a long and persistent educational effort—an effort for which, in many instances, a new generation of teachers will have to be provided, and one that will presumably have to proceed in the face of much instability in Russian life.

If the full seriousness of the problem is recognized and taken into account, and if the requisite patience and persistence can be mustered, there is no reason to preclude the possibility of eventual success. But the effort cannot be other than a long one; until it is completed, the prejudices and the forms of ignorance just described will continue to lie heavily across the path of Gorbachev's efforts at reform.

We come now to the third of the great elements in the process of change in which Russia is now involved: the readjustment of the interrelationships among the various national and ethnic elements that have heretofore made up the tsarist/Soviet state.

This readjustment is inevitable. The complete maintenance in any of its former forms of the multinational and multilingual empire of past decades and centuries is incompatible with the powerful force of modern nationalism. Most of the other empires of this nature have already been compelled to yield to that force. Russia, too, had begun to yield to it in 1917; but here, too, the process was interrupted and long postponed by the establishment of Communist power. Now the demand for it has reasserted itself with redoubled vigor, and not all of it, surely, is to be withstood. But this is a highly complex and even dangerous problem, which even the benevolently inclined outsider should approach only with greatest circumspection.

That the three Baltic states deserve their independence, and will eventually have it, seems beyond question. There are others that are demanding sovereign status but in whom the requisite experience and maturity of leadership, as well as other essential resources, have yet to be demonstrated. There are still other non-Russian entities where the demand for independence has not even been seriously raised and where the ability to bear the strains and responsibilities of an independent status is even more questionable. There is, in short, no uniformity in the needs and the qualifications that the respective Soviet peoples bring to any far-reaching alteration in their relationship to the Russian center. And no single model, not even one from the outside world, could possibly provide a useful response to all the problems such an alteration would present.

Very special, highly intricate, and full of dangerous pitfalls are those problems that present themselves in the case of the relationship between the Ukraine and Russia proper. Many Ukrainians can and do offer compelling reasons why their country should have at least a greatly changed if not fully independent status in the new era. But Ukrainians do not always speak with one voice. Some speak with a Polish voice, some with a Russian, and some with a more purely Ukrainian one. It will not be easy for them all to agree on how a future Ukraine is to be independently governed, or indeed even on what its borders should be. To which must be added the fact that so extensive is the interweaving of the Russian and Ukrainian economies that any significant detachment of the two governments would have to be accompanied by the widest possible arrangements for freedom of commercial and financial exchanges between them, if confusion and even hardship were to be avoided.

Pregnant with problems of equal, if not greater, gravity are the demands for a virtual independence on the part of the Russian center that now embraces nearly half of the population, and an even larger proportion of the material resources, of the Soviet Union. These demands, too, are not lacking in serious foundation. Russian national feeling, while not without weaknesses and distortions (notably in the tendencies toward xenophobia and intolerance), is deeply rooted in the culture, the religion, and the traditions of the Russian people. No less than the similar feelings of the other national parts of the Soviet Union do they deserve recognition and consideration. To which must be added the fact that the recent discussion within Russia proper of the separate future of that part of the country has been marked, notwithstanding all the handicaps noted above, by an encouraging level of seriousness and responsibility.

But here, serious complications present themselves. For were the process of designing an independent future for the Russian people alone to go too far, this would place in question the very *raison d'être* for any supranational center such as the Soviet government now presents. Were the Russians, in other words, to establish a separate sovereignty, or even a far-reaching degree of national independence, this, coming together with the similar detachment of other nationalities of the present Soviet Union, would raise the question as to whether enough would be left of the traditional tsarist/Soviet Empire to justify any great coordinating center at all.

The relationships that have existed between the many non-Russian parts of this traditional multinational structure and the Russian center have deep historical roots. Few would be prepared for the situation that would develop if all these ties were to be abruptly severed. The economic confusion would be enormous. Worse still is the growing evidence that certain of these non-Russian entities, if left suddenly to themselves, would either make war against each other or become subject to highly destructive civil conflicts within their own confines. Finally, there is the very serious problem that would be created by the fragmentation of responsibility for the nuclear weaponry now in Soviet hands.

Beyond this, there is the need of this entire region for a single voice—a mature and experienced voice—in world affairs. The importance of this problem is apparent in the commanding figure and present position of Gorbachev, a statesman of world stature and competence, without whose service as a spokesman for peoples of this entire area all would be impoverished. It is hard to think of any of the aspirants for independence who, trying to go it alone, could be as useful to world peace, or even to themselves, as this one common and enlightened voice in world affairs could be to all of them. The preservation of the Soviet government as a coordinating center will demand, most certainly, a far higher level of input on the part of these other entities into the development of a common foreign policy than they have enjoyed in the past, but to forfeit the advantages of this arrangement would be, for most if not all of them, to lose more than they would gain.

Of greatest importance in this connection would be the effect on international life of any complete breakup of the Russian/Soviet state. The abandonment of any general political center for the peoples of the region would mean the removal from the international scene of one of those great powers whose interrelationships, with all their ups and downs, have constituted a central feature of the structure of international life for most of this century. Experience has shown (not least in the sudden breakup of the Austro-Hungarian Empire in 1918–19) that any major change in the composition of the international community, although perhaps unavoidable or even desirable over the long term, is pregnant with possibilities for unpredictable complications and for grave dangers if it takes place too abruptly and without careful preparation.

It is clear, then, that no satisfactory solution to these problems will be found at either of the extremes of contemporary opinion in the Soviet Union—neither total independence for everyone nor a total preservation of the sort of subordination to a single central political authority that its component national entities have known in the past. Compromises will have to be found, restraint and patience will have to be observed on all sides.

All this would suggest the necessity for some sort of a federated interrelationship among those of the present components of the Soviet Union that are not to become entirely independent. This would have to be a highly flexible arrangement, and probably a looser one than that which Gorbachev now envisages. But the total absence of such ties would present dangers of great gravity for Russia itself, for the other Soviet nationalities, and for the peace of surrounding regions.

5

Let the following stand, then, as a summary of the considerations set forth above.

What is now emerging on the territory traditionally known as Russia will not be—cannot be—the Russia of the tsars. Nor can it be the Russia of the Communists. It can only be something essentially new, the contours of which are still, for us and for the Russians themselves, obscure.

The tasks to be encompassed are immense. A workable system of humane representative government—something of which Russian history provides only the most rudimentary experience—will have to be devised and rendered acceptable to a people among whom the principle of reasonable compromise, essential to its success, is largely foreign. A new economic system, compatible with Russian traditions but not limited by them, will have to be devised; and an essential feature of this new system will have to be a wholly new organization of the agricultural process, for which, in the main, there will be no precedent in Russian experience. And, finally, the immensely complex and dangerous process of political and institutional decentralization of the traditional Russian state will have to be in some way managed.

For the meeting of these demands the Russian people are today poorly prepared. The events of this century have, as we have seen, taken a terrible toll on their social and spiritual resources. Their own history has pathetically little to tell them. A great deal will have to be started from scratch. The road will be long, rough, and perilous.

How can we best relate to a people that finds itself in such straits, confronted with such tremendous and difficult tasks? The lingering tendencies in this country to see Russia as a great and dangerous enemy are simply silly, and should have no place in our thinking. We have never been at war with Russia, should never need to be, and must not be. As Gorbachev has often pointed out, we live in an age when other people's problems are essentially our own. This is the way we must come to view Russia's.

The Russians will need help from wherever they can get it. Some of that help, in our case, may from time to time take the form of economic assistance; but this will be of minor importance. The greatest help we can give will be of two kinds: example and understanding.

The *example* will, of course, depend upon the quality of our own civilization. It is our responsibility to assure that this quality is such as to be useful in this respect. We must ask ourselves what sort of example is going to be set for Russia by a country that finds itself unable to solve such problems as drugs, crime, decay of the inner cities, declining educational levels, a crumbling material substructure, and a deteriorating environment.

The *understanding,* on the other hand, will have to include the recognition that this is in many ways a hard and low moment in the historical development of the Russian people. They are just in process of recovery from all the heartrending reverses that this brutal century has brought to them. They are not, seen in the historical dimension, entirely themselves. We should bear this in mind. We, too, may someday have our low moments. And while we should beware of our American tendency to idealize those foreign peoples whom we consider to be particularly unfortunate, there is no reason why an understanding American attitude toward Russia at this juncture in its history should not include a reasonable measure of compassion.

Beyond this, while we speak of understanding, we can try to bear in mind that along with all the dark aspects of their development, the Russians have shown themselves historically to be a great people—a people of many talents, capable of rendering significant contributions, spiritual, intellectual, and aesthetic, to the development of world civilization. They have made such contributions at times in the past. They have the potential for doing it again—in a better future.

The obligation to respect and cherish that potential is primarily their own. But in another sense, it is ours as well. Let us accept that responsibility, and meet it thoughtfully, imaginatively, and creatively wherever we can.

Religion in Russia
(1992)

———··❮∞❯··———

I would like to remind you of what many people tend to forget: that Russia is essentially a Christian country. This is a very complicated matter. It would take a full hour to explain just what is meant by that one statement. But it is a fact; and it is one that should not be forgotten—particularly in this place and in this context.

The Communists spent seventy years trying to destroy the church, and indeed all religiosity, in the minds of the people. And they did indeed do great damage to it. But now that they are no longer running things, it is amazing to discover how much of religious faith has remained, and how important it still is as a factor in the lives of the people—and how important it should be as a factor in our view of the new Russia.

There are certain things we ought to bear in mind. First, the Orthodox Church—the former state church of the tsarist regime—continues, I am sure, to be the leading religious community in Russia. But it is not the only one. The various "sects" (as they are called), some of them Protestant, like the Baptists, others, like the so-called Old Believers, dissident branches of the orthodox faith: these sects embrace millions of people. And it is my impression that they survived the Communist period, in many instances, even better than did the Orthodox Church, largely because they were less dependent on property—on

Talk given at the Weekly Forum of Trinity Church, Princeton, New Jersey, January 12, 1992.

buildings, accoutrement, etc.—and less dependent on the formal theological training of their priesthood than was the orthodox establishment. In some instances, too, they were more accustomed to operating inconspicuously, sometimes even underground. They are not to be ignored when we think of religion in Russia.

But the Orthodox Church remains, as I say, the heart of the question. I expect many of you know a good deal about it. Because it drew its origins from Byzantium—that is, from Eastern Christianity—less, perhaps, in doctrine than in spirit, it is far less intellectualized (or so it seems to me) than our Western churches. For the Russians, faith is faith; and they see no reason to try to rationalize it. They are much more attached to the visual and audible symbols of faith—the icons, the ornamentation, the candles, the incense, the visual splendor, the clerical robes, and the magnificent singing of the orthodox service—than are we Westerners.

Striking, in particular, has been the very close association of the orthodox religion with Russian nationalism. To be a Russian did not invariably mean that you were an orthodox believer; but to be an orthodox believer normally meant that you were a Russian. Religion, rather than ethnicity, was the essential criterion of nationality. Baptism, that is, was more important than ethnic origin. If you were born a Jew but became baptized, you ceased, even in the eyes of the old Russian state, to be a foreigner and became a Russian.

This close association of religion with nationalism has had some positive sides. But it has also had, and still has, some dangerous ones. And we will do well to hold it in mind as the new situation there unfolds.

But for all this, I have found the Russian-orthodox religious faith in many instances very moving. It is marked by a great sincerity and, if you will, naïveté. It is the faith of people who have had a hard time, and are aware of their own faults and weaknesses as well as those of others. It is the faith of people who have seen, and sometimes participated in, a good deal of cruelty and brutality, and who have few illusions about their own virtue. But they have suffered a great deal. And the central appeal of their faith—an appeal that comes out a thousand times during their services, and not just from the mouths of the priests but from those of the laity as well, and with many repetitions—is the full-throated refrain "God, have mercy," *Gospodi pomilui.* And by this they mean: Lord, be kind to us. We know we are not perfect; we know our weaknesses. We are poor devils; we don't see all things clearly. Don't expect too much from us. But you know our sufferings. Be indulgent of us; treat us better than we deserve. This in the name of thy son, Jesus Christ.

That is the characteristic, strong, and moving appeal of Russian orthodoxy. I remember one Sunday some years ago, when I was in Moscow, and I went out to see what remained of one of the great old monasteries on the outskirts of the city. It was a windy morning; an icy cold wind was sweeping the whole landscape. The place seemed at first largely deserted, and the great church was closed. But there was a small church on the edge of the premises; and there people were coming and going, and something seemed to be happening. So I went in.

The building was packed—with people, all standing, in the Russian fashion, and with their winter coats on. The service was going on, but not just one service. Because, no doubt, of the lack of space and facilities, other things were taking place in various parts of the church. In one corner, babies were being baptized. In another one, a funeral service was being conducted over the open coffin of the deceased, lying on the floor. And in yet another corner right by the entrance door (I almost stumbled upon it when I came in), three little women in black were down on their knees before some sort of icon; and they were singing the service—singing it in harmony, like little angels, in their small, high-pitched voices, holding, in other words, a little service of their own. They were obviously old women, simple women, the lowest on the totem pole. No one could doubt that their life had been a hard one. But there they were, worshipping in their own way. They were not in the least self-conscious about it. They paid no attention to all the shuffling of the dirty boots of the people pushing past them. This was their way of worshipping. Their right to do it came from God. They had no need to apologize. This was the expression of a simple, but unquestioning and unbending, faith.

Well—that was real piety. And, taken together with many other glimpses of ordinary Russian life, this said something to me about the Russian people. It gave me a sort of ultimate confidence—a desperate and unreasoning confidence, if you will—in their ability to survive, somehow, the dreadful situation in which Russia now finds herself, to survive this crisis as they have survived so many others, and to play their part, once again, among the great peoples of the world. One can only hope that God's blessing will go out to them in this effort.

Part Two

COLD WAR IN
FULL BLOOM

Nuclear Weapons and
Christian Faith
(1982)

This habitat, the natural world around us, is, as you know, the house
the Lord gave us to live in. It's the house we were intended to
live in. It's the house in which man's spiritual struggle was meant to
take place and has taken place over the course of the ages. And it's the
house in which God's purposes will be fulfilled.

Now, we did not create this habitation. It was not given to us to
destroy or exploit for our pleasure, or in a mad effort to assure the safety
of our own generation. It is something placed at our disposal for us to
cherish and to pass on with all its beauty and fertility and marvelous-
ness to our children and to future generations—to those generations
yet unborn who have just as much right as we have to the privilege
and the enjoyment of this habitat God gave us all to live in. We have
no right to deny them either of those things.

Now all of this, of course, is placed in jeopardy by the very existence of nuclear weapons. And this is a situation to which, as I see it,
no Christian can be indifferent.

The problem of Soviet-American relations also has religious connotations. This is partly because it seems to conduce, in our country
at least, to an effort on the part of a great many people to externalize
evil, to attribute to the Soviet leadership and to the Soviet people every
sort of iniquity and indeed a sort of monopoly on iniquity. And what

Speech given upon receiving the Pacem in Terris Award of the Diocese of Dav-
enport, Iowa, May 11, 1982.

is worse, to see in *their* supposed total iniquity the proof of *our own* total virtue.

I would submit that in this monstrous oversimplification, which is what it is, conducive as it is to the most egregious sort of self-righteousness and self-idealization, you have something that is profoundly un-Christian. And it is something that we will not get away from until we learn to see both the Soviet leadership and the Soviet people, and ourselves, as we really are—as God's creatures, embodying both good and bad; each one of our hearts, if you will, the scene of a tiny part of the struggle between good and evil, which is the fundamental mark of all humankind. That is true in Russia no less than among us here.

And this has more than just a personal moral significance, because in the great question of nuclear weaponry there lies the deeper question of peace itself, at least among the great industrial powers. It will, I think, be a long time before we can ever hope to stop various primitive, underdeveloped peoples from squabbling with each other, attempting to settle their scores with whatever weapons they have at hand. But I find myself now, and only very recently, in my own older years, coming for the first time to the conclusion that it is not enough even to eliminate nuclear weapons from the national arsenals; that the day has passed when war itself in any form, conventional or otherwise, is permissible. I do not believe that Europe—and perhaps this goes for ourselves as well—would be able to endure a third world war in this century. What would be left would be not worth survival.

Now we cannot, of course, alone preserve the peace. Our Russian friends or adversaries will have to make their contribution, too. But what we can do is to do all in our power to preserve it and promote it. This we owe to the very preservation of civilization.

And this means to me that we must find another tone, not only for our discourse with the Russians, but for the discourse among ourselves about the whole problem of our relations with them—a tone marked by less tough talk, less militarization of rhetoric; a tone less penetrated with the assumption of war as something inevitable between the two of us, which I assure you it is not; a tone that involves less talk about what we could do to them and they could do to us with weapons in our hands. It would require a greater willingness to talk soberly and realistically about how we could peacefully solve our various problems, accepting the fact that neither of us is apt to be entirely right or entirely wrong all the time, and that sometimes even apparently insoluble problems, if treated quietly and persistently, do eventually yield to the laws of change and to the exercise of human patience.

Toward Peace on Two Fronts
(1982)

————··◦∞◦··————

When we speak of peace today, we normally have in mind the central international problem of our time: a dual problem, actually, consisting on the one hand of the alarmingly low state of Soviet-American relations, and on the other of the nuclear weapons race—a weapons race in which these two powers are the leading parties, and one that, I profoundly regret to say, is now rapidly running out of control.

These are two different problems. Each could exist without the other; and each, even alone, could give us great trouble. But they do exist together. They interact most unfortunately. And as this interaction multiplies, so does, of course, the danger each presents.

It is now sixty-five years since the Russian revolutions of 1917 brought into power on most of the territory of the traditional Russian Empire a regime profoundly antagonistic, in the ideological sense, to our system of government and prepared to do what little it could to stimulate a social revolution with a view to the overthrow of that system. That regime has endured to this day. It still does lip service to the ideology in question. But actually, it has undergone important changes over the years. The last of its leaders who had their political roots in the revolutionary decades of Leninism and Stalinism are now passing from the scene. The dream of world revolution has gone the way of so many other militant enthusiasms with universal pretensions:

Address delivered at Union Theological Seminary, New York City, October 25, 1982.

72

it has remained, that is, as a vague and remote ideal, wistfully clung to by a few zealots for ritualistic reasons but scarcely of any significance as a motivation for conduct among the bewilderments and necessities of the present day. On the other hand, the outcome of World War II endowed this regime, rather unexpectedly, with the military-political hegemony over the entire eastern half of Europe; and the subsequent intensive development of its military resources has placed it in most ways among the top ranks of the world's great military powers—nuclear as well as conventional.

Quite aside from the danger of a nuclear devastation of its own territory, the Soviet regime would have nothing to gain from a war, and does not want one. The elements of inherent unsoundness in its own political and economic system are beginning to catch up with it, and this is creating new problems, which are going to preempt most of its energies for years to come. In addition, its hegemony in Eastern Europe is in the process of gradual disintegration; and this disintegration, if it goes much further, is going to create for the Soviet leadership bitter problems of internal and external security. All this suggests a state of slowly developing but serious crisis within the Soviet system; and this, contrary to some superficial judgments one hears bandied about these days in the West, is not a crisis that could be relieved by another world war; on the contrary, war, as the Soviet leaders well know, could only make it worse.

On the other hand, precisely because of these internal weaknesses, and because of its own lack of sanction in freely expressed public opinion, the Soviet leadership suffers from a high degree of insecurity. Its greatest concern is for the integrity of its own dictatorial authority within the immediate orbit of its power. If it sees that authority seriously threatened by instigation or pressure from outside, and particularly from powers that, like China and the United States, it regards as military rivals, it could easily be moved to have recourse to violent measures that in other circumstances it would prefer to avoid.

The greatest danger this regime represents to us today is thus one connected primarily with its weaknesses rather than its strengths; and here, the degree of the danger will be importantly affected, for better or for worse, by the manner in which we handle our relations with it—and particularly by the impression we convey of what we are trying to achieve in the conduct of those relations. What is called "Soviet behavior" is, in far higher degree than seems to be realized in Washington, a reaction by the leaders of that country to the manner in which we ourselves treat them.

So much, for the moment, for the Soviet-American relationship. Let us now glance briefly at the nuclear weapons race. This dangerous competition is, as I have said, now effectively out of control. The arsenals of the two greatest nuclear powers have grown to dimensions far beyond anything that could conceivably be used in combat without producing a world catastrophe. Nevertheless, those arsenals are continuing to be increased rather than diminished. With this numerical increase, there is a corresponding increase in the danger of disaster by inadvertence—by human error, by computer failure, by misread signals, etc. And the danger is being further heightened by technological developments that tend to disrupt what little equilibrium might be said to have existed heretofore in the balance between the respective forces. There is powerful evidence that the rules of the game that were supposed to have prevailed thus far, and that were designed to rule out certain forms of destabilizing behavior, are now in the process of rapid disintegration.

It is true that negotiations are now taking place in Geneva and Vienna, with a view to bringing at least certain aspects of this competition under some sort of control. I wish I could see something hopeful in these negotiations. I cannot. Their desultory, intermittent, and dragging nature; the obvious skepticism and lack of enthusiasm with which our government entered into them; and the uninhibited striving of both parties for new technological breakthroughs even while the negotiations are in progress: all these leave little ground for hope that anything significantly positive will be achieved in these exchanges.

There are a number of ways in which, given sufficient good will and courage on both sides, this threatening and hopeless pattern could be broken up and the competition brought under a reasonable measure of control. There could be deep cuts—agreed and balanced cuts— in the numbers of missiles deployed on both sides. There could be a comprehensive test ban treaty. There could be a mutual renunciation of the option of first use of nuclear weapons. None of these measures would seriously jeopardize the security of either party. The Soviet side has declared itself unqualifiedly in favor of the renunciation of first use—has in fact even renounced it unilaterally and has called on the world community to do likewise; and such noises as it has made concerning the other two points have not been discouraging. Yet nothing very realistic and nothing very hopeful being done by our government to get on with any of these possibilities.

Meanwhile, the outward behavior of the two sides in all matters that could be seen to have any military significance is marked by the most extreme distrust and hostility. The two navies go chasing each other around and spying on each other in all the waters of the world in a manner that is not only ridiculous and not only incompatible with the relations between two powers nominally at peace, but is highly dangerous in the bargain. And this is only a single example of a much wider phenomenon. In many respects, the two powers are behaving in a way that could not be different if they knew for a fact that they were destined to be in open military conflict with each other in a matter of months.

The effect of all this has been to suggest to millions of people on both sides, in government as well as outside it, and by suggesting, to persuade them, that a shooting war is something inevitable. This is a frame of mind that, once adopted by influential people, does more than anything else to make war inevitable, whether or not it was really that in the first place; because whoever views war as inevitable tends to neglect the things that might have been done to prevent it.

Now, there has, of course, grown up in this country in these past years an antinuclear movement of extraordinary popular strength and intensity of feeling. It is not a unified movement, and it is probably best that it should not become one; for any effort to unify it and direct it from a single center would no doubt mean the sacrifice of some of its freshness and spontaneity. It is the reflection of a deep uneasiness among our people about the direction in which our present governmental course is leading us. It is now being attacked by its opponents as being Communist-inspired; and its adherents are being dubbed as the conscious or unconscious tools of Moscow. Some of this, I suppose, was inevitable; but I must say that I can think of nothing more contemptible than this effort to pin a Communist label on a movement that is actually overwhelmingly motivated by nothing other than a deep concern for the security of this country and this civilization in the face of a volume of weaponry quite capable of putting an end to both.

Not only has this antinuclear movement attained impressive popular strength, but it has been indirectly supported by what I view as a truly remarkable volume of searching critical literature from highly qualified professional sources, particularly in the medical, general scientific, and even military communities, all devoted to the analysis of the various courses our government is now pursuing, and most of it thoughtfully critical of the policies that have brought us where we are today—critical of their wisdom and of their necessity.

The Freeze: Symbol and Starting Point

As we all know, the issue the mass antinuclear movement has, for the most part, taken to its heart is that of the nuclear freeze. While a freeze of this nature is naturally open to criticism on the part of those who take seriously the various statistical comparisons between Soviet nuclear arsenals and our own, and while it would be only the merest beginning of what really needs to be done, the demand for it serves very well as a symbol and rallying point for the anxieties that inspire this demand. Widespread popular support for such a freeze might have some small effect in persuading the administration that the concerns of the public in the face of the weapons race have to be taken seriously.

But the fact is that to date, the powers-that-be in Washington have taken no serious notice of the antinuclear movement or of the critical literature by which it has been supported. I can think of no respect in which there has been any significant response from the official side to either of these challenges. The demonstrations of mass feeling have been absentmindedly brushed off like some annoying insect; and the government has not even deemed it necessary to reply to the many competent professional criticisms of what it is doing. It evidently feels that it could ride out challenges even stronger than these without bothering to take notice of them; and it probably has, as we shall see presently, some reason for this feeling.

Where, then, does this leave us? Have we not come up against some sort of a dead end in all these private efforts to deflect official policy into safer and more reassuring courses? Are we to give up in frustration, abandoning our efforts to influence official policy from the outside, and resigning ourselves to the position of helpless victims of a trend toward war that now seems to be quite out of control and has no visible outcome other than one of utter horror?

The answer, of course, is no, not at all. On the contrary, never was there a greater need for a strong critical scrutiny, and a clear expression of opinion, of what the government is doing in matters that affect the future peace of the world. The fact that efforts along this line have been ineffective to date is no sign that they must remain that way forever. Nor is it ever justifiable to abandon the right cause just because the odds appear, at any given moment, to be against it. But we *do* have to recognize, I think, that the problem is deeper than most of us have thus far believed it to be, and that it will take longer to solve than most of us have assumed.

Of the two parts of this problem—Soviet-American relations and the weapons race—it is the weapons race, and particularly our government's commitment to it, that is the more intractable. This is because the commitment has now become in a way institutionalized, and is very little responsive to public opinion or indeed to external pressures of any sort.

Millions of people in this country now have a personal stake in the maintenance and cultivation of this vast armed establishment, and of the Cold War psychology by which it is sustained. These include military people, industrialists, workers in defense industries, politicians, journalists, publicists, and many others who for one reason or another have locked themselves into characteristic Cold War attitudes.

The Cold War and the responses it engenders may in fact be said to have become an addiction for large parts of our society. And the long-term nature of many of our military-commercial and military-financial undertakings—the fact, for example, that many military programs and contracts represent commitments running several years into the future—make it clear that this is not an addiction that could be broken in a day. Even the most well-inclined president would find it hard, and indeed most unpleasant politically, to extract us from this dreadful institutional predicament in anything less than a number of years. Thus sporadic, one-time private efforts, designed to kick an unwilling and un-understanding government into modifying one part or another of this great military effort, are not apt to be crowned with any wide measure of success.

In the field of Soviet-American relations, the prospects are only slightly less discouraging. The dominant political circles in Washington have dug themselves deeply into a view of the Soviet Union that, while not wholly incorrect, is made up of so many, and such egregious, exaggerations and oversimplifications that it can hardly serve as a basis for any effort to arrive at a realistic and sensible relationship with the country; and not only have these circles committed themselves in the most irrevocable way to these distortions, but they have succeeded in peddling them to a good portion of our political, journalistic, and even religious establishments.

And as things stand today, I am afraid there would also be difficulties from the Soviet side. There are strong signs, it seems to me, that the Soviet leaders have given up on the Reagan administration, in the sense that they have concluded they have nothing to expect at its hands except a total, blind, and almost deadly hostility, and that not much is to be gained by trying to talk with it. I am inclined to doubt that anything this administration could now do in the way of trying to talk seriously with the Russians about the problems of war and peace, even if it wished to do this, would suffice to overcome, within the remaining two years of its incumbency, the suspicions and the defensive reactions that have already been aroused. Here again, we find ourselves up against the hard fact that very little is to be accomplished, in the short term, by outside pressures on our government for a sharp change in direction.

A Long, Hard Road

What, then, does all this suggest for those of us on the nongovernmental side who would like to use our influence as citizens to promote the prospects for a lasting peace?

It means, I think, that we have to recognize that we are farther from our goal than we thought; that the road is going to be longer and harder than it first appeared; that we must lay our plans with a view to their producing results in a matter of years, not months; and that the central element in these efforts must be an educational campaign of massive dimensions, designed to bring greater understanding not just to the voters of this country but also to those whom they elect—and also, incidentally, to those who, through the modern media of communication, have so great an influence on the shaping of our public opinion.

This will not be easy. It will require a great deal of leadership from those who have been given greater opportunities than others, either by education and professional preparation or by experience, to understand the problems at hand.

In the case of the nuclear arms race, the initial focus must be, it seems to me, not on that phenomenon itself but on those deficiencies in our society and in our political system that have made it so difficult for us to deal sensibly and constructively with it. By this I mean that we will have to look closely to determine, and then to make people understand, how it was possible that there could have been created in this country a gigantic institution—namely, the military-industrial complex with all its political and social ramifications—that is so extensively a power within itself, so inflexible, so little sensitive to public and even electoral opinion, so resistant to correction from outside, and capable of committing so large a part of our national effort, and this for so long in advance, to a cause so sterile and hopeless as that of the great all-out military competition of this present nuclear age.

If we wish to make headway against the nuclear danger, the first thing we Americans have to study and to understand is ourselves—how we could have wandered into this predicament, and what it would take to get us out of it. When it comes to the Soviet-American relationship, the required educational effort is less subjective and for this reason, perhaps, less difficult; and it offers, I think, greater hope for early progress. Still, it will be no easy task. For what is involved here, in the understanding of the Soviet Union as a problem in American policy, consists of many subtleties, many uncertainties, and not a few apparent contradictions. In essence, the task is that of exposing for what they are the many exaggerations and oversimplifications to which I referred earlier, and of teaching people to understand many things about our complex relationship with the Soviet Union.

People must be made to understand, for example, that just because the leaders of another country do not share our political ideals and do not appear to be nice people, that does not mean that one has to fight a war with them; that for individual Americans to have and to express their sympathy with oppositionists in another country is one thing, whereas for our government to espouse their cause and to try to support it publicly is another; and that there are things another government might be brought to do by gentle and private persuasion that it can never be brought to do if the pressure is mounted publicly and if its prestige is placed at stake. It is these lessons and a number of similar ones that will have to be brought home to our people and to their representatives if support is to be enlisted for a balanced, businesslike, and realistic policy toward the Soviet Union.

Until these various issues can be generally clarified and some sort of a workable consensus achieved on policy toward the Soviet Union, that policy will continue to be only too often the football of the extremists, the special interest groups, and all those good people who find it impossible to live without the image of a totally inhuman enemy, against the background of whose supposed infinite iniquity their own sense of total virtue can be indulged and gratified.

Fortunately, there has recently been a growing appreciation in influential circles in this country of the need for a reactivization of support for Russian and Soviet studies. Nothing could be more conducive to a balanced and constructive approach to the problems of our relations with the Soviet Union than a strong corps of Americans schooled in the knowledge of its life, its culture, its civilization. The people of that country are, after all, one of the world's great peoples, with a record of distinguished contributions to world culture—scientific, artistic, musical, dramatic, religious, and above all, literary. They have recently been through hard times, such as most of us could not imagine; and their civilization bears the marks today of all that suffering and sacrifice. But the long-term future of Western civilization depends very importantly upon our ability to live peaceably with them in one world, as we have done for several centuries. I am convinced that if we give to the study of their life the serious and unbiased attention it deserves, it will help us to ride out the conflicts of this age and to live successfully into a time when we can both contribute to the solution of each other's problems instead of trying to make them worse. And such is the gravity of the problems looming up for both of us, and for modern industrial society in general, quite aside from the danger of war, that we will need all of that sort of help we can get.

Let us therefore, instead of becoming discouraged by the darkness of the moment and by our sense of helplessness over the recent past, redouble our efforts on behalf of world peace, remembering that what is required from us first of all is the acquisition and dissemination of a greater understanding—a greater understanding of ourselves and of the inherent tendencies of our own society, a greater understanding of those whom so many of us have learned to regard as our enemies, but without whose increased sense of security, and without whose willing collaboration, no world peace will be conceivable at all.

Is this possible? I can only reply by repeating the answer that I gave in a similar address in Europe: "Why not?"

The State of U.S.–Soviet Relations
(1983)

——————◦⟨∞⟩◦——————

Soviet-American relations, in consequence of a process of deterioration that has been several years in the making, are today in what
can only be called a dreadful and dangerous condition. Civility and privacy of communication between the two governments seem largely
to have broken down. Reactions on both sides to statements and actions of the other side have been allowed to become permeated with
antagonism, suspicion, and cynicism. Public discussion of the relations
between the two countries has become almost totally militarized, in
this country at least—militarized to a point where the casual reader or
listener could only conclude that some sort of military showdown was
the only possible outcome, the only conceivable denouement of our
various differences, the only one worth considering and discussing.

I wonder whether anyone can mistake, or doubt, the ominous
meaning of such a state of affairs? These phenomena—the ones I have
just described—occurring in the relations between two highly armed
great powers, are the familiar characteristics, the unfailing characteristics, of a march toward war—that and nothing else.

I don't think I have to point out the immensity of the danger this
spells. The danger would be intolerable even if the two countries were
armed only with what are called conventional weapons. The history
of the past century has shown that the damages produced by armed
conflict between highly industrialized great powers in the modern age,

Address delivered at luncheon meeting of the American Committee on East-West
Accord, Washington, D.C., May 17, 1983.

even without the use of nuclear armaments, are so terrible that it is doubtful whether Western civilization could survive another such catastrophe. But this danger is multiplied many times over by the nature of the weapons the two countries hold in their hands. While either of these two factors—the nature of the weaponry or the state of the political relations—would be a danger in itself, the two in combination present a shadow greater than any that has ever darkened the future of Western civilization. I fail to see how anyone could be complacent about it.

Is this state of the Soviet–American relationship really necessary and unavoidable from the standpoint of the American policymaker—is there no way we could avoid it, no way we could cope with it, other than by a continuing and intensified weapons race of indefinite duration? And if this is not the case, what is there that we could do about it?

There are those in Washington who would argue that this situation flows automatically from the nature of the regime that confronts us in Moscow and is therefore unavoidable. And to support that view, they would point to a given image of that regime. It is an image, I suspect, largely of their own creation and cultivation. We are all familiar with it. It is an image of unmitigated darkness—the image of a group of men already dominating and misruling a large part of the world and motivated only by a relentless determination to bring still further peoples under their domination.

No rational motivation is suggested, by those who cultivate this image, for so unbounded and unquenchable a thirst for power. The bearers of it, we are allowed to conclude, were simply born this way— the products, presumably, of some sort of a negative genetic miracle. But in any case, being born this way and unable to help themselves, there is no way they could be reasoned with—so the thesis goes—no basis on which they could usefully be approached, no language they could be expected to understand, other than that of intimidation by superior military force. Only by the spectre of such a force—an overwhelmingly superior nuclear force, in particular—could these men be "deterred," as the phrase goes, from committing all sorts of acts of aggression or intimidation with a view to subjugating other peoples and eventually to conquering the world. There are allegedly no other inhibitions, no other considerations, no other interests, that could be expected to restrain them from such behavior.

Well, this image, if applied thirty to forty years ago to the regime of Joseph Stalin, might not have been so far from reality, but as applied to the Soviet leadership in the year 1983 it is grotesquely overdrawn, a caricature rather than a reflection of what really exists, one that is highly misleading and pernicious as a foundation for national policy, and one that is deeply and needlessly offensive to the people in question.

The Soviet regime was born in the agony of the First World War, and it has always reflected something of the profound estrangement of Russia from the Western world that that agony, and the resulting Russian Revolution, brought about. It is not surprising, then, that the regime has always been marked by a whole series of characteristics that complicate its relationship to the Western powers. Some of these were inherited from the tsarist empire of earlier centuries. Some betray, although in a much modified form, the militant ideological antagonism toward non-Communist countries that was so prominent a feature of the early revolutionary period. There are traces, too, unfortunately (also, thank God, now greatly modified), of the baleful influence once exerted on the Soviet regime by the years of Stalinist horror. But whatever their origins, these characteristics do exist; and I do not know anyone familiar with that government who would deny this.

I hope our friends from the Communist orbit will not take it amiss if I mention some of these complicating factors. In doing so, I am not unmindful of the fact that the American political system is also not invariably the easiest one in the world for foreigners to deal with.

Be that as it may, the Soviet regime has, for example, a relatively high general sense of insecurity, a marked sensitivity to conditions in border regions, a tendency to overdo in the peacetime cultivation of military strength, and above all, a positively neurotic passion for secrecy. And as one of the consequences of this passion for secrecy, it has what seems to be a veritable obsession with espionage, in both the offensive and the defensive senses—an obsession that often gets in the way of normal and relaxed relations with other countries.

Soviet negotiating techniques often appear, particularly for those not familiar with them, to be stiff, jerky, secretive, unpredictable, and above all, lacking in that useful lubrication that comes from informal personal association and exchanges among negotiators.

And then there are, too, specific Soviet policies that grate severely on Western sensibilities. The Soviet leaders do indeed make efforts to gain influence and authority among the regimes and peoples of the Third World; and while the methods they employ do not seem to me to differ very greatly from those of other great powers, including ourselves, and while their efforts have not met, generally speaking, with any great measure of success, I understand that these practices arouse alarm and indignation in large sections of our official community.

And then, of course, there is the fact that these Soviet leaders insist on maintaining a monopoly of political power in their own country and proceed harshly against those who appear to challenge or threaten that monopoly or even try to liberalize the political system; beyond which, they unquestionably use their military hegemony to support and to maintain in power in Eastern Europe regimes similarly inspired and similarly resistant or almost as resistant—to liberalizing tendencies. All this, admittedly, is a constant thorn in the flesh of much Western opinion.

And finally, while we are speaking of the difficulties, let us not forget the phenomenon, familiar, I think, to all foreign representatives and observers in Russia, of the curious dual personality the Soviet regime presents to the foreign representative: the facade, that is, composed of people—often amiable and charming people—authorized to associate and communicate with the outside world; but behind that facade, never visible but always perceptible, the other, inner, conspiratorial personality, of whose inscrutable attitudes and intentions the foreigner is never quite sure, and which for that reason probably incurs more suspicion than it deserves.

Now these, and others I could name, are formidable difficulties. Of course, they limit the relationship. And of course, they have to be taken into consideration by Western policymakers. But there are certain things I should like to say about them.

First, most of them are not new. Some have been there since the very outset of the Soviet-American relationship. All of us who have served in Moscow have had to contend with them. We were taught, in fact, to regard them as part of the problem. And General George C. Marshall, I recall, used to say to us: "Don't fight the problem." Second, most of these difficulties are actually less acute than they were many years ago. Perhaps with patience and understanding, they can become even less pronounced in future years. And third, those negative factors are counterbalanced by a number of more encouraging ones relating to both the psychology and the situation of the Soviet leadership.

Of these encouraging signs, the most important consist of the many persuasive indications that that leadership, however complicated its relations with the West, does not want a major war—that it has a serious and primary interest in avoiding such a war, and will, given a chance, go quite far together with us to avoid it. By an "interest," I do not mean an abstract devotion to the principle of peace as a moral ideal. I mean a consciousness on the part of these men that certain things they most deeply care about would not be served by another great war. I believe that anyone who tries to put himself in the position of the Soviet leaders will at once see the force of this point. Even if they should be as evilly motivated as they are sometimes perceived to be, these men are not free agents, wholly detached from the manifold complexities and contradictions that go, invariably, with the exercise of great power. They constitute the government of a great country. They have a direct responsibility for the shaping of the society and economic life of that country. It is from the successful development of this society and this economy that they derive their strength. They cannot play fast and loose with either. Beyond which, they live and operate in a highly complicated international environment.

There is no single consideration—there are a thousand considerations, and these quite aside from any so-called military "deterrence"— that would serve to dissuade these men from any thought that their interests could be served by opening the Pandora's box of another world war. The view that sees them as so totally independent, so wholly on top of all their other problems, and so madly riveted to dreams of world conquest that it is exclusively by the interposition of an overwhelming opposing military force that they could be dissuaded from striking out in any and all directions with acts of aggression or intimidation—this view, which, incidentally, seemed to me to permeate every page of the recent report of President Reagan's commission on strategic missilry (Star Wars), is simply childish, inexcusably childish, unworthy of people charged with the responsibility for conducting the affairs of a great power in an endangered world. Surely we can do better than this in penetrating, with our imagination and our powers of analysis, the true complexity of the forces that come to bear on the decisions of another great government, and in forming a realistic idea of the motivation of its conduct. And surely, if we were to make this effort, what we would then see would be more reassuring than what, in the absence of it, we are led by our fears to assume.

And the area of common interest between the Soviet Union and ourselves is not limited to the need of both these peoples to see world peace preserved. Both are great industrial powers. As such, they have a growing number of common problems. Prominent among these are the environmental ones. Both countries occupy major portions of the environmentally endangered Northern Hemisphere. The Soviet leaders are no less aware than we are of the extent to which this hemisphere, even if it should escape nuclear disaster, is still threatened by environmental pollution and deterioration. They know that these problems will not be mastered just by measures taken within any single country—that their solution will require international collaboration.

The environmental questions are only examples of the many problems and challenges that all the great industrial societies of this planet, including the United States and the USSR, have in common. And these problems—the familiar problems of the technological revolution that is coming to envelope us all—are the ones that unite, the ones on which we can collaborate; and they are the problems of the future. The others, those flowing from the ideological conflicts of earlier decades, are the problems of the past.

These, then, are some of the pros and cons of the Soviet-American relationship, as I see them; and if these pros and cons are stacked up against each other, what you get is naturally a mixed pattern, embracing serious differences of outlook and interest but also embracing positive possibilities that are more than negligible. It is a pattern that leaves no room for exaggerated hopes, or for fulsome and hypocritical pretenses to a friendship that does not, and cannot, fully exist. But it also affords no justification for some of the extremes of pessimism that we see around us today—no justification for the conclusion that it is only by some ultimate military showdown that our various differences can be resolved, and no justification for the overdrawn image of the Soviet leadership to which I have just pointed. We Americans lived for more than a century at peace with the empire of the tsars. Despite the addition of several seriously complicating factors, we have lived for some six and a half decades at peace with the Soviet Union. And I can see in this mixed pattern nothing to suggest that these two countries should not be able to continue to live at peace with each other for an indefinite number of decades into the future.

This cannot, of course, be assured by the state of relations we have before us today. While the true pattern of our respective interests does not, as I have said, suggest that the prospects for a peaceful development of Soviet-American relations are hopeless, they could easily become just that if we are unable to rise above some of the morbid nuclear preoccupations that now seem to possess us—if we are unable to see the positive possibilities behind the negative military ones, and unable to give to those positive possibilities a chance to breathe and to realize themselves.

I recognize the fundamental importance of the outstanding questions of arms control. I know that they represent the greatest and most urgent single problem we have before us in our relations with the Soviet Union. I know that without progress in this respect, there can be little hope of a peaceful future. But I would like the words I am speaking here today to serve as a reminder that there are other dimensions to the Soviet-American relationship than just the military ones; and that not only are these other dimensions of sufficient importance to warrant attention in their own right, but unless they, too, can be recognized and cultivated and their favorable possibilities taken advantage of, then the arms talks themselves are unlikely to have any adequate and enduring success. These two aspects of the relationship, military and nonmilitary, are complementary; and progress in the one is indispensable to progress in the other.

My plea, therefore, would be that we see what we can do to place this relationship as a whole on a sounder, more reassuring, and less frightening basis. I recognize that as of today, things are badly fouled up, and any effort to straighten them out is unavoidably going to take time. There are even those who believe that nothing that could be done from the American side over the next year and a half would suffice to restore the atmosphere necessary to permit such an effort to go forward. I cannot share that extreme pessimism. Of course, the process will take time. But precisely because this is so, it is never too early to begin; and there is nothing to prevent us from considering the sort of agenda that would be necessary to create a more normal state of affairs.

What might such an agenda look like?

Well, some of it flows, by implication, from what I have already said. We could try, first of all, to restore the full confidentiality and the civility of communication between our two governments. And we could cease treating the Soviet Union as though we were, out of one pocket, at peace with it, and out of the other, at war. We could lift the heavy dead hand off Soviet-American trade and permit that normal and useful branch of human activity to proceed in response to its own economic requirements. We have no need to be trying to set back the economy, or depress the living standards, of another great people; nor is it in keeping with the American tradition to be engaged in such an effort.

We could take a much bolder, more hopeful and promising stance in matters of arms control; and when I say that, I am not talking about unilateral disarmament. We could acknowledge— and it is high time we did so—that the nuclear weapon is a useless one, which could not conceivably be used without inviting catastrophe upon the people whose government initiated its use, along with untold millions of people elsewhere. Recognizing this, we could reject all dreams of nuclear superiority and see what we could do about reducing the existing nuclear arsenals, with a view to their eventual total elimination. A number of approaches have been suggested: the freeze, deep cuts, the so-called "build-down," a comprehensive test ban treaty, and others. These are not alternatives. They are complementary. Any or all of them would be useful. But to get on with them, I believe that we must learn to treat the problem as a whole in our negotiations with the Russians, not in a series of fragmented technical talks—and to treat it at the senior political level, as it should be treated.

And then, turning to the more positive and hopeful possibilities, we could set out to take advantage of those areas where the peaceful interests of the two powers do coincide and where possibilities for collaboration do exist. What have we to lose? If my memory is correct, we once made some twenty-two separate agreements for collaboration and personnel exchanges in a whole series of cultural and scientific fields. A number of these proved fruitful; some, I understand, did not. I hold no brief for the retention of those that did not. But most of them, including certain of the useful agreements, have been allowed to lapse. These could be restored, and others, I am sure, could be added. There are many possibilities in the scientific field—possibilities for collaboration on environmental problems, on the study of the Arctic and Antarctic, on oceanographic research, on public health, on nuclear fusion. The entire great area of the uses of outer space—this vast common umbrella that protects every man, woman, and child on this planet—ought to be not only demilitarized but genuinely internationalized; and these two great countries ought to be taking a major, if not exclusive, collaborative part in that internationalization, instead of speculating on how they might exploit this medium to the detriment of the other party—and perhaps to the detriment of humanity as a whole.

There are those who will say: yes, we once had such agreements, but we did not get as much information out of them as the Russians did. To which I can only say: if this—the acquisition of military intelligence—is the only reason we can see for entering into agreements with another country, then they had better be omitted altogether. But if we are prepared to place our hopes in their long-term effects—their effects in bringing people together in a collaborative relationship and helping them to see each other and each other's society as human beings and not as some species of demon—then I am sure we will find that many of these arrangements provide more hopeful perspectives than the most ambitious of our efforts to learn how to destroy each other.

These collaborative arrangements require, as a rule, formalized agreements; and there will be some who will question whether we can trust the Soviet government to live up to such agreements. Whenever I hear this question asked, I am surprised; for we now have six and a half decades of experience to go on, and the answer provided by this experience is reasonably clear. You *can* conclude useful agreements with the Soviet side; they *will* respect them—on the conditions, however, that the terms be clear and specific, not general; that as little as possible be left to interpretation; that questions of motivation and particularly professions of lofty principle be left aside; and finally, that the other contracting party show a serious and continued interest in their observance.

And then, while we are on the question of the objections that will be raised to what I have suggested, there is one more I must face: and that is the question of human rights.

I am afraid that my answer to this question must be brief—and to many, unwelcome. Of course our sympathies are engaged for people who fall afoul of any great political police system; and I see no need to conceal it. But if what we are talking about are the interrelationships of governments, a choice must be made between the interests of democratization in Russia and the interests of world peace; and in the face of this choice, there can be, as I see it, only one answer. Democracy is a matter of tradition, of custom, of what people are used to and expect. It is something that cannot be suddenly grafted onto an unprepared people—particularly not from outside, and not by precept and preaching and pressure rather than example. It is not a concept familiar to the mass of the Soviet people; and whoever subordinates the interests of world peace to the chimera of an early democratization of Russia will assuredly sacrifice the first of those values without promoting the second. By the nature of things, democratization must wait; world peace cannot. If what we want to achieve is a liberalization of the political regime prevailing in the Soviet Union, then it is to example rather than to precept that we must look; and we could start by tackling, with far greater resolution and courage than we have shown to date, some of the glaring deficiencies in our own society.

These, then, are some of the directions in which we could move and in which I should like to see us move. We have, I reiterate, so little to lose. At the end of our present path of unlimited military confrontation lies no visible destination but failure and horror. There are no alternatives to this path that would not be preferable to it. What is needed here is only the will—the courage, the boldness, the affirmation of life—to break out of the evil spell that has been cast upon us, to declare our independence of the nightmares of nuclear danger, and to turn our minds and hearts to better things.

Permit me now, if you will, one personal word in conclusion. These observations flow from an involvement on my part with Soviet-American relations that goes back, I believe, over a longer span of years than that of anyone now in public life on either side. In the course of these years (and there are actually fifty-five of them), I have seen this relationship in some of its better times: particularly at the time of the establishment of diplomatic relations just a half-century ago and again during our association with the Soviet Union in the waging of the Second World War. I have also seen it in some of the most bitter and disheartening moments it has known—have not only seen it in such moments but have felt some of their effects upon my own person. Precisely for this reason, I think I know as much as anyone about the difficulties the relationship involves. Yet at no time in the course of these fifty-five years have I ever lost my confidence in the constructive possibilities of the relationship. For all our historical and ideological differences, these two peoples—the Russians and the Americans—complement each other; we need each other; we can enrich each other; together, granted the requisite insight and restraint, we can do more than any other two powers to assure world peace. For this reason, the rest of the world needs our forbearance with each other and our peaceful collaboration. Our allies need it. And we ourselves need it—and can have it if we want it.

I wish I could convey something of this confidence to those around me here in Washington. I know that if this could be done, we would go forward without hesitation to face the challenges this view presents, and to shoulder, soberly but cheerfully, the burdens it implies.

America's Far-Eastern Policy at the Height of the Cold War
(1984)

——————⟡——————

Let me take up some of our main involvements in the Far East in the postwar period. And let me begin with Korea.

Remember the situation at the end of the war in the Pacific. We firmly, and I think rightly, refused to permit the Russians to play any part in the occupation of the defeated Japan. But on the Korean peninsula, we ended up, as we did in the center of Europe, with the Soviet forces taking the Japanese surrender in the northern part of the peninsula and our side taking it in the south, but with no agreement between the two powers about the future of that country.

Now General Douglas MacArthur, who was initially the most influential person in determining American policy toward the defeated Japan, seems originally to have envisaged a permanently disarmed and politically neutralized Japan. It was my own thought (and I still think there was good reason for it) that we should have stuck to that principle. I thought it possible that in return for our consent to a neutralized and demilitarized Japan, which would have meant that the country would not be used as a base for American military or naval forces in the postwar era, the Russians, for whom such a settlement held important advantages, might have been willing to consent to the establishment of a democratically elected and presumably moderate government in all of Korea.

But by the end of the year 1949, something had happened in

Excerpts from a lecture delivered at Grinnell College, Grinnell, Iowa, January 26, 1984.

Washington that was to have a profound effect on all our postwar policies. The concept of containment, which I had been so bold as to put forward in 1947, had been addressed to what I and others had believed was a danger of the *political* expansion of Stalinist Communism—and especially the danger that local Communists, inspired and controlled by Moscow, might acquire dominant positions in the great defeated industrial countries of Germany and Japan. I did not believe, nor did others who knew the Soviet Union well, that there was the slightest danger of a Soviet military attack against the major Western powers or Japan. This was, in other words, a political danger, not a military one. And the historical record bears out that conclusion. Yet for reasons I have never fully understood, by 1949 a great many people in Washington—in the Pentagon, the White House, and even the Department of State—seemed to have come to the conclusion that there was a real danger of the Soviets unleashing, in the fairly near future, what would have been World War III.

One of the most interesting subjects for historical inquiry would be, even today, the reasons why this conclusion became so current in Washington at that time. I opposed it. So did my colleague Charles Bohlen. But in both instances without success. I can attribute it only to the difficulty many Americans seemed to have in accepting the idea that there could be a political threat, and particularly one emanating from a strong military power, that was not also, and primarily, a military threat. Particularly powerful, especially in military quarters, seems to have been the temptation to leap to the conclusion that since the Soviet leaders of the Stalin period were antagonistic toward us, since they were heavily armed, and since they were seriously challenging our world leadership, they were just like the Nazis of recent memory: they wanted and intended, that is, to make war against us. Therefore, policy toward them must be in accordance with the model of what policy toward the Nazis *ought to have been* before the outbreak of hostilities in 1939. None of this was correct.

In any case, this change in American opinion did occur in late 1949 and early 1950. And one of its first consequences was the growth of a strong feeling in the American military and political establishments that we could not leave Japan demilitarized—that, on the contrary, we must garrison it for an indefinite period to come, even if this meant the conclusion of a separate Japanese peace treaty, not agreed to by the Russians. This view was made manifest publicly in a number of ways in early 1950, at a time when we were greatly reducing our military presence in South Korea. And the immediate Russian reaction to all this took the form of permitting, if not encouraging, the North Koreans to attack South Korea, with a view to extending Communist control to the entire Korean peninsula. If Japan, in other words, was to remain indefinitely a bastion of American military power, if there was to be no agreed peace settlement for Japan, and if Moscow was to have no look-in on the Japanese situation, then Moscow wanted, by way of compensation, to consolidate its military-political position in Korea— an area we appeared not to care too much about in any case.

This, of course, was the origin of the Korean War. You know the rest. Three years and 54,000 American casualties later, the conflict was terminated, but it was terminated by a stalemate on the Korean peninsula much like what we had had before—simply with a much heavier American involvement. And there it has remained to this day.

Now, what I think we should note about this episode are the following.

First, we Americans had little interest in negotiating with the Russians a political settlement of the problems of that region, and particularly one that would have put an end to our military presence in Japan. And why did we have so little interest? Mainly, I suppose, because we had already made up our minds that Moscow was determined to launch a new world war. To resist this, we needed Japan as a military outpost. But also because Russia was already identified as the epitome of evil; and it wouldn't look good, from the domestic-political standpoint, to be negotiating and compromising with evil.

The second thing I want to point out is that when the Russians reacted as they did, by authorizing—or acquiescing in—the North Korean attack, we were never willing or even able to recognize the connection between what we were doing in Japan and what the North Korean Communists were doing in Korea. On the contrary, when the North Korean attack came, the immediate conclusion in Washington was that this was indeed the first move in a Soviet program of worldwide military expansion, comparable to the Munich crisis of 1938, which was so often seen as the first Nazi move in the conquest of Europe. Again, both Bohlen and I challenged this interpretation, but we could make little headway against it. It was the military interpretation that prevailed.

Now, bearing all that in mind, let me turn to the other great involvement of this country in Far Eastern affairs in the postwar period, one that lasted twenty-five years instead of only three: the Vietnam War. I must assume here that all of you have some memories or some knowledge of that prolonged, expensive, unsuccessful, and in every way unfortunate effort on our part to defeat what we saw as the Vietnamese Communists (they were really primarily nationalists) and to install some sort of anti-Communist government in their country. This effort was obviously tragically misconceived. It is clearly recognizable today as a tremendous blunder of American policy.

And it raises two great historical questions to which we today ought to give the most careful attention. The first is how we got into the mess in the first place. And the second is why, since it was evident almost from the start that the effort could not be successful, we persisted in it for more than a decade.

Well, in each case, the reasons were complex; I do not want to oversimplify a complicated situation. But I might just say this: in the reasons why we got ourselves into this tangle in the first place an important part was played by the belief in Washington that the Russians, as part of their design for world domination, were bent on the military-political conquest of Asia, and that the effort of the Vietnamese Communists to establish their power in Southeast Asia was a part of this supposed "design." And essential to this scenario we had created for ourselves was the belief that Ho Chi Minh and his followers were only puppets of the Russians; and that therefore a takeover by them in Vietnam would be equivalent to a Soviet conquest. There was general disbelief in Washington that these Vietnamese Marxists could be more strongly motivated by nationalistic impulses than by their Marxist ideological views.

Both these assumptions were basically wrong. The Soviet leadership had no preconceived design for world conquest. Its psychology was primarily defensive. Moscow had little, if anything, to do with Ho Chi Minh's efforts to take power in Vietnam at that time. We know today that Soviet connections with the Communists in Southeast Asia were actually distant and rudimentary. Ho Chi Minh was indeed primarily a nationalist who, despite his Communist ideological rhetoric, would probably have been glad to keep a certain balance in his relations with the Communist world and with us, had we encouraged him to do so. Several of our best experts tried vainly to tell us this.

Let me expand a bit on this tendency of ours to insist on seeing as blind puppets of some other great power weaker or smaller factions or regimes whose relations with that great power are actually much more complicated and much less sinister than that. There seems to be a curious American tendency to search, at all times, for a single external center of evil to which all our troubles can be attributed, rather than to recognize that there might be multiple sources of resistance to our purposes and undertakings, and that these sources might be relatively independent of each other.

Let me give examples. In the patriotic emotionalism that overcame our country during the First World War, the unfortunate German kaiser came to be seen as the fountainhead of all that was bad and reprehensible in this world. And because the first thing the Russian Communists did when they seized power in 1917 was to take Russia out of the war, and because this benefited the Germans and was therefore disagreeable to us, the entire Russian Revolution had to be in some way attributed to the kaiser; many good people came to believe that Lenin and his associates were simply acting as German agents. And if we carry this inquiry down to the present day, we see the strong disinclination on the part of distinguished Americans to believe that the rulers of such countries as Nicaragua or Syria might be, despite their primitive Marxist utterances, in large measure independent political agents, acting primarily in their own interests as they see them, and not men deferring blindly to orders or ideological pressures from Moscow. Evil, in other words, must always be seen in many American eyes in the singular. Virtue, on the other hand, may be graciously allowed to appear in the plural case, it being understood, of course, that we Americans always stand at the center of it.

But let me get back to the Vietnam episode and take a glance at the second of the great questions it raises: namely, why we continued this effort for nearly two decades when it was clear to each of the successive administrations that the effort was a hopeless one. Here, the answer is no less significant.

All this was happening on the heels of the triumph of the Chinese

Communists in the Chinese civil war. And this development, let us remember, had been made the occasion for the most violent and reckless attacks on the Truman administration by a group of right-wing senators and others, generally known as the China Lobby, the charge being that the Democrats, and particularly the secretary of state, Mr. Dean Acheson, had, as the phrase then went, "lost China," and that they had done this under the influence of Communist sympathizers in their official entourage who wanted the Communists to win.

Never could there have been greater nonsense than this. The United States government had never *had* China. Not having had China, it could scarcely have lost it. The basic condition making possible the Communist takeover in that country was the weakness and corruption of the Chiang Kai-shek regime, and the tendency of that regime to lean on us instead of pulling its own socks up. And not only was the charge in itself absurd, but the political attacks launched in its name against Truman and Acheson were as vicious and irresponsible as any, I think, that American political history has to offer. These attacks were in fact closely connected with, and actually an early part of, the wave of anti-Communist hysteria that was soon to become known as McCarthyism—an episode of our public life so disgraceful that one blushes today to think about it.

I have the impression that the emotional background of that particular hysteria still awaits its historical analysis. But what I want to point out here is simply that not only the Truman administration but its Republican successor as well were so greatly intimidated by the violence of these attacks and by the extent of the response they evoked in Congress and in portions of the public that they could never bring themselves to confront them head-on, as questions of national interest and policy. The Truman administration, viewing them exclusively as partisan-political attacks, and ignoring the effect they had in distorting public opinion on foreign policy issues, tried to deflect them by professing some degree of sympathy for their premises and by appropriating to itself a certain amount of their rhetoric. The same was true of the Eisenhower administration, which even went so far as to throw to the wolves several of the best experts we had on Far Eastern matters, in the hopes of appeasing the authors of the attacks.

The results were appalling. Not only did these reckless vendettas set up traumas that have affected the American political establishment down to the present day, but they seriously distorted the understanding of a great many Americans about foreign policy, implying as they did that our policy was always the decisive mover of events everywhere in the world; that in any country of the world, including China, we had it in our power to prevent, if we only wanted to, the rise to positions of authority of people professing Marxist sympathies; and that therefore if a Communist takeover nevertheless occurred somewhere, this was always attributable to the faintheartedness or the remissness or the blindness or the lack of a suitable anti-Communist stance on the part of the American administration then in office. Because of the failure of successive administrations to challenge head-on these outrageous imputations, those administrations became themselves the attackers' victims

And so it was in Vietnam. Not only did neither administration, Truman nor Eisenhower, feel that it could afford to be seen as unwilling to make the effort to oppose a Communist takeover in Vietnam, but no administration, having once engaged itself in such an effort and having been obliged to recognize that the effort was hopeless—no administration, down to that of Richard Nixon, dared try to extract itself from the involvement at all, for fear of being pilloried by the silly charge that it had "lost Vietnam."

The failings we have been looking at were primarily those of what we might call popular diplomacy as opposed to professional diplomacy. The problems presented by these episodes could seldom be reduced to simple choices among only two or three alternatives. Like most great problems of foreign affairs, they usually involved a bewildering welter of conflicting considerations—considerations requiring, for their understanding, much historical background and much detailed study. Obviously, such complexities could not be fully taken account of in the oversimplifications to which political orators, newspaper reporters, and television announcers are almost unavoidably reduced. It is no wonder that in the face of this particular helplessness, the crude stereotype should regularly have prevailed over the sophisticated analysis, and that this stereotype should have lent itself, at every turn, to domestic-political exploitation rather than to the clarification of our international problems.

American Policy Toward Russia on the Eve of the 1984 Presidential Election

(1984)

I am sure all of you here recognize as clearly as I do the cruciality of this present moment from the standpoint of the view we take of the Soviet regime and the designing of our policy toward it. For a full ten years back, but particularly in the past five or six years, our public discourse has been racked by violent differences between two poles of opinion (which require no description) over just this question. I myself, looking back on some fifty-six years of professional involvement with this problem, have followed these debates and polemics with particular interest and sometimes, as you can imagine, with considerable agony of spirit; and I have tried to contribute usefully to them where I thought I could.

It seems to me that we are now approaching some sort of a denouement of this long battle of conflicting outlooks. Whoever wins this election is simply going to have to make an effort to overcome these divisions, to find a workable middle ground that gives some recognition to each of the opposing views, to devise a clear and simple policy that can be followed consistently over a long succession of years, and then to employ the great educational potential of the presidential office to mobilize bipartisan support behind this middle course. We cannot go on as we have been. To leave unresolved the violent conflicts that now divide our opinion on this most crucial of all our problems of foreign policy is to invite confusion and paralysis of policy in an area where we simply cannot afford it.

Remarks made at a private dinner, New York City, October 9, 1984.

It is essential from two standpoints that we achieve this middle ground. It is essential, first, from our own standpoint, because no policy toward Russia that moves too far either of the two extremes of opinion can assure the general support it requires. We have to recognize—at least, people like myself have to recognize—that there is an important segment of American opinion that is simply not prepared or inclined to accept any policy that leans too far in the direction of an effort to achieve any early intimacy or general understanding with the Soviet Union; and if the government gets too far ahead of these people in its efforts to develop intimacy and collaboration with the Soviet Union, it will provoke reactions that negate everything it was trying to accomplish. If, on the other hand, the government goes too far in the other direction of an unlimited confrontation with the Soviet regime, it will stir up the acute anxieties of millions of people who fear an intensification of the arms race and acceleration of the drift toward nuclear war. In either case, popular support for American policy becomes unbalanced.

But the achievement of an acceptable middle ground is also necessary from the standpoint of our competitors and our friends on the international scene. If one looks carefully at Soviet reactions over these recent months and years, one sees that what bothers them is not just the deterioration of relations that has taken place, but, even more, the question growing in their minds as to whether they can expect any stability at all in American policy—whether, that is, this polarization of American opinion will not continue to lead to such vacillations and zigzags and ups and downs in American policy that it becomes futile for them to try to adjust to us in any hopeful and constructive way, that there is nothing stable in our own policies on which such an effort could be based. And it is not just our Soviet opponents that are thrown off in this way. Our friends, too, who look to us to set the example of a steady and effective course of policy, are no less unsettled by it.

What this suggests to me in the way of the most desirable approach in this coming period is what I would call a low-keyed one—low-keyed both in its positive and its negative elements, an approach that accepts the obvious limitations on intimacy and understanding between two such drastically different societies and governments and does not try to force the pace, but is nevertheless so designed as to allow for a slow, cautious, but positive development of the relationship. Such a policy would permit a reasonable flow of private cultural, scientific, and intellectual exchanges, so long as these can be conducted in a serious and quiet and businesslike way, devoid of political exploitation. It would allow, assuming that reasonable security precautions have been observed, for normal, unrestricted trade (which does not mean long-term governmental credits). It would allow for, and encourage, extensive official communication between the two governments, but would avoid dramatization and attempts to put down the other party publicly. It would be designed to avoid raising either exaggerated hopes or exaggerated fears.

Now, that—the need for just such a low-keyed relationship—is the first of the two points I wanted to make. And the second is that there is no reason why it should not be possible, even within this narrow and subdued framework, to pursue and achieve understandings with the Soviet government, particularly in the crucial problems of arms control, that would greatly reduce the dangers of the present tense and jittery state of Soviet-American relations.

Consider for a moment, if you will, the condition and the situation of the Soviet leaders. As we all know, this is a group of men of whom it can only be said that they are well advanced in years. Of some twenty-three of the leading figures of the regime, ten are over seventy, another ten are between sixty and seventy; only three are under sixty, and these are all in their fifties.

This has, to me, two important connotations. First, these are, by and large, cautious and prudent men. They have to be. Such is the nature of political competition in the Soviet system that if they had not learned to tread cautiously and prudently, they would never have arrived at their present positions or have held them as long as they have. Second, they are extensively committed personally to the major policy decisions already arrived at, and cannot easily change them in any sudden or frivolous way. Add to this the built-in inertia of the vast and bloated bureaucracies over which these men preside—bureaucracies that are also highly resistant to drastic change and manned by people who know very well how to obstruct it—and you will see that this is a very ponderous and inflexible political system indeed, to which bold, imaginative, and far-reaching decisions do not come easily, particularly when they have to be initiated by elderly men who are decidedly set in their ways.

Now let us consider, in light of this background, the problems with which we know these men to be confronted—the problems that present themselves daily in one form or another.

First, there are the economic problems. Many of these have recently been well described in the press. There is the growing shortage of skilled industrial manpower. This shortage is made more serious by the continuing low rate of labor efficiency. It is rendered more serious still by the low state of labor morale: the lack of incentive; the lack of spontaneity; the indifference, the boredom, and, above all, the appalling alcoholism, which encourages absenteeism and cuts down labor productivity in many ways. And all this is, of course, connected with the disturbing demographic trends about which you have all heard: the alarming falling off, practically to the zero point, of the birthrate in the highly industrialized Russian center of the country, in contrast to the burgeoning increase in the population of the Muslim republics. Then, too, there is the perennial backwardness of Russian agriculture, with its deep roots in the general deficiencies of the collective farm system and in the many other abuses to which that sector of the Soviet economy has been subjected over the decades at the hands of doctrinaire experimentalists who know very little about agriculture and have no love or respect for it. And connected with all of the above and adding appreciably to the difficulty is the continued extremely low rate of efficiency in industrial investment.

What all this adds up to is the unmistakable fact that the Soviet economy, as developed to date, is simply not competitive with the economies of the great technologically advanced countries of other parts of the world—not only the United States and Western Europe, but even more the great arc of fantastic economic and technological growth that stretches along the eastern shores of the Eurasian landmass from Korea to Singapore. It is not that the Soviet economy is in any immediate danger of collapse or disaster; it is even growing, slowly. But it is not growing rapidly enough to overcome its backwardness with relation to the remainder of the technologically advanced world. This is becoming widely known; and given the pretensions of Soviet socialism, it presents a very serious problem indeed for the present leadership, for it undermines Soviet prestige precisely among the Marxist and pseudo-Marxist regimes and political parties of the Third World and elsewhere, among whom Moscow would particularly like to exercise leadership.

Nor are these economic and social problems the only ones these Soviet leaders have. There are the nationality problems. There is the perennial tension between the Russian center and the non-Russian nationalists situated around the periphery of that enormous country. And closely connected with this tension is the even more delicate problem of diminishing Soviet prestige and authority in the Eastern European satellite area. I regard this as potentially the most urgent and dangerous problem they face. Their hegemony in this region, while it looks strong, has worn thin—has become fragile and precarious. They have drifted into the classic dilemma of the waning colonial power—into the never-never land where problems can no longer be solved by cracking down with brute force but can also not be solved by yielding indefinitely to the forces of resistance, and where the colonial masters are thus reduced to maneuvering unhappily in the steadily narrowing margin between these two unattractive alternatives. And I think I should point out that the danger this presents for the Soviet leaders is every bit as much a danger to us as to them; because any abrupt and sudden breakdown of Soviet authority in that region would at once raise the German problem in ways that we, in the Atlantic community, are no better prepared to face than they are.

And finally, there are strong signs that these Soviet leaders are also confronting an incipient, but probably in the long run inevitable, constitutional problem centering around the uneasy relationship between the two great pillars of the Soviet power structure: the Party bureaucracy on the one hand, and the government on the other.

Now this is, as you see, a formidable bundle of internal problems these men face—enough to keep them busy from morning to night for many years, even if they had no problems of foreign policy on their hands as well. I stress this point, because these internal problems alone constitute to my mind convincing evidence that the leaders have no reason at all to wish to see Russia involved in any major armed conflict at this period in her history, and every possible reason to see such an involvement avoided. There is not one of the problems I have mentioned that could be alleviated by such a development; not one of them, in fact, that would not be dangerously aggravated by it, however the conflict might end. This would be true even if nuclear weapons were not in the picture at all—if what we were talking about were only a conventional war.

I emphasize this, because a great many people in the West, here and in Europe, have been persuaded that it is only the American nuclear potential that has restrained the Russians from launching an attack on Western Europe in these recent decades. I consider this sheer nonsense. There are many reasons why the Soviet leaders would not see such an adventure as being in their interests, not the least of them being the extreme military-political isolation in which their country finds itself at this period in history. Remember that the Soviet Union does not have a single ally among the great powers. Its only allies are secondary client states, generally resentful of their dependence on Moscow, weak and unreliable for any serious military encounter. To believe that men in this position would be panting to unleash another major war, and deterred from initiating it only by the fear that we would respond with the use of nuclear weapons—to believe this is to reveal so wild a misestimation of the condition and situation of the Soviet leadership as to suggest that what is envisaged is not a real human phenomenon at all but rather the product of someone's unrestrained imagination.

Now none of what I've been saying is meant to suggest that these Soviet leaders are going to be easy to deal with in any circumstances. But it does give us something to build on, particularly in the problems of arms control. There is no reason to suppose, given patience, consistency, and a certain amount of imagination on our part, that it is not possible to reach useful understandings with them in this area. This, to be sure, will not be accomplished merely by a resumption of negotiations at the technical-military level among people absorbed in the abstruse mathematics of potential nuclear destruction. The sterility of such an approach has been amply demonstrated. Not only must this sort of thinking be discarded, but any further such negotiations will have to be preceded and accompanied, or perhaps replaced, by a wholly different kind of communication, this time at the political level, if we are to get on with the problem at hand. But this, too, is not beyond the bounds of possibility; and it is precisely here that the background factors I have described can make themselves felt.

Beyond that, there are only those basic rules to be observed that have proved their value in dealing with the Russians over several centuries. One must recognize their way of doing business and have patience with it. One must never try to humiliate them before world opinion or before each other; and one must take pains not to frighten them. One must remember that they are basically insecure people, and can be driven by fear or concern for their prestige to do things that are not in their best interests or in ours. The externals—the appearances, that is—are often more important to them than the realities; and it sometimes pays to indulge them in that inclination where this does not affect our own interests too adversely. Above all, one must recognize, as I believe they do in their hearts, that war among advanced industrial powers is no longer an acceptable option for anybody in this age of high technology and vast destructive potential, and that other means will simply have to be found for the adjustment of those conflicts of philosophy and interest that inevitably affect the relations among great sovereign powers. Given that recognition, and the acceptance of certain elementary restraints, the problems I have been talking about are not at all insoluble.

First Things First at the Summit
(1985)

————··◦◇◦··————

As the date of the Reagan–Gorbachev meeting approaches, the world public is being increasingly assailed by high-level statements from one side or the other with a view, of course, to setting the stage for the final event. The statements forthcoming from the Soviet side have generally been greeted in Washington with expressions of scorn and disbelief, among them the charges that these statements were "not new," were "just propaganda," were designed exclusively to mislead world opinion and to sow division (particularly in NATO)—that they were inspired, in other words, solely by unworthy tactical motives, and reflected no serious interest in the mitigation of the dangers of the nuclear weapons race. It is about this reaction that a word or two of comment might be in order.

No one should underestimate the profundity of the skepticism in Mr. Gorbachev's mind concerning the sincerity of Mr. Reagan's professions of a desire to get on with the reduction and control of nuclear weaponry. This skepticism has its origins not only in the congenital tendency of the Russians to over-suspiciousness but also in a number of incidents that have marked the past three or four years and in a number of statements that have issued, evidently with the president's approval, from members of the Reagan entourage.

Given this skepticism, and given the circumstances surrounding all summit meetings, it is not surprising that the Russians should be di-

Originally published (in a different form) in the *New York Times*, November 3, 1985.

recting their statements, primarily at this stage of the game (and perhaps at Geneva as well), not to the U.S. government itself but to the world outside. The Reagan administration, for that matter, has been doing much the same thing. Beyond which, it is standard procedure for responsible statesmen, when they make public statements concerning their relations with a particular government, to shape their utterances with a view to their effect on the wider environment of opinion which the other government will have to take into account. In this sense, there is no difference between "propaganda" and statesmanship. Indeed, the great statesmen of earlier ages would have found it hard to perceive the distinction.

For this very reason, perhaps, it would be a serious mistake to suppose that just because the designing of Soviet statements was influenced by a concern for their tactical effect, they are not also the reflection of serious strategic considerations and attitudes. The two are not necessarily incompatible. All those who have given close attention to Mr. Gorbachev's internal pronouncements and personnel dispositions will have recognized that he has very serious reasons for desiring a moderation of both the dangers and the expense of the weapons race, nuclear and conventional. His principal purpose as a political leader will plainly be to find means of overcoming the various aspects of backwardness and uncompetitiveness that have hampered the Soviet system ever since Stalin's day and have damaged so much of Soviet prestige in the rest of the world. This is a task that demands concentration on domestic affairs and a shift in priorities in the allotment of Russia's limited resources—a shift away from expensive international political and military involvements and into the field of internal investment. So compelling is this requirement that it ought to be possible for our government to take advantage of it in the interests of a diminution of the military competition. Not only should this be possible, it would in fact be tragic in uttermost degree if Washington failed to make the effort; for one does not know whether the same opportunity will ever present itself again.

The meeting at Geneva is, of course, not where the highly complex problems of the weapons race are going to be faced and solved in detail. But it may have a decisive effect on the direction in which the future efforts to solve these problems will run, and on the prospects for their success. For this reason, it will be a great pity—indeed, more than a pity—if at Geneva the consideration of the weapons race is crowded out by wrangling over human rights issues and over the rights and wrongs of our respective involvements in Third World places and situations. Not only is the arms question of great—indeed of central—importance, but it represents, despite all the difficulty it presents, the more hopeful line of effort. Such are the variations in the form and intensity of centralization or decentralization of political power in the 150-odd political entities across the globe that they offer no firm lines of differentiation between despotism and self-government. The president will have a hard time making a plausible division of this confused spectrum into the sheep of "democracy" and the goats of tyranny. And there is no early victory to be won here in any case, for the partisans of what is considered to be democratic freedom. Better, surely, to concentrate on bringing the atom under control, and thereby keep civilized life as we now know it physically intact, with all its faults and blemishes, and to leave the cause of human freedom to the graces of a gentle and gradual historical evolution, which is in fact the only process by which lasting beneficial changes can be realized.

Of course, the Geneva discussions should not be limited to the problems of the arms race. Other aspects of the Soviet-American relationship, particularly the positive ones where possibilities of collaboration actually exist, should receive serious attention. But to these the questions of the form or the internal practices of government do not belong; rather the contrary.

If people in Washington, instead of crying out in alarm every time the Russians say anything at all, can be attentive to the hopeful implications their statements occasionally contain, and if then they can bear in mind the priority that the effort to avoid nuclear catastrophe obviously deserves, the Geneva summit, while not the culmination of the effort, may yet be one of the great steps along the road.

Containment: Then and Now
(1985)

————·◦∞◦·————

The word "containment" was, of course, not new in the year 1946. What was new, perhaps, was its use with respect to the Soviet Union and Soviet-American relations. What brought it to public attention in this connection was, as many know, its use in an article that appeared in 1947 in the magazine *Foreign Affairs* under the title "The Sources of Soviet Conduct," signed with what was supposed to have been an anonymous "X." This piece was not originally written for publication; it was written privately for our first secretary of defense, James Forrestal, who had sent me a paper on Communism and asked me to comment on it. It was written in December 1946 in the National War College, where I was then serving as a deputy commandant "for foreign affairs." To understand the meaning of "containment" as mentioned in that article, one must try to envisage the situation that existed in that month of December 1946.

The Second World War was only a year and some months in the past. Our armed forces were still in the process of demobilization; so, too, though to a smaller extent (because they proposed to retain a much larger peacetime military establishment than we did) were those of the Soviet Union. In no way did the Soviet Union appear, at that moment, as a military threat to this country. Russia was then utterly exhausted by the exertions and sacrifices of the recent war. Something like 25 million of its people had been killed. The physical destruction

Based on a talk given at a conference on containment at the National Defense University, November 6, 1985.

had been appalling. In a large portion of the territory of European Russia, the devastation had to be seen to be believed. Reconstruction alone was obviously going to take several years. The need for peace, and the thirst for peace, among the Russian people was overwhelming. To have remobilized the Soviet armed forces at that time for another war effort, and particularly an aggressive one, would have been unthinkable. Russia had then no navy to speak of, and virtually no strategic air force. She had never tested a nuclear weapon. It was uncertain when she would test one, and it was even more uncertain when, or whether, she would ever develop the means of long-range delivery of nuclear warheads. We had ourselves not yet developed such delivery systems.

In these circumstances, there was simply no way that Russia could appear as a military threat. It is true that even then she was credited by some with the capability of overrunning Western Europe with her remaining forces if she wanted to. But I myself regarded those calculations as exaggerated, and was convinced that there was little danger of anything of that sort. So when I used the word "containment" with respect to that country in 1946, what I had in mind was not at all the averting of the sort of military threat people are talking about today.

What I *did* think I saw—and what explained the use of that term— was what I might call an ideological-political threat. Great parts of the Northern Hemisphere, notably Western Europe and Japan, had just then been seriously destabilized, socially, spiritually, and politically, by the experiences of the recent war. Their populations were dazed, shell-shocked, uncertain of themselves, fearful of the future, highly vulnerable to the pressures and enticements of Communist minorities in their midst. The world Communist movement was at that time a unified, disciplined movement, under the total control of the Stalin regime in Moscow. Not only that, but the Soviet Union had emerged from the war with great prestige for its immense and successful war effort. The Kremlin was, for this and other reasons, in a position to manipulate these foreign Communist parties effectively in its own interests.

As for the intentions of the Stalin regime toward ourselves: I had no illusions. I had already served three tours of duty in Stalin's Russia—had in fact just come home from the last of these tours when I began at the War College. I had nothing but suspicion for the attitude of the Stalin regime toward us or the other recent Western allies. Stalin and the men around him were far worse—more sinister, more cruel, more devious, more cynically contemptuous of us—than anything we face today. I felt that if Moscow should be successful in taking over any of those major Western countries, or Japan, by ideological-political intrigue and penetration, this would be a defeat for us and a blow to our national security, fully as serious as would have been a German victory in the war that had just ended.

One must also remember that during that war, and to some extent into the post-hostilities period as well, our government had tried to win the confidence and the good disposition of the Soviet government by fairly extensive concessions to Soviet demands with respect, first, to the manner in which the war was being fought, and then to the prospects for the postwar international order. We had raised no serious objection to the extension of the Soviet borders to the west. We had continued to extend military aid to the Soviet Union even when its troops were overrunning most of the rest of Eastern Europe. We had complacently allowed Soviet forces to take Prague and Berlin and surrounding areas even when there was a possibility that we could have, if we had wanted to, arrived there just as soon as they did. They were refusing to give us even a look-in at their zone of occupation in Germany but were nevertheless demanding a voice in the administration and reconstruction of the Ruhr industrial region in West Germany. Now there seemed to be a danger that Communist parties subservient to Moscow might seize power in certain of the major Western European countries, notably Italy and France, and possibly in Japan. And what was meant by "containing Communism" in the article in question was simply this: "Don't make any more unnecessary concessions to these people. Make it clear to them that they are not going to be allowed to establish any dominant influence in Western Europe and in Japan if there is anything we can do to prevent it. When we have stabilized the situation in this way, then perhaps we will be able to talk with them about some sort of a general political settlement and military disengagement in Europe and in the Far East—not before."

One may wish to compare that situation with the one we face today, and to take account of the full dimensions of the contrast between them. For the situation we were confronting in 1946 is almost exactly the reverse of the situation today.

One saw at that time, as just stated, an ideological-political threat emenating from Moscow. No comparable threat is visible at the present time. The Leninist-Stalinist ideology has almost totally lost appeal everywhere outside the Soviet orbit, and partially within that orbit as well. The situation in Western Europe and Japan has now been stabilized beyond anything we at that time were even able to foresee. Whatever other dangers may today confront those societies, a takeover, politically, by their respective Communist parties is simply not in the cards.

One may say: yes, but look at Soviet positions in such places as Ethiopia or Angola. Fair enough. Let us look at them, but not exaggerate them. Aside from the fact that these places are mostly remote from our own defensive interests, what are the Russians doing there? With the exception of Afghanistan, where their involvement goes much further, they are mainly engaged in selling arms and sending military advisers—procedures not too different from many of our own. Can they translate those operations into ideological enthusiasm or political loyalty on the part of the recipient Third World regimes? The answer, surely, is: no more than we can. These governments will take what they can get from Moscow, take it cynically and without gratitude, as they do from us. And they will pay lip service to a political affinity with Moscow precisely as long as it suits their interest to do so and not a moment longer. Where the Russians acquire bases or other substantial military facilities, this has, of course, greater military significance. But it is not an *ideological* threat.

On the other hand, whereas in 1946 the military aspect of our relationship to the Soviet Union hardly seemed to come into question at all, today that aspect is of prime importance. But here, lest the reader be left with a misunderstanding, a caveat must be voiced.

When I say that this military factor is now of prime importance, this is not because I see the Soviet Union as threatening us or our allies with armed force. It is entirely clear to me that Soviet leaders do not want a war with us and are not planning to initiate one. In particular, I have never believed that they saw it as in their interests to overrun Western Europe militarily, or that they would have launched an attack on that region in these postwar decades even if the so-called nuclear deterrent had not existed. But the sheer size of their armed force establishment is, of course, a disquieting factor for many of our allies. And, more important still, I see the weapons race in which we and they are now involved as a serious threat in its own right, not because of aggressive intentions on either side but because of the compulsions, the suspicions, the anxieties such a competition engenders, and because of the very serious dangers it carries with it of unintended complications—by error, by computer failure, by misread signals, or by mischief deliberately perpetrated by third parties.

So there is now indeed a military aspect to the problem of containment as there was not in 1946; but what most needs to be contained is not so much the Soviet Union as the weapons race itself. And this danger does not even arise primarily from political causes. One must remember that while there are indeed serious political disagreements between the two countries, there is no political issue outstanding between them that could conceivably be worth a Soviet-American war or that could be solved, for that matter, by any great military conflict.

Nor is the weapons race all there is in this imperfect world that needs to be contained. There are many other sources of instability and trouble. There are local danger spots scattered about in the Third World. There is the dreadful situation in South Africa. There is the grim phenomenon of a rise in several parts of the world of a fanatical and wildly destructive religious fundamentalism, and there is the terrorism in which that sort of fundamentalism so often expresses itself. There is the worldwide environmental crisis; the rapid depletion of the world's nonrenewable energy resources; the steady pollution of its atmosphere and its waters. There is the general deterioration of the environment as a support system for civilized living.

And finally, there is much in our own life, here in this country, that needs early containment. It could in fact be said that the first thing we Americans need to learn to contain is, in some ways, ourselves: our own environmental destructiveness; our tendency to live beyond our means and to borrow ourselves into disaster; our apparent inability to reduce a devastating budgetary deficit; our comparable inability to control the immigration into our midst of great masses of people of wholly different cultural and political traditions.

In short, if we are going to talk about containment in the context of 1985, then we can no longer apply that term to the Soviet Union alone, and particularly not to a view of the Soviet Union drawn too extensively from the image of the Stalin era or, in some instances, from the even more misleading image of our Nazi opponents in the last great war. If we are going to relate containment to the Soviet Union of today, we are going to have to learn to take as the basis for our calculations a much more penetrating and sophisticated view of that particular country than the one that has become imbedded in much of our public rhetoric. But beyond that, we are going to have to recognize that a large proportion of the sources of our troubles and dangers lies outside the Soviet challenge, such as it is, and some of it even within ourselves. And for this reason, we are going to have to develop a wider concept of what containment means, a concept more closely linked to the totality of the problems of Western civilization at this juncture in world history—a concept, in other words, more responsive to the problems of our own time—than the one presented in the so-called "X" article in 1946.

Foreword to The Pathology of Power, *by* Norman Cousins

(1987)

----·•◦◦◦•·----

When the first nuclear weapon was exploded over Hiroshima, and in the years immediately following, a number of weighty and impressive voices could be heard, pointing out that the emergence of destructive power of this magnitude invalidated the greater part of traditional thinking about the relationship of war to national policy and calling for the adoption of a new mindset—a new way of looking at things, one based on the recognition that war was no longer a rational option for great industrial powers and that other means would have to be found to resolve the conflicts of interest that would always be bound to arise among them.

In some instances, these demands came from the great intellects of the day. Those of Albert Einstein and Bertrand Russell are well-known and have been frequently republished. Less well-known are the views of certain of the military leaders, particularly those mentioned in this volume—Generals Douglas MacArthur and Dwight Eisenhower (others, notably Lord Mountbatten, might also have been cited). All of these men perceived the suicidal quality of the nuclear weapon and the danger in allowing it to become the basis of defense postures and the object of international competition. All of them spoke with a great sense of urgency. All went to their death hoping, surely, that their warnings would not fall on deaf ears and that a new generation of leaders would recognize that we were all living in a world of new politi-

New York: W.W. Norton, 1987.

cal-strategic realities and would draw the necessary conclusions.

Unfortunately, this has not happened. For thirty years past, these warning voices have been disregarded in every conceivable respect. There has been no new mindset. There has been no recognition of the revolutionary uniqueness of the weapons of mass destruction—no recognition of their sterility as weapons, no recognition of the dangers of their unlimited development. On the contrary, the nuclear explosive has come to be treated as just another weapon, vastly superior to others, of course, in the capacity for indiscriminate destruction, but subject to the same rules and conventions that had governed conventional weaponry and its uses in past ages. The suicidal quality of these devices has been ignored. They have been made subject to the primitive assumption that the value of a weapon is simply proportionate to its destructiveness, and that the more you have of any weapon, in relation to the similar holdings of your adversary, the more secure you are. Coherent political purpose has been lost sight of behind the calculations of sheer destructibility and the fascination of numbers.

And all those psychological distortions that had been allowed to accompany armed conflict in the prenuclear age have come to be applied to the competition in the development of this form of weaponry: the same exaggerations of enemy iniquity and capabilities, the same excesses of chauvinistic self-righteousness, the same thirst for unconditional surrender and total victory, the same mad assumptions that out of vast destruction and suffering there could come something called "victory," and that this would ensure the emergence of a better world. People have gone on, in other words, behaving as though this were 1916 instead of 1986 and as though the nuclear weapon were only some new species of artillery. This was, of course, precisely what the Einsteins and the Eisenhowers had tried to warn about.

We can see today the result of this rejection. After the passage of some thirty years, the security of this country has not been improved; never, in fact, was it more endangered than it is now. The nuclear arsenals have grown to absurd and monstrous dimensions—far beyond anything that even the most sanguine military logic could justify. Their very numbers have made them a potential danger to the world environment. The proliferation of nuclear weaponry into other hands, some of them far less responsible than those of the original nuclear powers, goes on apace, as it was bound to do, so long as the superpowers placed no restrictions upon their own cultivation of it. And to this whole process—the nightmarish growth of the arsenals and the dangerous proliferation of nuclear capability—there is no limit in sight. So far as we, the civilian laymen, are allowed to see, the process is supposed to continue indefinitely, into a future where every sort of outcome is conceivable except a happy one—a future so remote as to reach into a time when those who are now promoting it will be long gone; and there can be no telling in whose hands this awesome responsibility will then rest.

And it is not only the external effects of this dreadful progression that we must take account of. Hand in hand with it has gone, and must continue to go, a serious weakening of American society and an impairment of American democracy. It has led to the emergence of a military-industrial establishment of such dimensions that it has become the greatest single factor in our economic life, overshadowing the peaceful and constructive elements of the American economy and in some respects encroaching on them and replacing them. It is an establishment largely outside the perimeter of democratic control, as Eisenhower so clearly perceived it might become. Constituting as it now does the greatest single purchaser in the American market, with all the power that implies, anchored in long-term contractual obligations that defy the normal annual budgetary discretion of Congress, its tentacles now reaching into almost every congressional district and distorting the electoral situations wherever they reach, this military-industrial establishment has become a veritable addiction of American society— an addiction from which American society could no longer free itself without the most severe withdrawal pains. Were the Soviet Union to sink tomorrow under the waters of the ocean, the American military-industrial complex would have to remain, substantially unchanged, until some other adversary could be invented. Anything else would be an unacceptable shock to the American economy. The truth of the matter is that the greater portion of American society that lies outside the defense establishment is rapidly falling into a position resembling that of much of civilian society in northern Europe toward the end of the Thirty Years' War: reduced to trailing behind the armies as camp followers, hoping to live off the remnants from the military stores and kitchens.

So vast a peacetime defense establishment has demanded, of course, as a counterpart indispensable to its rationale, an adversary proportionate to it—proportionate in its alleged iniquity, in the presumed intensity of its hostility, and in the immensity of the armed power with which it was supposed to confront us. This counterpart was found in the form of the Soviet Union; and the forbidding image has been assiduously built up and nurtured, as it had to be, over the course of several decades. It was not that the reality of Soviet power provided no sustenance at all for the development of this image. The Soviet Union did indeed present problems for the statesmen of the West. The apparently inordinate size of its armed forces; its postwar position astride the eastern half of the continent; its fading but still perceptible world-revolutionary rhetoric; the forbidding aspect of the Stalin regime, surviving down to 1953; its obsession with secrecy; the anxious isolation of its people from normal contact with the outside world; and the persistent presence within its political-military establishment of an element no less militarized in its thinking and no less inclined to think in terms of some ultimate military showdown than some of those who confronted it on our side of the line: all these were real phenomena. What was wrong was not that they should be taken into account, as they had to be. What was wrong was that they became subject, at the hands of those who cultivated this image, to a regime of oversimplification, exaggeration, misinterpretation, and propagandistic distortion that had the cumulative effect of turning a serious but not unmanageable problem into what appeared to many people to be a hopeless, insoluble one—insoluble, that is, other than by some sort of apocalyptic military denouement.

So assiduously was this image cultivated that it became with the years part of the stock-in-trade of the electronic media, subject to all their propensities for overdramatization and vulgarization, pounded into the public mind day after day by one visual impression after the other, until the wicked Russian became the common villain of the spy story and the common nightmare of children. Behind this curtain of self-delusion and self-hypnosis, the real image of Soviet society retired farther and farther into the shadows, remote from the vision and the attention of the wider reaches of American society. It was thus that a discriminating relationship between two of the world's greatest societies also fell victim to those same tendencies of thought—that same militarization, that same ignoring of the realities of the time, that same inability to relate military considerations realistically to the other concerns of our society—against which the warnings had been uttered.

This great distortion of vision was, of course, never the entire picture. The attitudes it produced have been flanked at every turn by other ones—more critically thoughtful, more penetrating and realistic. But these two tendencies, most unfortunately, have never been reconciled in official American thinking. They have been allowed to exist side by side; and such is the nature of the American political system that it has proved politically expedient for established authority not to try to reconcile them, for this would have implied an intellectual responsibility too heavy for most of those in political life. It was easier to try to appease both bodies of thought—one out of the right-hand pocket, the other out of the left-hand—while trying to let each think it was having its way. The result has been an attitude toward the Soviet Union that can only be described as half war and half peace. Summit meetings, the facade of normal diplomatic relations, cultural and scientific exchange programs, a little trade (where demanded by some domestic-political lobby), and a modicum of peaceful tourism: these have been permitted to proceed with at least a pretense of normality. But back of them all the machinery of the great military establishment and, above all, of the related intelligence and internal security systems has ground along in its own ponderous, relentless way, largely remote from political observation or control, basing itself daily on working assumptions that could not have been much different had one known with a certainty that all-out war with the Soviet Union was both inevitable and impending. To which fact must be added the recognition, so amply supported by historical example, that believing a war to be inevitable, and acting accordingly, is the best way to make it so.

The conclusion to which all this points is one of great gravity, but it is inescapable. The problem posed by the discovery and development of nuclear weaponry has proved to be too large for the normal political system of this country. The qualities of mind required—one cannot say for its solution (that goes too far) but for coping with it in ways that do not spell utter disaster—are not encouraged by active participation in the political process. Intellectual leadership as opposed to the catering to mass reaction; the long view as opposed to the short one; the readiness to accept immediate hardship and to take the immediate risks with a view to averting much greater risks in the distant future; the insistence on tackling the schizophrenia that now prevails in American attitudes toward Russia and working out an attitude that will have both soundness and consistency—these things are not for the legislator with another election looming imminently before him; they are not for the official caught up in the vast networks of modern governmental bureaucracies and subservient to the primitive assumptions on which these latter usually operate; they are not for the political leader daily measuring his popularity by the reactions of the television screens and the opinion polls, harried hourly by a thousand different duties and problems of his office, and beholden in countless ways to the impressive posture and the effective slogan for the success of his effort.

One can conceive of help coming, in these circumstances, only from some sort of a permanent outside body advisory to the president, a body of men and women (and not too many of them) made wise by natural aptitude and long experience in the ways of the world, people wholly disengaged (at least at this stage of their careers) from the political process, people enjoying sufficient public respect and confidence so that their views would carry weight—a body of senior statesmen, in short, capable of supplying the president with precisely that sort of thoughtful and measured advice in the great matters of war and peace that he is unlikely to get from the men normally around him in the turmoil of his office.

One must hope that there will at long last be some movement in that direction, as thoughtful people have repeatedly urged. But it would be unrealistic to suppose that anything of this sort could mature in the near future. In the meantime, we will remain dependent on the lonely individual thinker who has come to possess, by one means or another, the delicate but not wholly trivial power of the pen. To this category of persons Norman Cousins eminently belongs, as he has belonged for so many years; and it is this ineffable power, frail and yet not always so frail, that his book possesses.

When Mr. Cousins invited me to introduce this book, he observed that I might not be in agreement with all of it. This is true; but the areas of disagreement are secondary, the areas of agreement—decisive. It reflects the wisdom of an honest and courageous spirit, accumulated over many years of involvement with public affairs as editor, educator, and commentator. Were there to be a body of senior statesmen such as the one I have suggested, Mr. Cousins would be a charter member. For this, and for the depth of the concern that he shares with so many other thoughtful people, his book deserves the attention of the serious reader.

Threat Lies in Arms Race, Not Force

(1985)

To the Editor:

A November 15 news story on an academic symposium devoted to the history and present significance of the concept of "containment," conveyed the impression that in my contribution to the discussion I had said there was "a threat of Soviet military might" and that this was "of prime importance."

I did indeed say "the military aspect of our relationship to the Soviet Union . . . is of course of prime importance." But I did not say it was in "Soviet military might" that I saw the threat. Had the reporter listened further, he would have heard the following, showing that what I had in mind was close to the opposite of what he inferred:

"When I say that this military factor is now of prime importance, I do so not because I see the Soviet Union as threatening us or our allies with armed force. . . . I recognize that the sheer size of their armed force establishment is a disquieting factor for many of our allies. And, more important still, I see the weapons race in which we and they are now involved as a serious threat in its own right, not because of aggressive intentions on either side but because of the compulsions, the suspicions, the anxieties such a competition engenders, and because of the very serious dangers it carries with it of unintended complications— by error, by computer failure, by misread signals, or by mischief deliberately perpetrated by third parties.

Letter to the Editor, *New York Times*, December 8, 1985.

123

"For all these reasons . . . there is now indeed a military aspect to the problem of containment . . . ; but what most needs to be contained . . . is not so much the Soviet Union as the weapons race itself."

Princeton, N.J.
November 25, 1985

Part Three

COLD WAR,
ITS DECLINE
AND FALL

American Democracy and Foreign Policy
(1984)

·✦·

A s I pointed out when I spoke here last week, the lectures I gave
in 1950 at the University of Chicago were critical in nature; and
so was the talk I gave here last week. I attempted to identify the relationship between challenge and response in American diplomacy; and
where the response did not seem to measure up to the challenge, I tried
to spot the weaknesses of analysis or concept that led to the failure. So
full of criticisms of American diplomacy was the first of these lectures
that some of you must be asking: did we ever do anything right?

The answer is, of course we did. We did many things right. The
Marshall Plan was a great act of statesmanship. The generally non-
punitive treatment of our defeated enemies in the wake of the two
world wars stands to our credit. There were, I am sure, many cases of
reasonably successful economic aid programs. There were dozens of
cases, too, where we intervened helpfully and generously in the case
of unexpected misfortune or catastrophe elsewhere in the world: earth-
quakes, floods, famines, what you will. An example was the great
famine relief program we conducted in Russia in 1920 and 1921. And
I remember my pride, as American ambassador in Yugoslavia in 1963,
in the speed and efficiency with which an American field hospital, sent
by our army in Germany, moved down to help the victims of the
Skopje earthquake. Then, too, there were a great many stupid things
we could have done but wisely refrained from doing; and for that, also,

Second lecture delivered at Grinnell College, Grinnell, Iowa, February 1, 1984.

the respective American statesmen deserve high praise, although they seldom receive it.

So our record is far from being only one of failures. On balance, we have little to be ashamed about. The rest of the world can be thankful that if over the last three centuries a great world power had to arise on this magnificent North American territory (and the rise of *some* such power could not have been avoided), it was one as peaceably and generously minded as this one. The offenses we have offered to our world environment since the establishment of our independence have arisen as a rule not from any desire on our part to bring injury to others or to establish power over them, but from our attempts to strike noble postures and to impress ourselves. But just as it does the human individual more good to reflect upon his failings than upon his virtues, I think the national society, too, has more to learn from its failures than from its successes. The contemplation of the failures induces humility; and that is something we Americans could well use more of. The contemplation of the successes leads only too easily to the pride that goes before a fall. So I shall continue, appealing to your patience, to talk about one or two further places where our thinking was at fault and where we made mistakes.

I have talked, both at Chicago and here, mostly about our policies with relation to the non-European world. But there was a great difference between the situations I discussed back in 1950—the ones that existed before the Second World War—and those I mentioned here last week. Although jingoism and a yearning for dramatic military exploits played a part in the Spanish-American War, most of the faults to which I drew attention in the Chicago lectures were of the sort I just mentioned: a certain moralistic and legalistic posturing on our part—a desire to appear, particularly to ourselves, as wiser and more noble than we really were. In the case of the two *postwar* involvements of Korea and Vietnam, on the other hand, something much more serious was involved: namely, the impression we had that we were confronted, for the first time since the birth of this republic, with a great, terrible, remorseless enemy, dedicated to our undoing, and holding in his hands the wherewithal to do us immense damage, even right here at home. This brought out fears, resentments, reactions, overreactions, even temptations on our part, in comparison with which our rather childish posturings and pretensions of earlier decades look innocent and naive.

And this brings me, of course, to the great and very real challenge of this post–World War II period, a challenge consisting of the fact that when that war came to an end, all the traditional great powers of the modern age now exhausted and weakened, had fallen into a secondary military status—all, that is, but two, the Soviet Union and the United States. And whereas these two powers had previously been widely separated from each other, in a military sense, by the geographic interposition of other great powers, the outcome of the Second World War eliminated this separation and placed their respective military forces in close proximity to each other in the center of Europe and in the northern Pacific. There was now nothing between them, as there had been in earlier decades, to absorb the impact of any serious political differences they might have. To this there was added the unprecedented, and immensely disorienting, factor of the introduction into national arsenals of nuclear weaponry—a form of weaponry that, together with its delivery systems, made each of these so-called superpowers capable of reaching the homeland of the other and of inflicting upon it damages of an unpredictable but obviously horrendous order, so that each of these two powers became in effect hostage to the other. And the challenge this offered to American statesmanship was, then: how to respond to this utterly new and unheard-of challenge for which there was no precedent, either in our own history or in that of any other country?

I think it not surprising, in these circumstances, that mistakes were made. They were made, of course, not just on our side but on the Soviet side as well. The challenge was no less unusual, no less bewildering, for the Russians than it was for ourselves. And in dwelling on our own mistakes, I would not wish you to think that I am oblivious to those made by people in Moscow. I would also not wish it to be thought that I considered that our response consisted of nothing *but* mistakes. Here, too, no doubt, many necessary, well-pondered, and constructive things were done.

But it is my belief that there *were* mistakes, and far-reaching ones at that. One category of these mistakes consists of those I pointed to in the first of these lectures. These were the mistakes involved in attributing to the Soviet leadership aims and intentions it did not really have; in jumping to the conclusion that the Soviet leaders were just like Hitler and his associates, that they were animated by the same lusts for military conquest, that they had the same sort of timetables for external military aggression, and that they could be met and dealt with effectively only in the same way that Hitler had been.

This view was given sustenance, of course, by the fact that at the end of the Second World War the Russians did not demobilize their armed forces to anything resembling the degree we did. They left a ground force establishment in Eastern and Central Europe far greater than anything that confronted them on the Western side. They offended everybody, and justly so, by behaving with great ruthlessness and brutality toward the peoples of the Eastern and Central European countries they occupied. They were wily and secretive in their dealings with us. And it was clear that they hoped, by various devices of political influence and authority, to extend their dominant influence, if not their direct power, as far as they could into Western Europe—and this at the expense of the freedoms of the Western European peoples as well. The period I am speaking about was, after all, still the Stalin era.

All these things were evidence, indeed, of no friendly feelings toward ourselves on the part of the men in the Kremlin. They were evidence that we and the Western Europeans had on our hands a great and serious competitor for influence, and indeed for power, over the European continent and other parts of the world. But they were not proof that the Russians wanted another war. They were not proof that it was by the launching of their armed forces on some all-out attack against Western Europe or Japan that the Soviet leaders intended to extend their influence. Yet these were the conclusions we jumped to; and the consequences have been far-reaching.

The second of our great postwar mistakes had to do with embracing the nuclear weapon as the mainstay of our military posture, and the faith we placed in it to assure our military and political ascendancy in this postwar era. We made the primitive error of supposing that the effectiveness of a weapon was directly proportionate to its destructiveness—destructiveness not just against an enemy's armed forces but against its population and its civilian economy as well. We forgot that the aim of war is, or should be, to gain one's points with the minimum, not the maximum, of general destruction, and that a proper weapon must be not only destructive but discriminating. Above all, we neglected to consider the strong evidence that the nuclear weapon could not be, in the long run, anything other than a suicidal one, partly because of its very destructiveness, together with the virtual certainty that others would develop it, but also because of its probable environmental effects. And by this commitment to a weapon that was at the same time suicidal, unsuitable to any rational military purpose, and environmentally extremely pernicious, we incurred, in my opinion, a heavy share of the blame for leading large parts of the international community into the most dangerous and fateful weapons race the world has ever known.

It is from these two great mistakes that there has flowed, as I see it, the extreme militarization not only of our thought but of our lives that has become the mark of this postwar age. And this is a militarization that has had profound effects not just on our foreign policies but also on our own society. It has led to what I and many others have come to see as a serious distortion of our national economy. We have been obliged to habituate ourselves to the expenditure annually of a great portion of our national income for what are essentially negative and sterile purposes—the production of armaments, the export of armaments, and the maintenance of a vast armed force establishment— purposes that add nothing to the real productive capacity of our economy, and only deprive us every year of billions of dollars that might otherwise have gone into productive investment.

And this habit—the habit of pouring so great a part of our gross national product year after year into sterile and socially negative forms of production—has now risen to the status of what I have ventured to call a genuine national addiction. We could not now break ourselves of the habit without the most serious of withdrawal symptoms. Millions of people, in addition to those other millions who are in uniform, have become accustomed to deriving their livelihood from the military-industrial complex. Thousands of firms have become dependent on it, not to mention labor unions and communities. It is the main source of our highly destabilizing budgetary deficit. An elaborate and most unhealthy bond has been created between those who manufacture and sell the armaments and those in Washington who buy them. We have created immense vested interests in the maintenance of a huge armed establishment in time of peace and in the export of great quantities of arms to other peoples—great vested interests, in other words, in the Cold War. We have made ourselves dependent on this invidious national practice; so much so that it may fairly be said that if we did not have the Russians and their alleged iniquities to serve as a rationalization for it, we would have to invent some adversary to take their place—which would be hard to do.

And the problem is made worse by the unnecessary wastefulness of this entire exercise, by the interservice rivalries that cause so much duplication of effort, by the double standard we apply to costs and results in relation to the military economy and the civilian, by the lack of any coherent relationship between the criteria Congress applies to military expenditures and those it applies to nonmilitary ones. It sometimes seems to me that those of us not involved in this great military-industrial enterprise are in danger of becoming, in the figurative sense, a nation of camp followers, like the pathetic civilian stragglers who trailed along behind the European armies of earlier centuries in the hopes of picking up remnants from the relative abundance of the military resources of food and clothing over which the armies disposed.

And when this phenomenon of the military-industrial complex distorts our lives internally, the result, again, is an adverse effect on our foreign policy. So great a military economy, intensified by the interservice rivalries and by the fierce competition of the armed services for congressional appropriations, requires constant rationalization; and what more inviting form could this rationalization take than the overrepresentation of the military potential of the supposed adversary, designed to heighten the suspicion of that adversary and to arouse antagonism in our population? The figures on supposed Soviet military expenditures released in recent years from certain quarters within our government have been among the most shamelessly tendentious and misleading statistical manipulations I can recall seeing.

And the worst feature of all this is that it confuses and obscures the real dimensions of the external political challenge. It becomes impossible to know how much of our behavior is a justifiable response to the problem the Soviet Union presents for us, and how much is the product of our own commitment to our military-industrial addiction. I say these things simply to make the point that this great militarization of our view of the Cold War is not only an external danger for the country but an internal one as well, promoting pernicious habits to which great parts of our society become almost hopelessly committed. And much of this is traceable, once again, to those two great faults of analysis to which I have drawn attention: our misunderstanding of the nature of Soviet expansionist policies and intentions; and our failure to spot the terrible blind alley into which we bring ourselves, and much of the rest of the world, when we consign the leading role in our military policy to the nuclear weapon and other weapons of mass destruction.

Let me try, then, to sum up the main conclusions to which I am carried by the observations I have put before you here.

We have seen a wide variety of faults in American diplomacy as they have revealed themselves over the entire span of the twentieth century. Up to the Second World War, they were largely the faults of a young and somewhat naive people, overtaken by the heady and disorienting forces of modern nationalism, coupled with the unsettling consciousness of our own growing strength, which was rapidly elevating us into the ranks of the major powers. We were affected, in those years, by something of the relatively innocent erraticism of the adolescent who is becoming aware of his own strength and would like to use it, but lacks the maturity to know how best to do so.

Since this last great war, a wholly different situation has come into being. We have been put, as a nation, to different tests—obliged to deal with a wholly different order of demands, some of them involving greater and more baffling responsibilities than any statesmen anywhere have ever faced. Now, sometimes we have responded, I think, as well as any country could have to the various challenges implicit in these situations; but there are other instances where we have not. And if I look at the cases where we have not, and consider the apparent reasons for our failures, I think I see two factors that, taken together, give us the clue to the greatest of our difficulties.

The instances where we seem to have fallen down most frequently and most seriously seem all to have been ones in which military affairs were involved. Sometimes the fault lay in our analysis of situations elsewhere in the world: in our tendency to overemphasize the military factors at the expense of the political, and consequently to over-militarize our own responses. Sometimes, as in the cases of the two world wars, it has been a question of the use to be made of our own military potential—how and when to employ it, and then, when employed, how to relate it to the remainder of our national life. Sometimes, finally, as in the case of the nuclear weapon, the problem has been in our inability to think through the possible uses of weapons of mass destruction and, indeed, the uses of war itself between great industrial nations in this modern age. But in each case, it is the military factor that has tripped us up.

And when you stop to think about it, this is not surprising. We are a nation that has no traditional concepts of military strategy or of the place of military power in the structure of its national life. Except for our own Civil War, which was quite a different thing and was fought for a different purpose, our involvements with the use of armed force in the modern age have occurred primarily in the confusing and to some extent misleading experiences of the two world wars of this century. Both these wars ended in unconditional surrender, encouraging us in the mistaken view that the purpose of war was not to bring about a mutually advantageous compromise with an external adversary (now seen as totally evil and inhuman), but to destroy completely the power and the will of that adversary. In both those wars, but particularly the second, we erred again in departing increasingly from the principle, embodied in the earlier rules of warfare, that war should be waged only against the armed forces of an enemy, not against the helpless civilian population. It was by our wholehearted acceptance of the practice of waging war against civilians as well as against soldiers, and especially by our commitment to the so-called area bombings of World War II, that we were led into the terrible bewilderments we are confronting today. We are now finally being brought to recognize that to follow that practice to its logical conclusion is to destroy ourselves and probably civilization itself. We have, in other words, worked ourselves into a blind alley; and now, as we try to retreat from this dreadful trap, it is becoming apparent to us that we have no workable alternative theory of the uses of armed force to fall back on. Both of these errors— the commitment to unconditional surrender and the commitment to massive civilian destruction—have led us seriously astray.

And it is not surprising that we should have trouble relating military matters to the internal problems of our society. We have never had the tradition of maintaining standing armies in peacetime. We have never learned how to fit that practice in with the other habits and needs of our society in point of education, civic training, and manpower use. Even worse, we have not been able to find any very rational way to relate to the other processes of our society the industrial and financial effort required to maintain a great armed forces establishment in what is nominally a time of peace. No wonder, in the face of all this confusion, that our greatest mistakes in national policy seem to occur where the military factor is most prominently involved.

I wonder whether this confusion is not compounded by certain deeply ingrained features of our political system. I am thinking first of all about what I might call the domestic-political self-consciousness of the American statesman. By this I mean his tendency, when speaking or acting on matters of foreign policy, to be more concerned for the domestic-political effects of what he is saying or doing than about their actual effects on our relations with other countries. In light of this tendency, a given statement or action will be rated as a triumph in Washington if it is applauded at home in those particular domestic circles at which it is aimed, even if it is quite ineffective or even self-defeating in its external effects. When this is carried to extremes, American diplomacy tends to degenerate into a series of postures struck before the American political audience, with only secondary consideration being given to the impact of these postures on our relations with other countries.

This situation is not new. We have only to recall Tocqueville's words, written 150 years ago, to the effect that "it is in the nature of democracies to have, for the most part, the most confused or erroneous ideas on external affairs, and to decide questions of foreign policy on purely domestic considerations." Nor is this, in essence, unnatural. Every statesman everywhere has to give *some* heed to domestic opinion in the conduct of his diplomacy. But the tendency seems to be carried to greater extremes here than elsewhere. This may be partly explained by the nature of the constituency to which the American statesman sees himself as appealing. In the European parliamentary systems, the constituency is normally the parliament, because the ministry can fall from office if it loses parliamentary support. In our country, unhappily, the constituencies are more likely to consist of particularly aggressive and vociferous minorities or lobbies; and these, for some curious reason, seem more often than not to be on the militaristic and chauvinistic side, either because there is some particular nation or ethnic group abroad they want our government to support, militarily or otherwise, or because they like to wrap themselves in the national flag and beat the jingoist bell as a means of furthering their partisan-political purposes. American administrations seem to be particularly vulnerable to just this sort of intimidation, presumably because they do not want to be placed on the defensive by being charged with lack of patriotism. And the effects of this we have had occasion to note both in connection with our policies in Third World areas, such as Vietnam and Lebanon, and in connection with the problems of arms control and the relations among the great military powers.

If there is any substance to what I have been saying, then this is simply further evidence for the fact, to which many wise observers besides Tocqueville have drawn attention, that our political system is in many ways poorly designed for the conduct of the foreign policies of a great power aspiring to world leadership. I, in any case, believe this to be true; and I consider that the trend of events in these recent years has revealed deficiencies in this system that even Tocqueville could not have foreseen.

What are we going to do about it? It would be naive of us to expect, or even to hope, that these features of our governmental system are going to be corrected within our time. To try to correct them abruptly might well do more harm than good. In many respects, they represent the reverse side of the great coin of the liberties we so dearly cherish. And in this sense, I see no reason why we should be ashamed of them. If our political system with all its faults is the only way that a great mass of people such as our own, stretching from Florida to Alaska and from Maine to Hawaii and embracing individuals of the most diverse ethnic and cultural origins—if this is the only way such a mass of people can be governed without the sacrifice of their liberties, then so be it; and let us be thankful that such a possibility exists at all, even if it is not a perfect one.

But the one thing we *can* do, in the face of this situation, is to take realistic account of the unsuitability of our political system for the conduct of an ambitious and far-reaching foreign policy, and to bear its limitations in mind when we decide which involvements and responsibilities it is wise for us to accept and which would be better rejected. Obviously, a number of the responsibilities that we have already accepted, including some of the very greatest ones—NATO and our obligations to Japan, for example—represent solemn commitments of which we cannot divest ourselves at any early date. There is nothing for us to do but meet these commitments as best we can, recognizing that the peace and safety not just of our country but of much of the rest of the world as well depends on how we meet them, and trying to place them, whenever we can, above the partisan political interests every American administration is bound to have. But when it comes to the acceptance of new responsibilities, let us, at long last, try to bear in mind the limits of our national capabilities and the price we are obliged to pay for our liberties. Let us recognize that there are problems in this world that we will not be able to solve, depths into which it will not be useful or effective for us to plunge, dilemmas in other regions of the globe that will have to find their solution without our involvement.

This is not a plea for a total isolationism, such as our grandfathers and great-grandfathers cultivated. It is only a request, if I may put it that way, for a greater humility in our national outlook, for a more realistic recognition of our limitations as a body politic, and for a greater restraint than we have shown in recent decades in involving ourselves in complex situations far from our shores. And it is a plea to bear in mind that in the interaction of peoples, just as in the interactions of individuals, the power of example is far greater than the power of precept; and that the example offered to the world at this moment by the United States of America is far from being what it could be and ought to be. Let us present to the world outside our borders the face of a country that has learned to cope with crime and poverty and corruption, with drugs and pornography—let us prove ourselves capable of taking the great revolution in electronic communication in which we are all today embraced and turning it to the intellectual and spiritual elevation of our people in place of the enervation and debilitation and abuse of the intellect that television now so often inflicts upon them. Let us do these things, and others like them, and we will not need 27,000 nuclear warheads and a military budget of over $250 billion to make the influence of America felt in the world beyond our borders.

U.S.–Soviet Relations: Containment as a Prerequisite for Accommodation (1987)

M y own passage at the Policy Planning Staff in the old part of this building forty years ago has come to be connected in the public mind with the question of containment; and I am often asked where we stand with all this today. The answer is that this principle of containment, as conceived in 1946, has little to do with the problems we face today. The Soviet Union has no intention of attacking Western Europe or any other place far afield. It would be wholly incapable of even threatening Western Europe or Japan politically in the present circumstances. And as for its supposed adventurism in the Third World, I must confess that I was never able to understand what my good friends in either this administration (Reagan) or the Carter administration were talking about when they used this term. Soviet efforts to gain influence in those parts of the world, aside from being largely indistinguishable in method from our own, have seemed to me to be not a bit more ambitious, more successful, or more threatening, and certainly no more "adventurous," than the similar Soviet efforts of the 1950s, 1960s, and 1970s. Today the Soviet leadership has every reason in the world, in its own interests, to avoid anything that would destroy or undermine the stability of world relationships and thus interfere with its effort to master the immense internal problems that it faces at home. Thus the whole principle of containment, particularly

Address delivered at the fortieth-anniversary celebration of the Policy Planning Staff, Washington, D.C., May 11, 1987.

as that term was conceived when it was used by me in 1946, is almost entirely irrelevant to the problems we face today.

Now, many people seem to have difficulty understanding that the purpose of the concept of containment as put forward in the 1940s was to prepare the ground for a wider political negotiation and accommodation, designed to overcome, if only by sensible compromise, the extremely serious East-West misunderstandings that had been permitted to develop during the war and now threatened to grow into a full Cold War situation. But this, to my own great disappointment and consternation, proved to be a far more difficult problem than containment itself. There were a great many people, it appeared, who really preferred a military stand-off and a Cold War of unlimited duration to even the very effort to reach an accommodation with the Russians, because of the strain that any such effort might impose on the Western coalition. So it was; and so it has now remained for nearly forty years.

It is my impression that today—in Europe, at least—the period during which we could afford to avoid the effort to achieve a political settlement with the Russians and the various Eastern European satellites is coming to an end, or at least that the Cold War situation, based on the avoidance of negotiation along that line, is going to come under increasing strain. This is partly because the Brezhnev regime, with its greater flexibility, its greater openness, and its obvious commitment to an internal program of enormous scope and difficulty, has every reason to wish to see tensions reduced, has every reason to seek some sort of stable accommodation. It is also because the Eastern European satellite governments are gaining a wider measure of independence of policy, and are going to want to create new relationships with the countries of Western Europe.

Now here again, just as in 1947, there are many people who regard containment as an end in itself rather than as a prerequisite for negotiation; there will be, and already are, many who see NATO as an end in itself and who will continue to oppose any serious effort to come to terms with the Russians because they fear that it would put a strain on the unity of NATO. This will, I suspect, be the prevailing force of official opinion.

But I think we should beware of the assumption that this stand-off position is going to remain for long a viable option. This is partly because it seems to me to be becoming increasingly questionable whether any hopeful settlement of the problem of nuclear arms control can be arrived at otherwise than against the background of a better political understanding than exists today. But it is also partly because things are changing: a new wind is blowing from the East; a new generation is coming into power in both parts of Europe. There's going to be a demand for negotiating effort, and if we Americans do not take the lead in finding a way out of the Cold War rigidities and exploring the possibilities for an East-West political accommodation, others may begin to do so, and the course of events may be wrested from our hands.

And this consideration, I might remind you in conclusion, is exactly the same as was expressed to me by General George C. Marshall, precisely forty years ago this month, when he ordered me to set up the Policy Planning Staff and to confront the problem of European recovery. If we failed to take the leadership, others, he said, might do so; we would be thrust onto the defensive; and things might get wholly out of hand.

Well, the circumstances are, of course, entirely different today; but the situation is basically quite similar. If we are going to continue to exert any leadership in European affairs, aside from the part we play in the nuclear arms race, we are going to have to look more deeply at the trend of political developments on that continent and take some initiative of our own in the effort to weaken or dismantle the unnatural political division of Europe that has prevailed over these past forty years.

The Marshall Plan and the
Future of the West
(1987)

Let me first say what a privilege it is for me to be speaking tonight in Berlin a city in which five years of my life were spent, and much of that time in close proximity to this place where we are now meeting. It is a city I myself once loved. It is a city that, by virtue of its own geographic location and its own tragic experiences, is closer than any other city in the world to the matters I propose to talk about tonight; because what I want to do is to discuss the Marshall Plan not just as a single episode in the history of a period now four decades in the past, but also as a source of suggestions for useful progress in meeting of some of Europe's problems of the present day.

There is no need for me to recount at this time the principal historic circumstances of the Marshall Plan. But I would like, before turning to some of our contemporary problems, to remind you of the background of circumstances in light of which General Marshall's initiative of June 1947 was taken, and to tell you of certain thoughts from which it proceeded.

The crucial state of instability in which the Europe of early 1947 found itself was not of wholly recent origin. Its roots went deeper than that. Never since the First World War—never since the breakup of the Austro-Hungarian Empire—had Europe, and particularly Central Europe, enjoyed a fully stable status quo. The arrangements prevailing in Eastern and Central Europe in the period between the two wars

Address delivered at a conference to commemorate the Marshall Plan's fortieth anniversary, Berlin, June 25, 1987.

were ones with which neither Germany nor Russia, the two powers excluded from the Versailles Conference, was entirely happy and to which neither of them was fully committed. Thus the peace of those regions, and indeed of Europe as a whole, rested even as early as 1919 on uncertain foundations. But then in the early 1930s, the economic life of the continent, which had never found its full equilibrium after the war, was further and seriously disorganized by the worldwide economic crisis. On top of that, the new democratic Germany known as the Weimar Republic found its life disoriented by political extremism; and in the early 1930s, as we all recall, that Germany fell into the hands of a regime whose ambitions and undertakings were directed to everything else but European stability.

It was, therefore, upon a Europe already extensively destabilized that there were superimposed the immense physical and human strains of the Second World War. And we all have in mind the unhappy way in which that war ended: the continent split down the middle by the military operations of the final months of hostilities; the armies of the great extra-European powers encamped in uneasy proximity to each other along a line through the center of the continent; Germany herself largely destroyed, helpless and hungering; throughout the remainder of Europe, nothing but shock, bewilderment, and anxiety among exhausted, frightened, often even uprooted peoples; and finally, no agreement among the victorious powers as to the principles upon which the life of Europe was to be rebuilt. To restore economic life and to create a new and stable status quo in a continent so profoundly unsettled was, as you will readily see, no easy task.

During the brief year and a half that ensued from the end of hostilities in May 1945 to the winter of 1946–47, the European peoples did their best, though in sadly incoherent and uncoordinated ways, to get on with this task. The United Nations Organization also did what little it could. So to a limited extent, did the occupying powers in Germany and Eastern Europe.

But in the absence of any sort of agreement among those occupying powers about the future of the continent, none of this was enough. By the winter of 1947, it had become clear that the situation was desperate and was not to be improved merely by the continuation of the uncoordinated and partial efforts put forward to that point. There was a pervasive lack of confidence in the future. The European financial resources needed to create economic stability were largely in hiding and could not be brought to the surface. Political extremists here and there, not least in the great Communist parties of France and Italy, were taking advantage of the prevailing misery in ways that threatened the integrity of the traditional political institutions of those two countries. The European peoples, in short, were faced with the problem of repairing not only the effects of the earlier instability, but the damages of a vastly destructive war; and it was becoming clear that with their available resources alone, without new leadership, and without some arresting new initiative, they were simply incapable of doing so. So great was the resulting uncertainty and helplessness that it threatened to undermine for the Western powers the very meaning of the victory they, with the indispensable military help of Russia, had won on the field of battle.

When General Marshall attended the last of the meetings of the foreign ministers of the Big Three in Moscow in the spring of 1947, he perceived all this, and he instantly grasped its significance. He returned home greatly disturbed, filled with the realization that if any effective initiative was to be taken to correct this situation, it was the Americans who would have to take it. The Europeans, he recognized, could not do it alone. And, as he also realized, whatever measures might be undertaken would have to be initiated at once. There was no time to lose. "The patient," as he put it, "was sinking while the doctors deliberate." Unless action could be taken immediately, the situation might deteriorate to a point where it went wholly out of control, with consequences no one could foresee.

In the face of this situation, the general, immediately following his return from Europe, called me in and directed me to set up a Policy Planning Staff. And the first matter he desired that this staff should confront was the question of what could and should be done about Europe. He gave us not weeks but days to come up with the required recommendations. He made, at that point, no observations or suggestions of his own. The only advice he had to give me was expressed in two deeply serious and unforgettable words: avoid trivia.

Of what then followed—of our report, of the drafting of the Harvard speech, of the subsequent designing and promulgation of the Marshall Plan—others will soon be talking. But there are certain points I should like to emphasize, because they are relevant to the problems we face today.

When we in the Planning Staff first began to come to grips with the problem of Europe and tried to discuss with others some of the ideas that occurred to us and some of the approaches we thought might be adopted, we encountered a great deal of skepticism and pessimism. To every idea we put forward, weighty and often plausible objections were raised. The problem, we were told, was too great: the resources were not there; the Europeans would never consent to take the initiative; whatever help we might be able to offer would merely sink into the sands.

Our instructions from General Marshall did not permit us, of course, to listen to these pessimistic voices. We had to come up with something, and we did. But the response in Europe to the general's Harvard speech exceeded our greatest expectations. The mere knowledge that something serious was now to be undertaken, not just in individual countries but on an all-European scale, released important European resources—both financial and spiritual—before American assistance had even begun to arrive. Our principal function, it soon developed, had been to provide the impulse, and to offer a certain amount of help. The Europeans themselves, calling upon those qualities of mind and spirit that had made this continent the center of the greatest civilization the modern world had ever known, did most of the rest.

I do not need to tell you what then happened—what all this amounted to. The undertaking came to constitute a major watershed in the history of postwar Europe—the watershed between a Europe of uncertainty, doubt, hesitation, and near despair and a Europe of confidence and hope. This was the great turning point in the revival of the continent's life in the aftermath of two terrible world wars and of the painful political upheavals that had accompanied them. And it demonstrated that given the prerequisites of breadth of vision, boldness of concept, and determination to see the problem solved, great things could be done—could be done even in war-weary, sophisticated, skeptical, and in part cynical, Europe.

What was proposed in June 1947 was a plan for European recovery; and a part of General Marshall's approach was the insistence that the designing and drawing up of the plan should come from the Europeans themselves and not from the United States. It would be "neither fitting nor efficacious," the general said in his Harvard speech, for us Americans to attempt to draw up and to impose upon the Europeans a plan with the effects of which they, not we, would have to live.

And second, the approach to the Europeans was addressed, and the offer made, not just to the western portion of the continent but to Europe as a whole. Many historians, in writing about the plan in later years, have alleged that this offer was made cynically, in the hope and the confidence that it would be rejected on the Communist side. Well, there may have been persons in the American official community to whom this reproach might apply. But I can testify, as the person in whose mind this feature of the Marshall approach originated and who was obliged to insist upon it in the face of considerable opposition within the American government itself, that things were not really that way. The offer was made in good faith: had the Communist side—the governments, that is, of the Soviet Union and of the Eastern European countries—accepted it in the spirit in which it was offered, we would have been glad to sit down with their representatives and to inquire not only into their own needs for recovery, but into the manner in which they, too, might contribute to the general revival of Europe's economic vitality.

Now, both these features of the Marshall Plan are relevant to the problems we face today; but I stress the second one in particular, because it was the one point in General Marshall's offer that was not successful. The eastern countries, as you all know, did not respond favorably to that offer; and it was their refusal to respond favorably that laid the groundwork for what I believe to be Europe's greatest problem of the present epoch. This, of course, is its divided state: the tragic line of political and cultural division that runs from the Baltic to the Black Sea, which severs as though by a surgical knife the natural cohesion and integrity of European civilization, and the most vivid and tragic component of which is the ugly concrete barrier that passes within a few meters of this building where we are now meeting.

I have been tempted, as a historian, to talk about the subsequent history of this division of the continent. I would have liked to talk about how the division was deepened, about the various efforts to prevent that deepening, and, in light of the failure of those efforts, about what people have done to mitigate its worst effects. But all that belongs to the past. Our time tonight is short. What we must now concern ourselves with is not the past but the future.

Can we continue to accept with complacency the indefinite continuation of this unnatural division of the European continent? In my opinion, we cannot. The stultifying shadow this division casts upon the present life and ultimate future of Berlin alone is an argument why we should not content ourselves with it. But it is not just here that the unfortunate effects of the division are felt. Those effects project themselves all the way across the continent, cutting across natural cultural, political, and economic unities, denying to both sides a portion of the mutual fructification they have a right to expect, creating areas of misunderstanding, suspicion, and danger that ought not to exist. This division is out of accord, in particular, with the great revolution in communication that is the mark of our time—a revolution that ought to serve the uniting of cultures, not the walling off of one against the other.

I greatly welcome the measures that have been taken in recent years to mitigate some of the worst effects of this situation. I welcome the constructive agreements arrived at some time ago between the German governmental authorities in East and West for the improvement of the interaction between these two parts of Germany. I welcome the relatively relaxed and mature arrangements for cultural exchange and for movements of individuals along and across the border between Austria and Hungary. But I think that more could be done, and urgently needs to be done, along these lines. I shall try presently to tell you why.

But first let me assure you that I am well aware of the limits within which any further movement in the direction of a more closely united Europe must proceed. First of all, I am under no illusion that everything that needs to be done could be done suddenly and completely, in one fell swoop. It is clear that the generations now reaching maturity on the two sides of this dividing line have been brought up in different spirits and have been subjected to varied social and political disciplines. The effects of these differences are not trivial. They have left deep marks. Some of those marks must be expected to endure.

It is also clear to me that any further progress that might be made toward weakening this division would have to proceed under very dif-

146

ferent conditions, and within different limitations, from those that prevailed when the division first came into existence. The time is plainly not ripe today for any abandonment, or even any drastic modification, of the prevailing military alliances. This is also not the time to consider schemes for German unification or any extensive modification of the political boundaries now subsisting across the continent. Whatever might be done today to promote greater unity throughout Europe would have to be conceived and carried out within the framework of these restricting conditions.

Finally, one must also not expect that the initiative for such changes, or even the ideas from which they might spring, could come from either or both of the extra-European superpowers. In anything that might be contemplated along these lines, the interests and reactions of those superpowers would, of course, have to be consulted and considered; in part, in anything that might be done, their collaboration would be necessary. But remember: both have serious problems of their own. Both have interests in parts of the world other than Europe that are inevitably going to preempt much of their attention in the coming period. Both are immersed in what I view as a sterile and tragic long-range military rivalry—a rivalry predicted on the existence of Europe's divided conditions and not conducive to the exploration of possibilities for its removal. Just as General Marshall said in 1947 that the initiative for great changes in Europe must come from the Europeans themselves, so today it is the European countries themselves, acting not individually and in nationalistic selfishness but collectively in recognition of their community of fate, who will have to discover the paths of escape from their unfortunate divided state, if these paths are to be discovered at all.

These, then, are some of the limits within which, and within which alone, modifications of Europe's division can usefully be considered at this time. But what I am here to express tonight is my belief that even within these limits there are now coming into existence new conditions and possibilities for such modifications—possibilities that were not present forty years ago, possibilities that cry out for recognition, possibilities that, if ignored or neglected, might not present themselves again.

A new wind, after all, is blowing from the east, and not just from the east, at that. On both sides of the line, a new generation is coming to maturity and to positions of authority—a generation in whose minds the fateful fixations of the Cold War are no longer so active as they were in the minds of the people who were responsible for creating Europe's division in the first place so many years ago. This continent and the world at large now find themselves confronted with new problems that have little or nothing to do with the East-West differences—environmental problems, economic and financial problems, problems of North-South relations—problems that are not to be alleviated, and certainly not to be resolved, by the outcome of a nuclear weapons race. These problems are beginning to overshadow, in all but the most rigidly militaristic minds, the Cold War fixations of the earlier generation. The anxieties and aspirations that caused that earlier generation to split the continent often seem to the emerging generation, and rightly so, scarcely relevant to the questions in which its members are most interested. And with that loss of relevance, the rationale for Europe's division is beginning to become undermined. Demands are being raised for greater attention to the positive possibilities of international relations—for greater response, that is, to Europe's hopes and less to its fears. Surely, in light of these circumstances, one can afford to begin to think more boldly about what could be done to reunite this so tragically divided continent. And surely, one could fall back here on the truth that, to my mind, the experience of the Marshall Plan also demonstrated: namely, that when something must be done in the field of human political and economic affairs, there is always a way to do it. One need not take no for an answer.

In saying these things, I am well aware that at the heart of this entire European question, both symbolically and in reality, there lies the fate of the great city in which we find ourselves this evening. No alleviation of the division of Europe would be worth even the attention we are now giving it if it did not include at least some measure of progress toward the disappearance of that sorrowful affront to Europe's past, its present, and its hopes for the future that runs within a few meters of this building and that we know by name of the Berlin Wall.

I hope that no one in this room imagines that I am unaware of the full weight and complexity of the interests and commitments that stand in the way of the reunification of this city. I know that what are involved here are not just the interests of the Berlin population and of

the two parts of Germany, but also those of the four occupying powers. I know in what unhappy preconceptions and decisions of earlier
years and in what subsequent constitutional arrangements the claims
and the positions of the respective parties are now imbedded.

But when all this is said, we are left with the fact that the situation
we have before us and all around us in Berlin today is a wholly abnormal one, which no great urban population should be asked indefinitely to endure. The burden it imposes both upon Berlin itself and
upon the stability of Europe is all the greater for the fact that this city,
as history has shown, has the capability to be one of the great inspir-
ing cultural centers of Europe and the world. There was a time, some
sixty years ago, when it did indeed occupy just that position. I lived
here then, and I remember it. And if it is true that in neither portion
of the city has that capacity been entirely lost today, it is also true that
the city's division represents a grievous burden on the possibilities for
cultural development open to both sides and prevents each of them
from unfolding to the full the real sources of strength that it possesses.

Here, too, it seems to me that developments are moving in the direction of a weakening of the conditions that gave rise to the division
of the city in the first place. These changes do not suggest the possibility of any sudden solution. What they do suggest is the possibility
of a continued gradual relaxation of the wholly abnormal rigidities that
have so long held the city in their grasp. Some progress in this direction would seem already to have been made. More ought now to be
possible. Such progress will, of course, not be aided by violent demonstrations, by confrontational tactics, or by rhetorical demands not supported by serious negotiation. But if people on both sides will continue to exert themselves in the right direction, recognizing the
anxieties and hesitations of the other side and endeavoring to meet
them in a spirit of accommodation even when they cannot share the
ideological commitments from which they flow, then I would not despair of the sort of changes that would eventually deprive the Wall of
all justification and make possible the removal that we all desire. I am
well advanced in years; but I have not lost hope that I may yet see the
day when this city can again breathe a normal breath and resume its
place among the great cultural centers of Germany, of Europe, and of
the world.

Now: one more last thought.

Berlin is only the most dramatic manifestation of the far wider problem of Europe's division. When, many years ago, I lightheartedly used the word "containment" in a manner that attracted much attention then and later, what I had in mind was, as many of you know, not a response to a military danger (I saw in fact no such danger), but a response to what I saw as a political danger, flowing from the abnormal conditions that then prevailed in Europe. I did not expect that the need for this sort of "containment" would last forever. Last of all did it occur to me that it could serve as the rationale for a weapons race of unlimited duration and unprecedented danger. What I did hope was that it would create a species of provisional stability in Western Europe and that this stability would make possible the negotiation of a general European political settlement—a settlement that would correct the imbalances flowing from the outcome of the war and would place the continent on the path of peaceful and hopeful development. Such a settlement, needless to say, would have made unnecessary and unthinkable anything like the division of Europe that now exists.

Well—this negotiation never took place. The fact that it never took place was, I think, the greatest disappointment of my professional life. But it cannot now be helped. And if I were asked whether I thought it would or should take place today, I would have to say no. That chance was missed. The conditions that might have made it possible then no longer exist. Anything that may be done today will have to be done in a different way.

But the heart of the problem is now, as it was then, this question of Europe's division; and I wonder whether conditions are not now coming into existence that would permit a new attack. The success of any such effort would depend, of course, on how far the East was willing to come to meet us. It has already come some slight distance, and the signs would seem to indicate that it might, if we encourage it, venture further. New ideas will also be required, and we might hope that these would be even better ideas than the ones we once came up with. For we are sadder people than we were in 1947; sadder people are supposed to be wiser, and that ought to help. But if these ideas, and their reciprocation in the East, actually came into being, if our military enthusiasts would stand aside long enough to permit some constructive things to be undertaken, and if the effort were to be pursued with the same boldness of concept, the same refusal to be discouraged, and the same recognition of the need for a strong, flourishing, and reasonably united Europe that underlay the Marshall Plan, then what was a dream in the period 1947–1950 might still become the reality of 1987–1990.

This conference encourages me to hope that it will.

Is the Cold War Over?
(1989)

------··-<∞>-··------

Is the Cold War over? And if so, what does this mean for American policy toward the Soviet Union?

This is not a bad time, at the beginning of a new year and of a new administration, to stand off for a moment and to look at these questions from a longer historical perspective. It might be worth recalling, as a starter, that traditionally, in the days of the Russian Empire, Russia was never seen by Americans as an enemy of the United States—on the contrary. The tsarist autocracy, to be sure, was distasteful to most Americans as a form of government. But we felt no responsibility for it. We were prepared to take it as it was, to maintain normal relations with it, and to make the best of these relations so long as Russia posed no threat to our national security.

All this changed with the Russian Revolution in 1917. There seems to be a widespread impression in this country that the Cold War, as something signifying a state of sharp conflict and tension between the two governments, began only in 1945, after the Second World War. The impression is erroneous. Never were American relations with Russia at a lower ebb than in the first sixteen years after the Bolshevik seizure of power in 1917. Americans were deeply shocked by the violence of the revolution, by the fanaticism and cruelty of the new rulers, by the refusal of those rulers to recognize the debts and claims arising out of the recent war, and above all by the brazen world-rev-

Originally published (in a somewhat different version) in the *New York Times* Magazine, February 5, 1989.

olutionary propaganda they put out and the efforts they mounted to promote Communist seizures of power in other countries. Over all those sixteen years, as many of us can today recall, we had no official relations whatsoever with the Soviet regime—no diplomatic representation, no formal communication. Even after the exchange of diplomatic relations at the end of 1933, the relationship continued to be, over the remainder of the 1930s, a distant and troubled one. The Stalinist tyranny was, after all, not a form of government with which it was easy for anybody else to coexist. And the cynicism of Stalin's pact with Hitler at the outset of the Second World War did nothing to improve the attitudes of most Americans toward the Soviet regime.

From 1941 to 1945, when both the Soviet Union and the United States were at war with Germany, the basic antagonism of the two political systems was muted in the interests of their military collaboration against the common enemy. But this outwardly professed friendship never went very deep on either side; and no sooner were hostilities over than new and serious sources of friction began to emerge.

The war, after all, wrought fundamental changes in the entire background of the relationship. The interest in world revolution, which had long been fading in Moscow even before the war, almost totally disappeared as a feature of Soviet policy and rhetoric. But new sources of difficulty arose to replace it. The outcome of the hostilities placed the Soviet Union in military and political control of most of the eastern half of the European continent. This constituted a major displacement of the balance of power in Europe. Alone, this was bound to be disturbing for the Western allies.

But the seriousness of the change was magnified by several other factors. One was the failure of the Soviet government to match, by any extensive demobilization of its own forces in Europe, the extensive demobilizations promptly carried out there by the Western powers. Another was the cruel suppression at the hands of Soviet police and Party authorities of every trace of independent democratic government in the countries of Eastern and Central Europe the Soviet forces had overrun. On top of this, it soon became evident that the Soviet leaders were trying to take advantage of the war-shocked, exhausted, and confused state of several of the Western European peoples with a view to fastening upon them Communist minority regimes similar to those Moscow was already busy installing in the part of Europe under its authority. And finally, there was injected into all of this a new and highly confusing factor—a factor without precedent in human history, overthrowing all traditional military concepts and inflaming all military fears and ambitions: the nuclear weapon and its introduction into the arsenals of both the United States and the Soviet Union.

It was out of this witches' brew that the post–World War II phase of the Cold War emerged, as the symbolic expression of a new, highly antagonistic Soviet-American relationship. It represented at the outset a curious realization of Trotsky's famous formula "No war, no peace." Diplomatic relations were to be continued, to be sure; and the guns, including the nuclear ones, were for the moment to remain silent. But the threshold of actual hostilities was, at that time, never remote. Many people, including Stalin himself, thought it likely, if not inevitable, that this threshold would soon be passed. On both sides, great military establishments began to be trained and taught to think as though war, or some form of military showdown, was the way the conflict was bound ultimately to end. In many ways, in everything except the silence of the weapons, war already became a reality in the minds of millions of men, military and civilian.

Although there were to be successive later crises, the high point of the Cold War was probably reached during the Korean War. And we all know the further course of events. Fortunately for all of us, war between the United States and the Soviet Union did not break out. The crisis was surmounted. And in the ensuing four decades, down to the middle of the 1980s, each of these components of the Cold War, while often retaining its initial validity in the perceptions of people in both countries, diminished in sharpness and often in reality. The peoples of Western Europe soon recovered their political balance, their prosperity, and their self-confidence. After the success of the Marshall Plan in 1948, there could no longer be any question of dangerous communist penetration in that region. Both sides, furthermore, soon began to learn to live, after a fashion, with the nuclear weapon, at least in the sense that they came to recognize that this was a suicidal weapon that must never be used—that any attempt to use it would lead only to a disaster in which all concepts of victory or defeat would become meaningless. And as for the relationship of conventional military forces in Europe: not only did the development of the NATO alliance restore an approximate military balance in the heart of the European continent, but, more important still, it became increasingly clear with the passage of the years that neither side had either the incentive or the desire to unleash even a conventional war, much less a nuclear one, in that region.

One might have thought that in light of these changes, the highly militarized view of East-West relations that the term "Cold War" signified might have faded. But military preparations and weapons races are stubborn things. They engender their own patterns of habit and suspicion. They ride along on their own intrinsic vitality even when the original reasons for them have largely faded. So in this sense, the Cold War, as a state of mind on the part of a great many people, lived on through the 1950s, 1960s, and 1970s, even after most of the justification for it had faded. And it was only in the middle of the 1980s, with the emergence onto the world scene of a Russian leader intelligent enough to recognize that the rationale of the Cold War was largely unreal and bold enough to declare this publicly and to act accordingly, that the world was brought to realize that one epoch—the epoch of recovery from the enormous dislocation of World War II—had passed and that a new one was beginning, an age that would, to be sure, create new problems, as all great changes in international life are bound to do, but would at the same time also present new possibilities.

This is the point at which we now find ourselves. The initial sources of contention between the two governments—the prewar ones, that is—no longer have serious significance. Those flowing from the outcome of the Second World War have been extensively moderated, and Mr. Gorbachev has shown every evidence of an intention to see them substantially eliminated. Where do we go from here?

The Russia we confront today is in many respects like nothing we have known before. The last vestiges of the unique and nightmarish system of rule known as Stalinism are now in the process of disappearance. What we have before us is in many respects the freest period Russia has ever known, unless it be the few years of feverish change that just preceded the outbreak of the First World War in 1914.

But we must be careful when we use the term "freedom." This does not mean that Russia is becoming like us. This it is not doing, could not do, and should not be expected to do. Forms of government and the habits of governments tend over the long run to reflect the understandings and expectations of their peoples. The Russian people, like a number of other peoples of the Soviet Union, have never known democracy as we understand it. They have experienced next to nothing of the centuries-long development of the discipline of self-government out of which our own political culture has evolved. If you presented them tomorrow with our political system, most of them would not know what to do with it; and what they did do might be far from our expectations.

It is clear, then, that whatever happens, and whatever may be the fate of Mr. Gorbachev's efforts at the restructuring of Soviet society, Russia is and is going to remain a country very different from our own. We should not look for this difference to be overcome in any short space of time. Beyond which, Russia, as a great modern country in a unique geographic position, and the heir to extensive involvements flowing from that position, is bound to have political interests quite different from our own. These are, fortunately, for the most part not interests that conflict seriously with ours. Such differences as remain should not preclude a normal relationship, and particularly when leadership on the Russian side is in the hands of a man such as Gorbachev. But this disparity between our countries does mean that one should not look, over the long term, for quite the same sort of political intimacy with Russian regimes that we might expect from a country that had inherited more of our own legacy of political outlooks and institutions.

All that being said, we are faced with the fact that Gorbachev has given every evidence, for his part, of an intention to remove as many as possible of the factors that have hampered Soviet-American relations in the past; and a number of the bold steps he has taken in that direction give testimony to the sincerity of his effort. To the extent he is able to carry these efforts to conclusion (and that depends to some degree on the response they meet with from our side), they present the most favorable opportunity the United States has had for the past seventy years to develop a normal, constructive, and hopeful relationship with his country.

Gorbachev's position, on the other hand, is obviously an extremely difficult one. The burdens he has assumed are almost superhuman. His efforts at internal economic reform have served thus far mainly to reveal that the damages done to Soviet society economically, socially, and spiritually by fifty years of Stalinist terror and Brezhnevist corruption and stagnation are greater than any of us supposed. It is going to take longer than anyone realized to repair those damages and build a healthy society.

Whether Gorbachev will be given the time to do this, no one can say. His difficulties are heightened by the fact that his reforms have had the unintended and unexpected effect of inflaming nationalistic feelings in several of the non-Russian ethnic communities of the Soviet Union, thus rendering acute a political problem—namely, the relations of the non-Russian periphery to the Russian center—that many of us had thought was only a problem of the more distant future. Particularly in the case of the three Baltic countries, this has led to a situation of great potential instability; for what goes on in those parts of the Soviet Union interacts with what goes on in the so-called satellite countries of Eastern and Central Europe, farther afield; and if things get further out of hand in this entire region, situations could easily be produced that would engage the defensive military interests of the Soviet Union, with unpredictable consequences.

For all of this, too, Gorbachev must accept the responsibility. How long he will be able, or permitted by his colleagues, to bear these burdens, we cannot know. His position has important elements of strength: his great reputation as a statesman, plus the fact that whoever might succeed to his powers would also have to succeed to his problems, something of which all his opponents must be painfully aware. The pressures, on the other hand, are cruel.

It is equally impossible to make predictions about what, were Gorbachev to be removed, would follow. That conditions could not revert to what they were before he took power is one of the few things on which almost everyone agrees. The intellectuals, released now from their long decades of repression, have been given their head; and it is unthinkable that this generation of intellectuals should ever again be bottled up as they were before. Not only that, but the Gorbachev economic reforms, unproductive as they may have been to date, have been formally accepted by the highest bodies of party and government; and this stamp of approval is not apt to be withdrawn until and unless someone can come up with a better alternative, which no one yet has shown any sign of doing. One must suppose, therefore, that whoever might replace Gorbachev would have to follow extensively in his footsteps, though possibly at a slower speed and without his boldness of leadership.

Particularly is this true in the field of foreign policy, which should be of greatest interest to us. This has been, within Russia, the least controversial of Gorbachev's fields of activity. Hard-liners, military and civilian, might like to retract, if they could, some of the more conciliatory steps he has taken in the area of arms control; but they would soon find that they faced the same financial stringencies he has been attempting to master, and they would presumably have little room, here too, to maneuver. One must suppose, therefore, that a good portion of what Gorbachev represents would survive him, even if he were to be removed at an early date. Meanwhile, to our good fortune, he hangs on, suspended precariously in mid-air to be sure, supported mainly by his incomparable qualities of insight, imagination, and courage, and by the relative mediocrity and intellectual poverty of most of his opponents.

To the policymakers of a new administration, the Russian scene of this particular moment presents, then, a series of tremendous uncertainties—uncertainties greater than Russia has ever known since the fateful year of 1917. If one were to be asked, what is it that is most likely to happen in the coming period? one could only reply—the unexpected. These uncertainties are unquestionably reasons for great alertness, caution, and prudence in American policy toward that country. They are not, however, reasons for neglecting the opportunities offered by Gorbachev's policies for the easing of military tensions and for improving the atmosphere of East-West relations generally. If realistic and solid agreements are made now, while the iron is hot; if these agreements are, as they should be, inherently self-enforcing; if, as is to be expected, they are seen in Moscow as in the Soviet interest; and if they are sealed in formal undertakings—then they are not apt to be undone simply by changes in the Soviet leadership.

What, then, should be the objectives of American policy toward the sort of international partner Gorbachev is trying to make out of Russia? What could we, from our side, do to promote the normalization of this relationship and to shape its future in a manner commensurate with its positive possibilities?

It would seem obvious, to me at least, that our first concern should be to remove, insofar as it lies within our power to do so, those features of American policy and practice that have their origins and their continuing rationale in outdated Cold War assumptions and lack serious current justification. To some extent, this has already been done. Cultural exchanges and people-to-people contacts are proceeding briskly, no longer seriously impeded from either side. The same may be said of scholarly exchanges in the humanities and the sciences. In all these areas, the initiative has normally and properly to come from private parties. The government's task is primarily not to stand in the way when this can be avoided, but to lend its support whenever this is really needed. That things have gone as well as they recently have in these forms of contact is encouraging testimony to the private demand for them and to their usefulness as components of normal relations between two great peoples.

In the commercial field, too, progress has been made; but here, obstacles remain— obstacles for which there is no present justification and the removal of which should present no problems. One hears a certain amount of discussion about whether we should or should not give aid to Gorbachev. The entire question is misconceived. One must bear in mind the difference between trade and aid. Mr. Gorbachev has not asked us for anything in the nature of loans or special credits or other abnormal forms of assistance; he is most unlikely to do so; and we, in my opinion, would be ill-advised to give it even if he did. What the Russians are asking for, and deserve to be given, are only the normal facilities for trade, facilities that include, of course, the extension of the usual commercial credits by both parties in specific business deals.

For the rest, once minimum security precautions have been observed, let Soviet-American trade proceed as it will. The prospects for it are not open-ended. The Soviet side has at this time little to offer in export items, and has sharply limited amounts of foreign exchange available for imports. But these prospects are also not insignificant, and they should not be curtailed by unnecessary official restrictions.

The most serious of the factors weighing on the Soviet-American relationship and impeding its improvement is unquestionably the problem of arms control, including the continuing competition in the development of strategic nuclear weaponry and the stand-off in the deployments of conventional forces in Central Europe. This exorbitant confrontation of military strength, out of all reasonable proportion to the political differences that are supposed to justify it, constitutes an inexhaustible source of mistrust and suspicion between the two parties, distracts public opinion from more serious aspects of the relationship, and preempts vast quantities of resources that could well be used for more creative purposes.

What can be done about it?

Obviously, not everything depends on us. It takes two, at every point, to perform this tango. But since Mr. Gorbachev has given impressive signs of his intention to do his best in this respect, and has taken a number of conciliatory and even unilateral steps in that direction, this would be a good time for us to review our own record and to see whether it could not be improved.

We have, of course, had one significant success in recent years: the so-called INF (Intermediate Nuclear Force) agreement, eliminating intermediate-range nuclear weaponry from the forces of both sides stationed in Central Europe. This success was made possible by the willingness of both Mr. Reagan and Mr. Gorbachev to override all the intricacies of negotiation at the technical-military level and to take the bold steps, each giving reasonable credit to the good faith of the other side. But it has carried us only a small distance along the path of general arms reduction. For the rest, our record may well stand questioning.

We could certainly have had by this time, had we wished to, a comprehensive nuclear test ban; and nothing, surely, could have gone further to assure extensive, if gradual, reductions in nuclear weaponry. We do not have it.

We could in all probability have had by this time, had we wanted to, the 50 percent reduction in long-range nuclear missiles that both Mr. Reagan and Mr. Gorbachev recognized as desirable and that, once achieved, would presumably have changed the whole climate of the arms control problem. We do not have it. We chose, I gather, to give higher priority to the Strategic Defense Initiative, and to the modernization and consequent buildup of our strategic nuclear arsenals.

The maintenance of the present American conventional deployments in Germany absorbs, we are told, some 40 percent of our great military budget. Nothing within the realm of practical possibility could have contributed more directly and importantly to the reduction of the federal budget than a significant reduction in these expenditures. For years, we have been toying timidly with negotiations over the possible reductions of these forces and have gotten nowhere. These negotiations having now been moved to a much wider forum (that of the Atlantic-to-Urals talks, embracing a greatly expanded number of participants), the prospects for any success in the coming period would seem to have been diminished rather than improved.

Mr. Gorbachev, in the meantime, has announced important changes in Soviet doctrine affecting the mission and the composition of the Soviet forces in Germany, changes envisaging in particular the removal from the forward positions of forms of weaponry that would lend themselves to employment for sudden aggressive purposes. This change of doctrine has been accompanied by a number of specific suggestions from the Soviet or Warsaw Pact side for confidence-building measures of one sort or another, and by extensive unilateral Soviet measures of restraint. The responses with which these initiatives have been met on our side have been, for the most part, reluctant, embarrassed, and occasionally even surly. These responses have caused a great many people elsewhere in the world to wonder whether we really have any serious interest in arms control at all. Can we not do better than that?

The hesitations underlying these unenthusiastic responses seem to have been largely connected with the impression, so frequently propounded and supported in official American circles, that there has been an "overwhelming" Soviet superiority in conventional forces in the Central European theater and that this situation would continue to prevail even after completion of the unilateral Soviet withdrawals Gorbachev has announced. There are many of us who would strongly dispute that thesis, and dispute it on the basis of statistics fully available to, and even recognized by, official Washington circles. The confusion seems to arise from several more fundamental miscalculations. There has been the use of the unrealistic and seriously misleading NATO–versus–Warsaw Pact comparisons for measuring Soviet and American forces in Central Europe. There has been the persistent assumption that the American tactical and short-ranged nuclear weapons in Germany are an essential element of "deterrence," without which there would be serious danger of a Soviet attack in that region. Finally, and in close connection with this assumption of aggressive Soviet designs, there has been the insistence of our military authorities that the extent of the "threat" presented to us by any foreign power must be measured solely by our estimate of that power's capabilities, ignoring its interests and intentions.

A new administration in Washington owes it to itself to reexamine these assumptions, and others like them, and to ask itself whether, considering both the dangers and the expense of the maintenance by both parties of these enormous and inordinate arsenals, we could not find more realistic means of measuring the problem and more hopeful ways of promoting its solution.

If, in this way, some of the more obvious and extensive impediments to a better relationship with the Soviet Union could be overcome, the greater part of what needs to be done would have been accomplished. Bilateral relations between sovereign governments are not the area in which great positive things are to be achieved; rather, they are a way in which conflicts of interest are to be composed and negative things are to be avoided. The first duty of every country is to itself, and this duty must be met by its respective government within the area of its own competence. If we succeeded in doing no more than eliminate the greatest sources of conflict prevailing between the United States and the Soviet Union, this alone would be a great accomplishment, worthy of all the effort and enthusiasm we put into it.

But this would not be the end of the story. There are limited possibilities for useful collaboration even between governments so different in traditional and in ideological inspiration as the Soviet and American ones. These possibilities relate to a number of fields; but the greatest and most important, without question, is that of environmental protection and improvement on the planetary scale. The dangers now beginning to overshadow us all in this respect are confirmed not only by many of the findings of the scientists but in some instances by the perceptions of our own vision and senses. The greater part of what we could and should be doing to ward off this disaster has to be done within the national framework; and here, both we and the Russians have a great deal to catch up on before we can say that we have done all that it lay within our power to do. But environment recognizes no national boundaries, and efforts to come to terms with it within those boundaries can never alone meet the total problem. To achieve their maximum effectiveness, the national efforts need to be supplemented by international ones. This fact is now coming to be widely recognized in Russia as well as here; and environmental movements are springing up all over the Soviet Union.

There are no two countries that could, if they wanted to, contribute more by joint effort in this field than the United States and the Soviet Union. Some measures of Soviet-American collaboration have already been put in hand. More could surely be proposed and promoted. The same applies to the area of space research. If we could get over the idea that outer space, the common umbrella of the entire planet, is there primarily to be exploited by us for our military advantage, there would clearly be important possibilities for collaboration with the Soviet Union in the whole great field of space research.

Such collaboration would be justified if only by the direct effects it was designed to achieve. But the probability ought to be recognized that to the extent the two countries could join their efforts in this manner, the remaining impediments to a firm and useful relationship between them would be the more easily overcome. Because in the very process of collaboration in a necessary and peaceful process, useful to all humanity, the neurotic impulses of military and political rivalry would be bound to be overshadowed; eyes and attention would have to be removed to other and more hopeful undertakings; and the peoples might find, in the intermingling of their own creative efforts in a common problem, a firmness of association no other intergovernmental relationships could ever assure.

What we are seeing today is in effect the final overcoming and disappearance of the Russian Revolution of 1917, as we have witnessed it and attempted to deal with it over the seven decades of its existence. The present Soviet leaders are the first of that sort who, in trying to shape their society, will have to relate themselves not just to the post-1917 revolutionary period but to the entire span of Russian history. What they are creating, and what we must now face, is another Russia, entirely identifiable neither with the revolutionary period nor with the centuries of tsarist power that preceded it. Just as the designing of this new Russia calls for innovation on the part of those in Moscow who are responsible for it, so it calls for innovation on the part of an

American government that, more perhaps than any other of the world's governments, must relate to it.

This is the challenge the Bush administration will have to meet. In their attempt to meet it, they will not be able to ignore the immediate past, but they cannot be successful if they allow themselves to be its captives.

Just Another Great Power
(1989)

———————···⟨∞⟩···———————

What we are witnessing today in Russia is the breakup of much, if not all, of the system of power by which that country has been held together and governed since 1917.

Fortunately, that breakup has been most pronounced in precisely those aspects of Soviet power that have been most troublesome from the standpoint of Soviet-American relations, namely:

• The world-revolutionary ideology, rhetoric, and political efforts of the early Soviet leadership. (Fortunately, these are no longer a significant factor in Soviet behavior.)

• The morbid extremism of Stalinist political oppression. This factor began to be greatly moderated soon after Stalin's death in 1953. Further extensive modifications of it have been proceeding under Mikhail Gorbachev; the remnants are now being dismantled at a pace that renders it no longer a serious impediment to a normal Soviet-American relationship.

There remain, however, three factors that do indeed trouble the relationship and have to be considered when one confronts the questions of its future: what many in the West consider to be the inordinate size of the peacetime conventional armed-force establishment; what remains of the Soviet political and military hegemony in Eastern and parts of Central Europe; and the rivalry between the two powers in the cultivation and development of nuclear and conventional weaponry.

Originally published in the *New York Times,* April 9, 1989.

To these factors might be added the unstable and in some respects dangerous internal-political situation that now prevails in the Soviet Union.

I would like to comment, briefly, on each of these factors.

First, the maintenance of what appear to be numerically excessive ground forces in peacetime has been a constant feature of Russian/Soviet policy for most of the last two hundred years. The reasons have been partly domestic and partly defensive. Never in all this time have these forces been employed to initiate hostilities against a major military power. Under Mr. Gorbachev, the size of the establishment is now being somewhat reduced. Altogether, this should not be a serious complication of the Soviet-American relationship.

Second, since roughly the time of the increased troop movements into Czechoslovakia in 1968, Soviet political hegemony over the other Warsaw Pact countries has been slackening. Since Mr. Gorbachev's advent to power, there has been a marked advance in the effective independence of these satellite governments. In the shaping of their economies and of their relations with Western countries, those regimes now have essentially a free hand, provided only that they do not challenge their obligations of membership in the Warsaw Pact and that they do not depart from use of the term "socialist" as the official designation of their economies. So tenuous is the Soviet hold over these countries today that I personally doubt that military intervention along the lines of the action in Hungary in 1956 would now be a realistic option of Soviet policy. Not only would it be in crass conflict with Mr. Gorbachev's public commitments, but the consequences in the remainder of the satellite area, and among non-Russian nationalities of the Soviet Union, would be unpredictable.

Third, our government has not made the efforts it could and should have made to reach acceptable agreements with the Soviet side for the reduction of either nuclear or conventional weapons. While this question is too complex for detailed treatment in this statement, I would like to offer some general comments.

There have been, in recent months and years, several interesting and encouraging initiatives and suggestions from the Soviet side to which we have been essentially unresponsive. Obviously, these initiatives and suggestions could not be taken at face value. They all called for explorations, in discussions with the Soviet side, of their reality and practical significance. But this exploration has not been seriously undertaken. I think it should have been.

The problem of reductions in conventional armaments has been needlessly complicated and distorted by the egregious exaggeration of the existing Soviet superiority in such weapons that has marked the public statements, and apparently the official assumptions, of our government. This, obviously, should be corrected.

The arsenals of nuclear weapons now in the possession of the Soviet Union and the United States are plainly vastly redundant in relation to the purpose they are supposed to serve. Owing to their over-destructiveness and their suicidal implications, these weapons are essentially useless from the standpoint of actual commitment to military combat; and whatever "deterrent" function they might usefully serve could be effectively served by far smaller forces. The statements and policies of our government appear to reflect an assumption that the maintenance of these excessive arsenals presents no serious problem, and that there is no urgency about their reduction. I cannot share this complacency.

Not only is there the danger that these weapons might come into use by accident, misunderstanding, or other inadvertence, but there seems to be a real and immediate danger of further proliferation in the coming period. This danger calls urgently for a vigorous attack on the whole problem of proliferation; and a prerequisite for such an attack would be, as I see it, extensive reductions in the holdings of the two superpowers.

As to the fourth point, the domestic-political personal situation of Mr. Gorbachev is indeed in certain respects precarious, particularly in view of the meager results to date of his program of *perestroika*. But his position also has had important elements of strength, as does his program; and both have now been further strengthened by the results of the recent election. His initiatives in foreign policy have not met with serious internal resistance. There is therefore no reason to suppose that agreements entered into with his government under his leadership would not, if properly negotiated and formalized, be respected by his successors.

In summary, it appears to me that whatever reasons there may once have been for regarding the Soviet Union primarily as a possible, if not probable, military opponent, the time for that sort of thing has clearly passed. That country should now be regarded essentially as a great power, like other great powers—one, that is, whose aspirations and policies are conditioned outstandingly by its own geographic situation, history, and tradition, and are therefore not identical with our own but are also not so seriously in conflict with ours as to justify any assumption that the outstanding differences could not be adjusted by the normal means of compromise and accommodation.

It ought now to be our purpose to eliminate as soon as possible, by amicable negotiation, the elements of abnormal military tension that have recently dominated Soviet-American relations, and to turn our attention to the development of the positive possibilities of this relationship, which are far from insignificant.

NATO and the Warsaw Pact
(1989)

The changes that have recently come over, and are continuing to come over, Central and Eastern Europe are momentous, irreversible, and epoch-making. They mark the end of a status quo that has existed in most of this region for four decades, and in Russia for a full seven. Whatever else may be said of them, it is safe to say that Europe will never again look as it has looked in all these years since the end of the last world war. And how this future Europe *will* look is going to depend upon the quality of statesmanship—of thoughtfulness, of insight, of the balance of prudence and courage—that the many governments prominently involved, including our own, are able to bring to the shaping of it.

For ourselves, and for the other major powers of both NATO and the Warsaw Pact, this situation presents two great and complex problems; and it is of utmost importance for the solution of both of them that they not be confused.

The first is the short-term problem: that of preserving sufficient stability throughout the Central and Eastern European region over the coming weeks and months to give all those concerned time to address themselves in a careful and orderly way to the second and long-term problem, which will require much more time for its successful treatment and should not be approached in haste or under pressure.

This second problem cannot be described in a single sentence; it

Originally published (in a different form) in the *Washington Post*, November 12, 1989.

is too vast and too many-sided. In essence, it involves not just the designing of a new status quo for this part of Europe but also the working out of a new political, economic, and security framework for much of the remainder of the European continent, to replace the one, so deeply impregnated with Cold War concepts and assumptions, that has prevailed since the last great war and is now no longer applicable. This, as former German prime minister Helmut Schmidt recently observed, is primarily a problem for the Europeans themselves. They are the ones who will have to live with the solution of it. We cannot replace them in this primary responsibility; nor should we wish to. But a central component of this long-term problem will be the future of the North Atlantic alliance; and we, as the leading power in that grouping, cannot avoid a measure of involvement. To meet that responsibility is going to take a great deal more in the way of thought and discussion—discussion among ourselves, but also with the Europeans, including the Russians—than we have given it to date.

What this problem entails is tremendous in scope and difficulty. It involves the relationship of Eastern Europe, economically and politically, to the European community. It involves the future of both NATO and the Warsaw Pact. It involves the military arrangements now pertaining in the center of the European continent. It involves the various negotiations now in progress over the conventional arms balance in Europe. It involves the relationship between the two parts of Germany, and the attitudes to be taken toward the possibility, and desirability, of their unification.

These problems are all of a part. None of them can be solved, or usefully treated, independently of the remainder. Their solution will require a great deal of study, of preliminary discussion, and ultimately of negotiation. The questions at hand are ones of great historical depth. Whoever undertakes the study of them (and that means all of us) is going to find himself confronting situations to which better answers should have been found but weren't at the end of the last world war, and even some (arising from the breakup of the Austro-Hungarian Empire) to which the same could be said about the years 1918 and 1919. Such problems go to the heart of the political structure of European society; and their successful treatment will require both an awareness and respectful consideration of what history has to tell us, together with a recognition of the peculiarities of our own age, in the face of which, of course, none of the possible solutions of earlier years would be entirely adequate or even relevant.

So complex and so profound in its implications is the task of designing this new Europe that it will not be accomplished at any one time, or subsumed in any single document or settlement. We are talking here of an edifice that will have to rest on many foundations. The erection of it will take years, not months. We will be lucky if the task is substantially accomplished before the end of the century. It is none too early to start the thinking that will have to go into this great effort. But it is important, at the same time, that the excitements of the moment do not rush us into hasty and un-thought-through decisions, or even discussions, that could prejudice an ultimately sound resolution of any of the major questions involved.

The best example of this danger is found in the loose talk that has marked the discussions of recent days about German unification. Many people talk about this as if it were something that would or could easily and naturally flow from any extensive liberalization of conditions in East Germany. This view takes little account of the true depths of the problem. There must now be well over a million armed men on German territory, with all their elaborate modern equipment and, in the case of ourselves and the Russians, with nuclear as well as with conventional weapons. These forces are there not by the will of the German authorities alone but by elaborate and long-standing agreements with other powers, and particularly with other groups of powers organized in the two alliances. The Germans could not unilaterally disarm these forces or cause them to disappear in the physical sense. Even less could they unilaterally disregard, nor would they want to disregard, the contractual framework by which the presence of those forces is supported. Beyond which, the very profiles of these great armies, in East as in West, are now under negotiation among some twenty-eight countries. No German unification would be even thinkable without widespread agreement among all these parties, in their individual capacities or in their collective capacities as members of one or the other of the alliances, about the dispositions and the political control of these forces.

Few would deny that the system of alliances on which European security has rested in these last three and a half decades, rooted as it is in Cold War assumptions that most of us would recognize today as extensively undermined, is rapidly becoming obsolescent. This implies the necessity of an alternative framework of security for the entire continent. At the center of the search for this alternative there must stand—Germany. That country is now the gathering point of by far the greater part of the armed strength of the continent. Its geographic position and its economic capacities will give it the central position in any new framework of security that may be devised. The problems that present themselves in the relationships of the two parts of Germany to each other and to their neighbors are not ones that can be solved other than in the context of that new, and presumably wider, security framework.

The principle by which most of us were guided when we found ourselves faced, forty years ago, with the problem of Germany's future was this: that there must not again be a united Germany, and particularly not a militarized one, standing alone in Europe and not firmly embraced in some wider international structure—some structure that would absorb its energies and, by doing so, give reassurance to Germany's neighbors. But if Germany is to be embraced in some wider structure (and the possibilities of this seem greater today than they did four decades ago), there then arises the question, should Germany enter this larger structure as a united entity? Or would it not be better, and even more reassuring to others, if the two parts of that country, while culturally and economically united, were to enter it as separate political entities as they are today?

It is precisely these questions whose answers will depend upon the nature of the wider security arrangements for Europe that will have to be worked out; and the one process must not precede the other. Anything else could create complications that no one would wish to invite but that no one might see the way to avoid. It is for this reason that even if the liberalization of political conditions in East Germany were to progress in the near future to a point where they were little different from the conditions prevailing in the German Federal Republic, this would of itself be no reason for an immediate German unification; and this is, therefore, not the time to raise that subject.

Our immediate problem is to see how the process of change now overtaking the countries of the eastern part of Europe, and the adjustment of their relations with Russia that these changes involve, can be eased in a manner conducive to the peace and security of the continent in the immediately forthcoming period, so that time can be won for the far more arduous and lengthy process of finding a new European order. The best contribution this country and our leading NATO allies can make to this immediate task will be to intensify our efforts to achieve far-reaching reductions of conventional arms in Europe. If, pending wider agreements, the two alliances and their respective military establishments must be kept in existence until they can be examined under a wider focus than the conditions of this day permit, there is no reason why the forces they now have deployed in the center of Europe, already grossly exorbitant with relation to any demonstrable need, should not be greatly reduced. That in itself would improve the atmosphere for the more wide-ranging explorations of the requirements for Europe's future security that await our attention. A major prerequisite for progress in this direction would be, however, a departure by Washington and its leading NATO allies from the silly belief that NATO's most urgent task is to frustrate an attack on Western Europe by a militant Soviet Union, accompanied by its supposedly faithful and equally militant Warsaw Pact allies, and the preparation, instead, for a searching examination of the ways in which Europe's security is to be achieved in an age where the great enemy is not the Soviet Union but the rapid deterioration of our planet as a supporting structure for civilized life.

A New Age of European Security
(1989)

————··⟨∞⟩··————

W e are living through one of those great moments of change that
have punctuated the history of modern Europe for the last two
centuries, at roughly generational intervals, marking the transition
from one clearly definable epoch to another. But this present transition is a particularly confusing one. It has in it something of a number
of these past great moments of change. What has been happening in
the streets of various Eastern European cities reminds me, for example, in its spontaneity and in the contagious quality of its mass enthusiasm, of the waves of revolutionary fervor that swept over so many
of the European capitals in 1848. But in the problems it presents for
the peoples in question and for us, this present crisis reminds me more
of some of the great historic moments of decision in the ordering and
reordering of Europe, as, for example: the Congress of Vienna of
1815; the Peace of Frankfurt concluded in 1871, after the Franco-Prussian War; the Congress of Berlin of 1878; and the Versailles Peace Conference, which brought to an end the First World War. What was at
stake on each of these occasions was, I repeat, a reordering of much
of the political structure of Europe's life, a new determination of how
the European community was to be constituted, what was to be the
quality and status of individual states, and how they should relate one
to another. What we are now going through, and will continue to go

Remarks delivered before the Council on Foreign Relations, New York, December 20, 1989.

174

through for at least the next couple of years, resembles all these other great moments.

But there is one way in which it does not resemble them. You may have noted that these other moments of decision occurred just after the ending of great wars. Yet there was one such ending I did *not* mention. That was the ending of World War II, forty some years ago. And the reason I did not mention it was that this moment, in contrast to the others, marked the solution of nothing at all. It yielded no agreed concept of a new order in Europe. There was no peace conference at which the map of Europe could be redrawn. All this was made impossible by a number of factors: by the nature of the regime—the Stalin regime—then in power in Russia; by the fact that the armed forces of that regime were already in effective military occupation of one-half of Europe; and by the futility of coming to any agreement with that regime about how life should now be reordered in Europe to take account of the lessons of the two world wars, of the outcome of the last one, and of the demands of the modern age.

In the absence of any such agreement, things have been held together after a fashion over these past forty years by the continued political division of the continent and the stand-off between two great military alliances. This had its usefulness, of course. Despite the fact that this division of Europe constituted, itself, the greatest of artificialities, it served to repress, or to put on hold, a number of smaller abnormalities of international life—situations that would have been faced, and should have been faced, forty years ago had circumstances permitted. The stand-off of the two military alliances kept the lid on a number of potentially explosive situations. But this represented a cumbersome and undesirable way of doing it: expensive, precarious, and essentially uncreative. It involved the unnatural political oppression of millions of people in the eastern part of the continent. It led to economic stagnation and backwardness in all those countries. The limited stability it offered was not a real stability. It was a way of postponing problems, not of solving them.

And now, as we all know, this status quo has broken down—broken down on its own unnaturalness, its own artificiality. And here we are: suddenly faced today with all those problems that should have received attention forty years ago but couldn't, plus a number of new problems that, forty years ago, nobody could have foreseen. And we (by which I mean the Western Europeans and ourselves) are poorly prepared, it seems to me, to confront these problems. Our attention has been concentrated, too closely and for too long, on the sterile and hopeless mathematics of a military rivalry that was in part the product of our own feverish imagination and of our own inspiration. As little as a year ago, it would have seemed futile to us to be thinking of the future of a united Europe—a Europe without the Cold War—of what Gorbachev has called "a common European home."

Some of you may think, perhaps, that I am exaggerating the scope of this present crisis. Why, you may be asking, do I speak as though what was needed was a reordering of the entire life of the European continent? Is not the life of the greater part of that continent already reasonably well ordered under the benevolent umbrella of the NATO alliance? And is the problem not simply one of reintegrating into the life of the remainder of the continent the economies of a number of countries that were hitherto behind the Communist Iron Curtain?

Well, the problem is that, of course. But it is unfortunately more than that.

It is more than that, in the first place, because these changes, while putting an end to a false stability, have not yet created a new and sound one. The peoples of these liberated countries are, generally speaking, poorly prepared to face the challenges and responsibilities of political freedom. In certain of them, the institutions of democratic government were shallow and thinly rooted even forty-five years ago, before they fell under Communist power. And in all of them, the generation that is now going to have to take political responsibility is composed of people who, by no fault of their own, have never had day-to-day experience with the modalities of self-government. They have never learned, or have forgotten, even all that their parents knew about it. The aptitude for democracy is not something just born into people. It comes, alas, only from experience, from long encounter with reality. To be useful, it has to attain the quality of a habit. And freedom, as I believe Goethe said, is something that must be reconquered daily. It is not achieved, and certainly not preserved, by a series of emotional street demonstrations.

Another reason why the problem we now confront is more than just one of economic adjustment is the fact that this process of liberation is not confined to northeastern Europe but is beginning to affect the peoples of that great breeding ground of wars and troubles: the Balkan peninsula. There has never been any very firm status quo in that region since the breakup of the Turkish and Austro-Hungarian Empires. And here, as elsewhere in Eastern Europe, there is the possibility that the removal of the Russian hand will release not only the thirst for freedom but also renewed outbursts of that romantic and intolerant and dangerous nationalism that has been the scourge of the relationships among those peoples for more than a hundred years. That will not be easy for the rest of Europe to handle.

And finally, among the reasons why what we face is more than just a problem of integrating three or four smaller economies into the life of the remainder of the continent is the fact that the liberation of a single one of these countries, namely East Germany, brings to the fore an unsolved question that has plagued Europe for more than a century, a question that has had a central place in the causality of two world wars, a question to which many Germans themselves have never found a fully satisfactory answer: whether an independent and united Germany, situated as it is in the heart of the continent and outranking all its neighbors in population, in economic strength, and in military power, existent or potential—whether such a Germany can be rendered compatible with the peace and stability of the European continent at large. Upon the answer to this question there depends not only the security of Germany's eastern neighbors, and in the first instance that of the Soviet Union, but also the security of a number of Germany's western neighbors as well.

For all these reasons, what is now done, or is not done, by way of response to the changes now in progress in Eastern Europe is bound to affect the life of the entire continent for many decades to come. And it will affect us, too.

In the political and economic sense, the problems I have mentioned are primarily European problems; and it is, of course, the Europeans who must take the initiative and provide the leadership in seeking out the solutions. Even here, we cannot be wholly uninvolved; and it is not the desire of most Europeans, I believe, that we should be. We are too much of a factor in their lives for total uninvolvement. But the primary responsibility must continue to lie with them.

A wholly different situation prevails when it comes to military affairs and the questions of international security. The two alliances, of course, still exist. Their great armies and garrisons are still in place. And while originally aimed against each other, they bear between them, for the moment, by far the greater part of the burden of the security of the European peoples. For this reason, they should not be allowed to go out of existence before something has been created to take their place. But let there be no mistake about it: they will themselves not be adequate to the needs of the longer future. No security structure predicated on an assumed mutual hostility of two great groups of European peoples, and of the two semi-European superpowers, will be adequate—indeed, as no such structure will be suitable—for the Europe of the future. In one way or another, a new all-European security structure, a structure resembling nothing that has ever existed in the past, will have to be created. And we Americans, at the present time one of the four greatest military powers on the European continent, will inevitably have to be heavily involved in its creation.

This will not be easy for us. The relating of military power to political purpose has never been our forte. It will not be easy for us to get it into our heads (as a few others, including Gorbachev, seem to have done) that the maintenance or employment of great offensive forces can no longer be a rational factor in the relations between great advanced industrial countries. This does not mean, however, that there will be no place at all for military forces in their proper scheme of things; it means only that the function and structure of such forces, and their relationship, respectively, to national or to international authority, will have to be quite different than it has been in the past. In this respect, Europe, the new Europe that must proceed from this present crisis, will need to be, as Europe has so often been in the past, the innovator, the pioneer, the pathbreaker for people in other parts of the world. And we Americans, poorly prepared as we are, will have to summon up, out of the great but scattered resources we possess, the information, the thoughtfulness, and the originality to play a worthy part in this great act of international creativity.

Remarks for the Milwaukee Forum
(1990)

———∞———

Never has there been a moment of greater uncertainty in the relationship between the United States and the Soviet Union.

In the first years of Soviet power, before World War II, the chief
factor in the relationship was the ideological and political conflict between the two countries. After the war, this factor was largely overtaken by the military-political competition; and the whole relationship was dominated by that.

Now, the changes that have taken place in Russia under Gorbachev's rule have made both of those factors unsubstantial. They are
no longer there to overshadow all the other aspects of the relationship,
as they did for so long. And we are forced to look for a new set of
guidelines in our approach to our relations with that country. You
might be tempted to say that we are back where we were in 1917, confronted again with the old Russia we had known before that time.

In some ways, that would be correct. But in other ways, it would
not be; because the seventy years of Communist power have changed
Russia very greatly, and not always for the good. It is true that the
Communist regime is disintegrating and can probably never be restored. In particular, I am glad to say, there is no possibility of returning to that dreadfully distorted version of what went by the name of
Communism that prevailed under Stalin. But a return to that Russia
of the old first regime in the centuries before the revolution would

Excerpts from a talk given at the Annual Forum of the Milwaukee Institute of
World Affairs, May 12, 1990.

also, for many reasons, be impossible. And the fact is that the country we think of as the Soviet Union, the successor to the old Russian Empire with its central core of Russian people and its surrounding belt of non-Russian peoples, is right now in a state of change, instability, and uncertainty—a time of turmoil and confusion more extreme than anything it has experienced since the Revolution of 1917, and perhaps greater than any crisis it has faced since the so-called Time of Troubles, a crisis of the monarchy and of the Russian state that occurred at the beginning of the seventeenth century.

Let me point out the three major ingredients of this situation of instability and uncertainty, just to show you how serious they are.

First, there is the state of the economy. The Soviet economy had begun to decline even before Gorbachev came in. He thought he had diagnosed the main reasons for the decline; and his *perestroika* was a program of reform intended to correct the deficiencies and to halt the process. Unfortunately, for reasons too numerous and complicated to be discussed here, it has not had this effect. To date, *perestroika* has only heightened the difficulties, particularly in the supply of consumer goods for people in the great cities. Gorbachev has tried to introduce, gradually, the principle of free enterprise as a means of increasing and improving distribution. The idea, I think, was quite sound. With time, it may yet begin to show its effects. But up to now, it has not. And what we see before us today is a country where the old Communist system for operating the economy has been extensively disrupted, whereas the new system has not yet taken hold. The country is falling, uncomfortably, between two chairs. And this has undermined a great deal of people's confidence in Gorbachev himself, particularly in the cities.

Second, Gorbachev, finding that the Communist Party was not very useful in helping him with his reforms, has been trying, and with some success, to shift the center of gravity of political power from the Party apparatus, where it had rested for seventy years, to a properly elected governmental apparatus in which the Party would no longer have a monopoly of power but would be, like political parties in other countries, only one of a number of contenders for popular support. This is a historic and fundamental change in Russia's political life, one that was greatly needed and was greatly to be welcomed.

But at the present moment, this change, too, is only halfway completed. The new and largely democratically elected Parliament seems to have taken over much of the power in the great cities; but in large sectors of the countryside, the local Party committees seem still to be in control and to be operating relatively independently. The result is that there is, at the moment, no clear center of political authority. No one knows where to turn to get an answer. And in a country where people are used to knowing where the seat of power is, to whom you can appeal, and from whom you can obtain an answer, this is very unsettling—even in some ways dangerous.

Finally: one of the things Gorbachev succeeded in doing was to abolish the old system of censorship and police terror—to concede, in most essential respects, freedom of speech, of thought, of the press, and of political demonstration and action. Now this was fine and, again, a great step forward. But it proved to be a contagious development, and had the effect of spreading not only to the countries of Eastern Europe, where it led to the overthrow of the Communist regimes right down the line, but also to certain of the non-Russian nationalities within the Soviet Union as well. Here, as one sees in the case of Lithuania, the result has been a sudden and impulsive demand for immediate and complete secession from the Soviet Union. And Lithuania, as you all know, is not the only place where this effect is being felt. Other Soviet nationalities, too, aspire to independence; and they are watching the Lithuanian conflict to see which way they, too, should jump.

Now, the Soviet Union is the last of the great multinational and multilingual empires to feel the disintegrating effects of modern nationalism. The others, like the old Turkish Empire and the Austro-Hungarian Empire, had already long since gone by the boards. Modern nationalism, which is the most powerful emotional-political force of this modern age, has proved simply incompatible with the holding together of a variety of national groups under a single imperial center. And the Soviet Union, too, is vulnerable to these centrifugal tendencies. In the end, I am sure, it will have to make way for them, at least to a considerable extent; and several of its national components, particularly the Baltic countries, will have to receive, sooner or later, their sovereign independence.

But this is not a simple problem. It is not a problem that can be solved from one day to the next just by this or that nationality's declaring itself independent. For one thing, not all the non-Russian nationalities want compete independence or are in any way prepared for it. Their situations vary. And beyond that, there are many things to be talked out, in every instance, if the process is to go forward peacefully and successfully. An abrupt, disorderly disintegration of the Soviet Union could be dangerous for the stability of the whole European continent, and even for some of these restless Soviet minorities themselves.

Now, all these forms of violent change—the attempted economic revolution, the shift of the political center from party to government, and the partial dissolution of the empire—are today coming together and interacting. And altogether, they create a situation the future of which is absolutely unpredictable. Anything might happen: a partial breakup of the Soviet Union, a complete breakdown of government in parts of the country, a split of the Communist Party, civil war, temporary regimes here and there—conditions such as those that prevailed during the Russian civil war, in the years just after the revolution. I am not predicting that any of these things will happen; they don't have to; but none of them can be excluded, and no one can tell you what *will* come.

And the result is that our government does not know, and cannot know, at this point with what sort of a Russia it is going to have to deal in the months and years just ahead. The uncertainty of the situation in Russia inflicts an equal uncertainty on American policy toward that country. Gorbachev may, of course, remain in office for a long time. It is not impossible that he will succeed in mastering his present difficulties and creating some sort of a stable situation. If so, so much the better. He is a great man; his efforts lead in the right direction; he deserves our good wishes. But whether or not that will happen is, again, something we cannot know. And it will be a fairly long time, even in the best of circumstances, before we can see what the final outcome of these uncertainties will be.

Well, what does all this mean for American policy toward Russia at this time? It seem clear to me that our policy should be, above all, a cautious one, which avoids involving this country or taking sides in the many tensions and conflicts that have already begun to mark, and must continue for long to mark, the state of high instability in Russia. We should maintain our detachment. We should use what little influence we have to see that developments proceed peacefully. But we should do so as a helpful, distant friend, not as an involved party.

That, so far as I can see, is what President Bush is doing; and I can only commend him for it. He is right, I think, for this and other reasons, to refrain from involving this country in the Lithuanian conflict. The Lithuanian demand for independence will not be the last demand of this sort with which we will be faced. And it would be a very unwise procedure to commit the policies of this country to a general breakup of the Soviet Union and to offer our support to any group that wants to separate itself from the Soviet state. Any policy of that sort might land us in strange and embarrassing company. We have troubles enough of our own these days without multiplying them by that sort of involvement. Mr. Bush is also quite right, in my view, to go ahead with the forthcoming summit meeting. And there is no reason why the present efforts at arms control and reduction should not continue to be pursued at all levels, vigorously, boldly, and with good will.

But back of all this, and through it all, we will be well advised to bear in mind the long-term aspects of the relationship. It is just about two centuries since the official relationship between Russia and America came into existence. For most of those two centuries, especially up to the Russian Revolution of 1917, the two peoples have lived together and have related to each other quite amicably, even though our systems of government were very different. We have never been at war with each other. In our respective national temperaments, we have certain things in common. So there is something to build on.

It is true that so long as Moscow appears to be holding in subservience against their will other peoples who want their independence and seem to be ripe for it, this is going to constitute, as it has constituted at various times throughout this century, a disturbing factor in the relationship. For this reason, the sooner the Russians come to terms with this problem, the better it will be for Russian-American relations. And we have every reason to hope that things will move successfully in that direction.

But to hope that a certain thing will happen in a region of the world far from our shores is one thing. To try actively to bring it about is another. This is Russia's problem, not ours. It is in some respects a complicated problem. No country ever understands perfectly another country's affairs; and none is likely to do much good by interfering in them. Let us wish them all well, and be helpful where we can. But let us not make ourselves a part of the problem.

The outstanding question of military security in Europe—of NATO, of German unification, and of the future of the various alliances and armed forces of that continent—is something else again. Here, our involvement and our responsibility are obvious. And here, I am not so sure that we are entirely on the right track. We are rapidly locking ourselves into an insistence that NATO should continue to exist and that a united Germany should not only be a member of it but should continue to figure as one of the continent's two greatest military powers (the other being France). That this does justice to the military anxieties of French and British friends seems evident. That it does equal justice to the security concerns of the Soviet Union is not apparent.

It is Gorbachev, I believe, who once said that if peace is to be preserved, you must learn to see the other fellow's security as just as important to you as your own. We would do well to bear that in mind. I have read of its being suggested in NATO circles that we don't need to be too concerned about Soviet feelings in the matter of Germany's military future because people in Moscow are today preoccupied with their own troubles, and even if they don't like the arrangements we propose, there is little they can do about it. I would like to say that it never pays, in my opinion, for one great power to take advantage of the momentary weakness or distraction of another great power in order to force upon it concessions it would never have accepted in normal circumstances. In the short term, this may seem to have advantages. Over the long run, it almost always revenges itself. The Russians are justly proud of their great war effort; and they will expect to see due recognition given to it in the dispositions that are under discussion today.

To some extent, this seems to have been recognized in Washington; and I have the impression that we are trying to persuade the French and British to join us in meeting the Russians—not halfway, but about 20 percent of the way. I doubt that this is enough, and I hope we will give this matter very careful thought before we go further. For this is a highly sensitive issue; and it can cause us a lot of trouble if we take the wrong course.

Republicans Won the Cold War?
(1992)

The suggestion that any American administration had the power to influence decisively the course of a tremendous domestic-political upheaval in another great country on another side of the globe is intrinsically silly and childish. No great country has that sort of influence on the internal developments of any other one. As early as the late 1940s, it was visible to some of us then living in Russia that the Soviet regime was becoming dangerously remote from the concerns and hopes of the Russian people. The original ideological and emotional motivation of Russian communism had worn itself out and became lost in the exertions of the great war. And there was already apparent a growing generational gap within the regime itself. These thoughts, it may be recalled, found a place in my so-called "X" article of 1947. They were even more clearly expressed in a letter written in 1952, when I was ambassador in Moscow, to a senior official in the State Department—a letter that has been subsequently widely published. There were some of us to whom it was quite clear, even at those early dates, that the Soviet regime as we had known it was not there for all time. We could not know when or how it would be changed. We knew only that the change was inevitable and impending.

By the time Stalin died, in 1953, even many members of the Communist Party had come to see his dictatorship as grotesque, dangerous, and unnecessary; and there was, in the wake of his demise, a general

Originally published (in a somewhat different version) in the *New York Times,* October 28, 1992.

impression that far-reaching changes were in order. It was Nikita Khrushchev who took the leadership in the resulting liberalizing tendencies. He was, in his crude way, a firm Communist. But he was not wholly un-open to reasonable argument. His personality offered the greatest hope for internal political liberalization and the relaxation of international tensions. It was the U-2 episode in 1960 that, more than anything else, put an end to this hope. It humiliated Khrushchev and discredited his relatively moderate policies. It forced him to fall back for the defense of his own political position on a more strongly belligerent anti-American tone of public utterance.

The U-2 episode was the clearest sort of example of that primacy of military over political policy that was soon to become an outstanding feature of American Cold War policy. The extreme militarization of American discussion and policy, as promoted by hard-line circles in this country over the ensuing twenty-five years, had the consistent effect of strengthening comparable hard-line elements in the Soviet Union. The more American political leadership was seen in Moscow as committed to an ultimate military, rather than political, resolution of Soviet-American tensions, the greater was the tendency in Moscow to tighten the controls by both party and police, and the greater the braking effect on all liberalizing tendencies within the regime. Thus the general effect of Cold War extremisms was to delay rather than hasten the great change that overtook that country at the end of the 1980s.

What did the greatest damage was not our military preparations themselves, some of which (not all) were prudent and justifiable. It was rather the unnecessarily belligerent and threatening tone in which many of them were publicly carried forward. For this, both of our great political parties deserve a share of the blame.

Nobody "won" the Cold War. It was a long and costly political rivalry, fueled on both sides by unreal and exaggerated estimates of the intentions and strength of the other side. It greatly overstrained the economic resources of both countries, leaving them both, by the end of the 1980s, confronted with heavy financial, social, and—in the case of the Russians—political problems neither had anticipated and for which neither was fully prepared. The fact that in Russia's case these changes were long desired on principle by most of us does not alter the fact that they came, and came far too precipitately, upon a population little prepared for them, thus creating new problems of the greatest seriousness for Russia, her neighbors, and the rest of us—problems to which, as yet, none of us have found effective answers.

All these developments should be seen as part of the price we are paying for the Cold War. As in most great international conflicts, it is a price to be paid by both countries. That the conflict itself should now be formally ended is a fit occasion for satisfaction, but also for sober reexamination of the part we took in its origin and its long continuation. It is not a fit occasion for pretending that the end of it was a great triumph for anyone, and particularly one for which any American political party could properly claim credit.

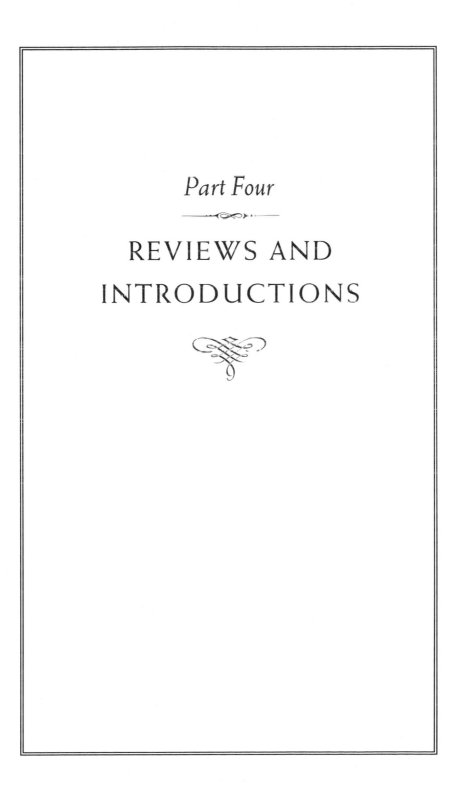

Part Four

REVIEWS AND
INTRODUCTIONS

The Balkan Crises: 1913 and 1993
(1993)

————————⌀————————

1

At the outset of the present century, there emerged in the United States, England, and other parts of northern Europe a vigorous movement for strengthening and consolidating world peace, primarily by the developing of new legal codes of international behavior. The movement was given a significant fillip when Tsar Nicholas II of Russia in 1899 issued a call for an international conference on disarmament. This curious initiative, largely the product of the immature dilettantism of the tsar and elaborated by the characteristic confusion of the Russian governmental establishment of the time, was not a serious one. But it was at once seized upon with enthusiasm by adherents of the peace movements and had consequences the tsar himself had not anticipated. Of those, the most important were the two Hague Peace Conferences of 1899 and 1907, resulting in a modernization and renewed codification of international law and in a significant elaboration, in particular, of the laws of war.

Beyond that there was, especially in the United States, a marked surge of interest in and enthusiasm for the negotiation and adoption of treaties of arbitration and conciliation. And these governmental efforts were supported by a number of private institutional initiatives, of which one of the most lasting and notable was the founding, in 1910,

Originally published in the *New York Review of Books,* July 15, 1993. Introduction to *The Other Balkan Wars* (Carnegie Endowment for International Peace, 1993).

of the Carnegie Endowment for International Peace. That institution was only one of the several creative initiatives of Andrew Carnegie on behalf of world peace, another being the erection of the great "Peace Palace" at the Hague.

It is both sad and ironic to reflect that these so far-seeing and commendable efforts on behalf of international peace were proceeding simultaneously with the intensive pursuit by the great European powers of what were, whether so intended or otherwise, preparations for the First World War. As recently as 1894, the French and Russian general staffs had linked the fates of their countries in a secret treaty of alliance, so worded as almost to ensure that there could be no further minor complication in European affairs that would not lead to wider hostilities among the great powers. In 1898, there was inaugurated, for the first time in earnest, the unnecessary and dreadfully misguided effort of Kaiser Wilhelm II's Germany to compete with Great Britain in the development of naval power. And throughout all of it, the great powers were busy with other military preparations that, however defensively conceived, simply diminished whatever small possibility of avoiding a general conflagration might still have existed.

In the face of all the preparations, the strivings and enthusiasms of the peace movement of those first years of this century might appear, in retrospect, unrealistic, naive, and pathetic. But they were, in addition to being—as we see today—profoundly prophetic in the concerns they reflected, deeply, almost desperately, believed in by those who experienced them. And they were not wholly without justification. Nearly a hundred years had then elapsed since the last great all-European military conflagration, that of the Napoleonic wars. An entire generation had intervened since the last great bilateral intra-European conflict, the Franco-Prussian War. Was there not then, people could ask themselves, a possibility that the great European powers could now be brought, with sufficient outside encouragement and pressure, to perceive the folly of war among highly industrialized powers in the modern age and then to retire at the brink?

It was in the entertainment of such hopes, fears, and aspirations that the protagonists of the American and European peace movements were struggling along as Europe entered the second decade of the twentieth century.

A hundred years before that time, the entire Balkan peninsula, from the Aegean Sea and the Turkish straits to the borders of the Russian and Austro-Hungarian Empires, had been, with minor exceptions, embraced by the Turkish Empire. But in the course of the nineteenth century, the Turks had been compelled to withdraw southward and eastward, to a point where all that remained of their European dominions were the southernmost parts of the peninsula, primarily Thrace and Macedonia. By the beginning of the twentieth century, a number of new states—notably Bulgaria, Serbia, Montenegro, and Romania—had sprung up in the area thus liberated from Turkish control. Those states were, without exception, monarchically governed; and the monarchs were, as a rule, somewhat more moderate and thoughtful than their subjects. But their dynasties were not well established. Their powers were usually disputed by inexperienced and unruly parliamentary bodies. Borders were in many instances vague and lacking in firm acceptance. The entire peninsula was, in short, devoid of international stability.

It was, of course, a time when the powerful forces of modern nationalism were achieving everywhere, but particularly in nations new to the experience of political independence, their greatest intensity. And nowhere did this have a more violent, intoxicating effect than on the politicians and military leaders of the newly founded Balkan countries. If, initially, the leading impulses for the expulsion of the Turks from European Russia had come from the neighboring great powers, Russia and Austria-Hungary, the political leaders of the newly established Balkan states were now beginning to take matters into their own hands. And it was hard for people who had recently achieved so much, and this so suddenly, to know where to stop. Dreams of new glories to flow from territorial expansion bemused many minds. The air was clouded by visions of a greater this or that: a "greater Serbia," a "greater Bulgaria," and so on. And while the remaining areas of Turkish control in the southern Balkans, Thrace and Macedonia, were by no means the only objectives of such aspirations, it was no more than natural that they should have been the principal ones. Turkey was regarded, in the common phrase of the time, as "the sick man of Europe." If this "sick man" had now been expelled from most of the peninsula, was there any reason why he could not be similarly expelled from the remainder as well? For that, however, alliance and common action were required. "Let us unite to complete the expulsion of the

Turks," was the general feeling. "And then, when we are free," as one Bulgarian revolutionary put it, "each shall have what belongs to him."

Vague impulses of that nature, hastily linked together by a flimsy patchwork of secret and poorly thought-out military engagements, led the Serbs, Bulgarians, Greeks, and Montenegrins to launch conjointly, in the early autumn of 1912, a military action against the Turks. That was the first of the two Balkan wars of 1912 and 1913. The Turks, as it happened, proved to be considerably weaker than had been generally supposed. Within a few weeks, they had been driven to the gates of Constantinople, and the war was over.

But never, surely, did any coalition of powers launch a war on the basis of flimsier understandings among them about what it was they were fighting for than did the participants of this military action against the Turks. The relations among the supposed allies, and particularly the most prominent of them—Serbs, Bulgarians, and Greeks—had even before this been of the worst kind, ridden by rivalries, suspicions, and conflicting aims. The result was predictable. The defeat of the Turks ended with forces of Serbia, Bulgaria, and Greece occupying portions of the helpless Macedonia. Each had aspirations with relation to the territory that could be satisfied only at the expense of the others. It was not surprising, therefore, that in June 1913 war broke out among them. It was this that was known as the second Balkan war.

This second fracas centered upon the fighting between the Serbs and the Bulgarians, long-standing rivals for preeminence in that southern part of the Balkans. Hostilities were furious but brief, lasting only over the midsummer of 1913. The Bulgarians, already overextended by their action against the Turks, were decisively defeated. A species of peace treaty (like many such arrangements, in essence a provisorium) was signed in Bucharest on August 10, 1913.

The news that war had broken out in the Balkans naturally came as a shock to the adherents of the European and American peace movements. The shock was modified, to be sure, by the fact that in Britain and America public opinion, and in particular the liberal opinion so prominently represented in the peace movements, had for years been strongly, sometimes fulsomely, sympathetic to the Balkan Slavs in their struggle for liberation from Turkey. Many well-meaning people in the West found it easy, in light of this enthusiasm, to forget that the hostilities had been inaugurated in the first war by the Balkan Slavs themselves, in ways that constituted violations not only of international law but of existing contractual agreements of one sort or another.

In the case of the second war, the situation was different. The Turks (although they took advantage of the occasion to recover a small part of the territory they had lost) were no longer a principal party to the hostilities. Not only that, but reports were now coming in of the extreme savagery of the fighting that had marked the first war and of the many atrocities against war prisoners and innocent civilian populations that had accompanied it. It was becoming evident that by no means all of the atrocities had come from the Turkish side. Altogether, it was now being realized that the continuation of the Balkan hostilities constituted a serious challenge to the peace movements of the time.

By no institution in the West could that challenge have been more keenly felt than by the Carnegie Endowment for International Peace. Only three years had elapsed since its founding. What was happening was plainly in flagrant conflict with its commitment. But what could be done? What action could it take? Disturbing as the situation was, the information coming in from the area of hostilities was still for the most part fragmentary, indirect, and unsatisfactory. Little of it was fully reliable. It was hard to know how to distinguish fact from fiction, reality from exaggeration, the known from the merely alleged. Before far-reaching decisions could be made, one had to gain a clearer picture of what was happening.

This was the background for the decision of the Carnegie Endowment, made immediately upon the outbreak of the second war, to set up a prestigious international commission and to charge it with the task of establishing the facts and giving to Western opinion a clear and reliable picture of what was going on in the affected region. Once this picture was available, it would be easier, one felt, not just for the endowment itself but for the many others as well who were committed to the cause of international peace to determine what might be done to set things to rights.

The commission, then, was duly established. It consisted of seven members: one each from the United States, Britain, Germany, Austria-Hungary, and Russia, and two from France. They were all men of some prominence in their respective countries, chosen particularly for their interest in the peace movements. The presidency of the commission was exercised by a French senator, Baron d'Estournelles de

Constant, a man of much eminence who had not only taken a prominent part in the peace movement, serving as the French representative to the Hague conferences, but had considerable familiarity with at least one area of the Balkans.

Four of the men were designated to serve as a special fact-finding subcommittee charged with visiting the region of the Balkan hostilities on behalf of the commission. Three included the American, Dr. Samuel T. Dutton, professor at Teacher's College, Columbia University; the French lawyer and member of the Chamber of Deputies M. Justin Godart; and the well-known Russian professor, historian, writer, and liberal political figure Paul Milyukov (destined later to play so prominent a role in the provisional government of 1917). The fourth was a British journalist, a man whose distinction was also to reach its acme in later years: Henry N. Brailsford. A person of outstanding intelligence, literary talent, and scholarly diligence, Brailsford would appear to have had extensive previous experience in the Balkans and was conversant with at least two of its languages. He had lived in both Greece and Macedonia and had written, some six years earlier, an excellent book on the Macedonia of that day. Milyukov had also had earlier experience in the Balkans, particularly as a dilettante archaeologist in Bulgaria and Macedonia between 1897 and 1899.

These men set forth from Paris on August 2, 1913, shortly before the ending of the second of the two wars. Their journey took them, together or severally, to Belgrade, Salonica, Athens, Constantinople, and Sofia. Although the commission's report includes no account of their experiences, reason tells us that it must have been, to say the least, an eventful journey; and that supposition is confirmed by several hints given us in Baron d'Estournelles' introduction to the report. From these hints we may conclude, for example, that the Serbian government, resenting (for different reasons in each case) the inclusion of Milyukov and Brailsford in the delegation, not only declined to give any official recognition to the commissioners but also was initially reluctant to assist them in practical ways. The commissioners persisted, however, and in the end the government provided them "with every facility for reaching the frontier and Salonica."

The Greek government, similarly motivated, officially denied permission for Brailsford (who had once fought with the Greeks against the Turks but had later been critical of the Greeks in certain respects)

to come to Kilkich, and limited his movements while he was in Salonica. As a result of these reactions, Milyukov curtailed his participation. But the other three commissioners, undismayed by the rebuffs,
pushed on with their mission; and after nearly eight weeks of strenuous travel, they returned to Paris on September 28. They had seen little of the actual hostilities, which ended at roughly the same time the
commissioners arrived. But they had seen much of their immediate aftermath, and had tapped the fresh memories of many survivors, military and civilian. That, in the circumstances, was quite enough.

The report of the commission consisted of seven chapters beginning with a long historical introduction leading up to the outbreak of
the first war but no further. There followed three chapters, comprising 135 of the report's long and finely printed pages, forming the very
body of the document. Those chapters dealt exclusively with the excesses, and particularly the atrocities, that marked the hostilities and
their aftermath: in short, the abundant evidence of violations not only
of international law but of the minimum dictates of common humanity. While the final report, issued unanimously in the names of all the
members of the commission, did not identify the authors of the various chapters, the Carnegie Endowment's archives clarify the matter,
without indicating the degree of collaboration among the principal authors. The first chapter, the historical résumé, was written by Milyukov. The following three, concentrating on the atrocities, were
from the pen of Brailsford (chapter two) or Milyukov (chapters three
and four).

There followed a chapter on the precise relationship of the two wars
to the principles and accepted provisions of international law—a document that also came from Milyukov's pen. A further chapter, on the
economic consequences of the two wars, was written by the French
authority, Godart. The brief final chapter of conclusions, written by
Dutton, was a sad and penetrating document, not hesitating to recognize the two wars as "a ghastly chapter of horrors," declaring that the
commission's members could "indulge in no optimism regarding the
immediate political future of Macedonia" in particular, and confessing that for the region in general the case for the future seemed "well
nigh hopeless" in the light of prevailing conditions.

Following the return of the three commissioners who visited the
affected area, the report was rather laboriously put together—labori-

ously because the several members of the commission were living in widely dispersed geographical locations; and it was not completed and made public until the early summer of 1914. It was, of course, destined to be at once blanketed, in the attention and reactions of the world public, by the more sensational event of the outbreak of the First World War—a circumstance that offers all the more reason for its republication today, when the attention of world opinion is once more so unhappily drawn to the still unsolved problems of the region with which it dealt.

Examined from a distance of some eighty years, the report makes today, in some respects, an odd impression. There seems to be little unity among its various parts. In the narrative chapters, those describing the atrocities, no effort seems to have been made to relate the happenings to the political and military events that supplied the background for them—not even noting the beginnings and endings of hostilities in the various wars and regions. There was no attempt to analyze the political motivations of the governments participating in the wars, or to suggest what might be done by the peace movements to prevent the wars' recurrence. But the document is replete with interesting and often penetrating passages on individual matters; and it may stand, in its entirety, as one of the most eloquent and compelling pleas for recognition of the folly of modern war and the essential need for international peace, not just in the Balkans but everywhere in the civilized world, ever penned.

2

All of the above having been said, the importance of the report for the world of 1993 lies primarily in the light it casts on the excruciating situation prevailing today in the same Balkan world. The greatest value of the report is to reveal to people of this age how much of today's problem has deep roots and how much does not. It will be easier to think of solutions when such realities are kept in mind.

The measure of historical continuity should not be exaggerated. There are significant differences between the Balkan situation of 1913 and that of the present day. There has been since that time a revolution in weaponry. In 1913, even the machine gun was in its infancy. There was no air power. Motor vehicles were so scarce that they played no significant part in military transport. For the most part, the atrocities recounted in the report were committed by the bayonet, the rifle butt, the cudgel, and the whiplash.

The revolution in communication, so predominant in daily life in our day and strongly affecting military affairs, would have been not only implausible but probably wholly unimaginable to the peoples and the soldiers of 1913. The outside world knew of the horrors of that day only from the reports of itinerant journalists. The report of Carnegie's Balkan commission was, in its capacity as a thorough survey of at least one outstanding aspect of those wars, a unique phenomenon. Today, the evidence of all the excesses, and in some instances the excesses themselves, is seen on the television screens of hundreds of millions of homes across the globe. And the publicity has had much to do with the prominent involvement of Western governments and other outsiders in the hostilities, an involvement taking the form of the presence of many thousands of Westerners—U.N. and Red Cross personnel, reporters and photographers for the press, representatives of private charitable organizations, and official conciliators—at or near the scenes of hostilities. The commissioners of 1913 were almost alone in their effort to bring to the attention of the world the truly alarming aspects of Balkan violence. Today, they would have had a host of collaborators in such an effort.

But even more significant than those differences are the many and depressing evidences of similarity between what was occurring in the Balkans in 1913 and what is going on there today. There are too many to be listed here, but a few examples will suffice.

Let us take just the general manner in which warfare is being waged. The common feature of Balkan wars, the 1913 report stated, is that "war is waged not only by the armies but by the nations themselves. . . . This is why these wars are so sanguinary, why they produce so great a loss in men, and end in the annihilation of the population and the ruin of whole regions." The object of armed conflict, the report continued, was "the complete extermination of an alien population." Villages were not just captured; they were in large part destroyed. The inhabitants were driven out (where they had not already fled), and their houses burned. Woe betided the man of military age, or the woman of "enemy" national identity, who was found alive in the conquered village. Rape was ubiquitous, sometimes murderous.

Victims, now wholly dispossessed and homeless, were obliged to take to the roads or the mountain trails by the thousands, in a frantic search for places where they could at least lay their heads. Great streams of pathetically suffering refugees could be seen on many of the roads of the peninsula. Little pity was shown for the sick and the wounded. Prisoners of war, if not killed outright, were sometimes driven into outdoor compounds or ramshackle buildings and left there to die of hunger and exposure. There was in general a total hard-heartedness toward the defeated, whether military or civilian. Some of this was carried beyond the level of neglect and indifference and into the realm of sickening and deliberate cruelty.

The similarity of all this with what is happening today is inescapable. And comparisons of who, statistically, has committed the most atrocities are idle. A single person's painful death under such treatment is always alone a measureless tragedy. That there were any such horrors at all in the Balkan wars was an abomination. Often, as the 1913 commissioners discovered, the rumors of the scale of the atrocities turned out, upon careful examination, to be exaggerations. But the commissioners were also obliged to point out, in many such instances, that the residue of reality discovered to lie behind the quantitative exaggerations was in itself enough to turn the stomach of any reasonably decent person.

It was often similarly charged in 1913 that those who ordered the excesses were not the regular governments and commanders—that the atrocities were carried out by armed bands of like political sympathies, but operating semi-independently under their own chieftains. The 1913 commissioners found this a lame excuse. If the behavior in question was not ordered by the regular commanders, they pointed out, it was certainly tolerated and winked at, sometimes actually encouraged, by them. Again, the comparison with what is going on today is obvious.

The 1913 commissioners found it hard, in investigating all the excesses, to distinguish comparative degrees of guilt among the various belligerents. The Serbs, indeed, figured as major offenders, particularly for the manner in which they treated the Macedonians in the liberated territory they occupied in the aftermath of the first of the two wars. But the Serbs happened to be, as they are described in the hostilities of 1992 and 1993, the strongest party. And who could say with certainty or even plausibility that the other parties, had they been in the driver's seat, would have behaved any better? None, after all, was entirely innocent in that respect. The commission's report emphasized that "there is no clause in international law applicable to land war and to the treatment of the wounded, which was not violated, to a greater or lesser extent, by all the belligerents."

The question arose in the minds of the commissioners of how much the ferocity of these hostilities could be properly attributed to religious fanaticism. That religion played a part in the animosities that motivated the fighting was clearly recognized. This was particularly the case in the first of the wars, which found the mostly Christian parties ranged together against the Muslim Turks. And similar situations occurred in the second war as well, there being Muslim elements in both the Bulgarian and Macedonian populations.

But to conclude that those differences were the principal cause of animosity would be to go too far. The Turks, for one thing, appear to have been, in the centuries of their onetime ascendancy in the Balkans, relatively tolerant in their treatment of non-Muslim religious institutions. Their treatment of such institutions was in any case not the leading grievance against them. And as the future was to demonstrate, the Christians were capable of being just as violent and savage in their conflicts with other Christians as they were with the Muslims. In the period of these Balkan wars, the Croats, as the only Roman Catholic people, were still, with minor exceptions, living in areas belonging to or under the occupation of the Austro-Hungarian Empire. They were not, therefore, directly involved in these two Balkan wars; and the Eastern Orthodox versus Roman Catholic religious antagonisms that were to play so unfortunate a role in later years were not at that time prominently involved.

No, the strongest motivating factor involved in the Balkan wars was not religion but aggressive nationalism. But that nationalism, as it manifested itself on the field of battle, drew on deeper traits of character inherited, presumably, from a distant tribal past: a tendency to view the outsider, generally, with dark suspicion and to see the political-military opponent, in particular, as a fearful and implacable enemy to be rendered harmless only by total and unpitying destruction. And so it remains today.

In attempting to reason with the respective governments about these matters, the 1913 commissioners found themselves up against blank walls. What was called in the report "the megalomania of the national ideal" had room for neither reason nor compromise. Statistics used to support a government's case were distorted to the point of sheer absurdity. Those invoked by different governments differed so widely so as to afford no conceivable basis for reconciliation. Yet anyone who challenged a given government's version of the truth documented himself thereby, in the eyes of that government, as a committed enemy. "It is," wrote Baron d'Estournelles in his introduction to the report, "impossible to avoid the reproach of a party, if one does not take sides with it against the others, and conversely." In the face of extreme nationalistic self-admiration and suspicion of every neighbor, there was little room for anything resembling conciliation.

One cannot end this summary of the similarities between yesterday and today without noting some of the reminiscences and reflections of the president of the Balkan commission, Baron d'Estournelles, as recorded in his introduction to the report. He had served many years before as a member of the international commission set up to delineate, on the spot, the Balkan boundaries described in the Berlin Treaty of 1879–1880. He had taken advantage of those duties to travel independently through much of Albania and Macedonia. Those countries were then very little known. They "were then, and are still, unlike Europe," he wrote, "more widely separated from her than Europe from America." Such were the impressions he had gained that he had, "as a matter of professional discretion, scarcely dared" to publish any of them.

Even then there had been hesitations about the desirability of sending a commission to investigate the circumstances of the Balkan wars. What if the commission should find "that the atrocities were inevitable, inseparable from the condition of war . . . ? What an exposure of the powerlessness of civilization!" And would its efforts not merely stimulate the animosities? It was that anxiety, "the fear of compromise, the fear of displeasing one or another of the nations, the terror, in short, of intervening reasonably and in time, which has brought about a crisis, the gravity of which is not only of yesterday and of today, but also of tomorrow."

Others were saying, of course, why go further afield to seek troubles and duties? Have you not enough to do at home? "Yes," was

Baron d'Estournelles' answer. "We have plenty to do at home." But "my own imperfection," he argued, "need not prevent me from doing my utmost to be useful." And, after all: "All this horror will not cease to exist as long as Europe continues to ignore it. . . . The spectacle of destitute childhood in a civilized country is beginning to rouse the hardest hearts. What shall be said of destitution of a whole people, of several nations, in Europe, in the Twentieth Century?" And then came this paragraph:

> This is the state of things which the Americans wish to help in ending. Let them be thanked and honored for their generous initiative. I have been appealing to it for a long time. . . . We are only too happy today to combine our strength, too willing to raise with them a cry of protestation against the contempt of skeptics and ill-wishers who will try to suppress it.

Well, here we are, in 1993. Eighty years of tremendous change in the remainder of Europe and of further internecine strife in the Balkans themselves have done little to alter the essence of the problem this geographic region presents for Europe, for our own country, and for the United Nations. Obviously, it is a problem with very deep historical roots. Those roots reach back, clearly, not only into the centuries of Turkish domination but also into the Byzantine penetration of the Balkans even before that time.

One must not be too hard on the Turks. The atrocities attributed to them in this report were no worse than those that the Christian peoples were inflicting both on the Turks and on each other in these wars. The report makes reference to the fact that there were those in Macedonia, in the period of Greek and Serbian occupation, who began to long for the return of the Turks. But that this effective separation from Europe during three centuries of immensely significant development in the civilization of the remainder of the European continent had profound effects on the development of the Balkan peoples cannot be denied. The author of the first historical résumé in the 1913 report referred to the Turkish conquest as "leveling all the nationalities and preserving them all alike in a condition of torpor, in a manner comparable to the action of a vast refrigerator." And it is worth noting that the events of the second part of the present century, most prominently the thirty years of Communist power, were not helpful in thawing out that congealment; in a sense, they may be said to have prolonged it.

What we are up against is the sad fact that developments of those earlier ages, not only those of the Turkish domination but of earlier ones as well, had the effect of thrusting into the southeastern reaches of the European continent a salient of non-European civilization that has continued to the present day to preserve many of its non-European characteristics, including some that fit even less with the world of today than they did with the world of eighty years ago. It will be argued that these states of mind are not peculiar to the Balkan peoples—that they can be encountered among other European peoples as well. True enough. But these distinctions are relative ones. It is the undue predominance among the Balkan peoples of these particular qualities that seems to be decisive as a determinant of the troublesome, baffling, and dangerous situation that marks that part of the world today.

3

What, then, can be done?

That question has already been the subject of extensive discussion and altercation in Western opinion; and this is not the place for any attempt at a definitive answer. But there are two or three observations that might serve as a suitable termination for this introduction.

First of all, let it be noted that while this Balkan situation is one to which the United States cannot be indifferent, it is primarily a problem for the Europeans. It is their continent, not ours, that is affected. They have the physical and military resources with which to confront the problem. And if they claim, as many of them do, that they lack the political unity to confront it successfully, the answer is that perhaps this is one of those instances, not uncommon in the lives of nations as of individuals, when one has to rise to the occasion.

Second, it is clear that no one—no particular country and no group of countries—wants, or should be expected, to occupy the entire distracted Balkan region, to subdue its excited peoples, and to hold them in order until they can calm down and begin to look at their problems in a more orderly way. Conceivably, such an occupation might be momentarily helpful; but even that is not certain; and in any case, any effort along that line could be only the most tenuous and temporary of improvisations. In the long run, no region can solve any other region's problems. The best the outsider can do is to give occasional supplementary help in the pinches.

And finally, there is the question of the more distant future. When the present hostilities are ended (as someday they must be), there will still remain the question of how the Balkan peoples are to interact with each other in the years that lie ahead.

Let us glance at what will presumably be the formal international structure of the Balkan community in the post-hostilities period. We may start by leaving aside two of the possible actors on that scene: the Slovenes, who are really an alpine people and who will, let us hope, remain remote from Balkan political affairs; and the Montenegrins, who have so extensively identified themselves with the Serbs in the recent unpleasantness that we may regard them as effectively subsumed by the Serbian state. There will then presumably remain eight countries actively involved in Balkan problems: Greece, Albania, Macedonia, Serbia, Croatia, Romania, Bulgaria, and Bosnia (or as much of it as survives). That is three more than there were before the breakup of Yugoslavia.

If there is to be followed the modern custom of conferring upon any body politic of whatever size or quality that demands membership in the United Nations the status of a fully sovereign state, theoretically equal to every other state in its proud, independent quality, then each of the Balkan states will presumably be given that status, if it does not already enjoy it. And each of them, we might note, will then have the right to develop whatever armed forces its resources and circumstances will permit.

Now, the practice of conferring that status on Balkan peoples is not new. The same practice was followed more than a century ago when the first of them were liberated from Turkish rule. Even then, the result was not a happy one, as is so clearly shown in the Carnegie report of 1914. It soon became evident that the new states had great difficulty in relating to one another in a mature and peaceful manner. In a sense, there was more peace when they were still under Turkish rule than there was after they gained their independence. (That is not to say that the Turkish rule was in all other respects superior to what came after.)

Eighty years have now passed since the Carnegie commissioners paid their visit to that region. And I know of no evidence that the ability of the Balkan peoples to interact peaceably with one another is any greater now than it was those eighty years ago. If proof of that were needed, it would be abundantly there in the appalling state of hostilities that now prevails in the region. And the difficulty of such interaction can only have been heightened by the fact that the number of players at this tragic game has now been significantly increased.

A further complication exists in the question of the future relationship of certain of those peoples, and particularly the Serbs, to the United Nations. The Serbs, just to take them as the leading example, have violated in every conceivable way the one and only requirement for membership in the United Nations as specified in its charter: "to accept the obligations contained in the present Charter, and, in the judgement of the Organization, [to be] able and willing to carry out these obligations." Not only have the Serbs consistently and contemptuously flouted, for months on end, the obligations in question, but they have repeatedly exerted themselves to frustrate the U.N.'s efforts to relieve the sufferings of the civilian population in the region of hostilities. In some instances, they would appear even to have opposed U.N. efforts by force of arms. And there could have been no behavior more fundamentally contrary to the first principles of the U.N. Charter, not to mention the provisions of international war and the laws of war, then the persistent artillery bombardment over weeks and months on end of the helpless civilian populations of entire cities. Something of the same could be said, no doubt, of the behavior of certain of the other parties; but if so, it would be true in far lesser degree.

What account is to be taken of such conduct, one wonders, when it comes to a peace settlement and the determination of future international relationships in the region? To date, no one has suggested that the membership of Yugoslavia in the U.N. should even be suspended in light of the behavior of the Serbs in the theater of hostilities. Are we to assume that when it comes to designing a post-hostilities settlement, all this is to be forgotten and the Yugoslavs (read: the Serbs) and the other parties are to be welcomed back to their normal position and role in the United Nations, as though none of this had ever happened? And if so, what would that say to any other U.N. member that found itself in some sort of military conflict and thought it to its advantage to ignore and flout its obligations as a member of that organization?

And what, indeed, would it say to the world as a whole about the U.N. as the only living and accepted symbol of the community of fate that links all the peoples of this planet? Are we to understand that membership involves no significant obligations at all? That the charter's provisions on membership are meaningless and that the persistent and contemptuous disregard of them has no effect on a country's membership?

Those are questions that are bound to present themselves when the necessity arises of devising some future status quo for international life in the Balkans to replace that which has now broken down so disastrously. If all these countries are to be established or reestablished as fully independent and sovereign states, members of the United Nations, with no serious obligations to flow from U.N. membership and without any other significant restraints on their conduct, what are we to expect, on the record of the more remote past and of the immediate one, of their future interaction? Let us recall, as just one example of the potential instability, that at least three of them, the Bulgarians, Greeks, and Serbs, and possibly a fourth, the Albanians, have political or territorial designs on one of their neighbors, Macedonia—designs that are sure to come to the surface of their interrelationships as soon as attention is withdrawn from the present hostilities.

It is relentlessly obvious that when the present military conflict is over, the international community, and particularly the European community, is going to find itself up against a very ugly problem in this southeastern part of the European continent. Two things will be necessary: the first, a new and clearly accepted territorial status quo; the second, certain greater and more effective restraints on the behavior of the states of the region. It would be naive to suppose that the first of those requirements could be met solely by negotiations among the various parties themselves. Their views should, of course, be heard and seriously considered; but it will take outside mediation, and in all probability outside force, to devise a reasonable settlement and to bring the parties to accept and observe it. As for the second, the restraints on the Balkan parties, in the exercise of what they view as their unlimited sovereignty and freedom of action, will clearly have to be greater than those that are now normally applied in the international community.

There will, therefore, be two necessities to confront those who, from the outside, try to be helpful in the solution of this great problem. One will be a capacity for innovation with respect to the rights and duties implicit in the term "sovereignty." The other will be force—minimum force, of course, but force nevertheless—and the readiness to employ it where nothing else will do.

Those will, I repeat, be necessities confronting in the most immediate way the European community; but the wider international community will also have a serious interest in seeing them met. Is there any reason to believe that in either of those communities the necessary resolve to tackle this problem, and the necessary readiness to accept the attendant agonies of effort, will be forthcoming? The answer is that there is only one reason; and that is the fact that the alternatives, for anyone who looks realistically at the problem, will clearly be worse.

In the American Mirror
(1986)

———··◦◦◦◦··———

Schlesinger sees two profoundly rooted but conflicting strains in the way Americans view themselves—in the role, that is, in which they cast themselves—as a nation among other nations. Sometimes these two strains do battle with each other in the same American breast; more often, large segments of opinion lean decisively one way or another, with the result that each of the strains has had its period, or periods, of ascendancy in American public life.

One of these views, strong initially among the Founding Fathers themselves, saw Americans as essentially no different from the general run of human beings: subject to the same limitations; affected by the same restrictions of vision; tainted by the same original sin or, in a more secular view, by the same inner conflicts between flesh and spirit, between self-love and charity. This view in its original eighteenth-century form was also informed by the recognition that history had had, to that time, few examples to show of a solid and enduring republic, whereas one could point to a number of examples of empires and monarchies that answered reasonably well to this description. Against this background of perception, the Founding Fathers tended for the most part to see the establishment of the national independence and unity of the United States as an experiment—not an easy one, not one whose success was automatically assured; rather, as Schlesinger describes

Review of *The Cycles of American History,* by Arthur M. Schlesinger, Jr. (New York: Houghton Mifflin, 1986); originally published in the *New York Review of Books,* November 6, 1986.

it, an experiment "undertaken in defiance of history, fraught with risk, problematic in outcome." With this question mark lying across its future, the fledgling republic could obviously not appear as a guide or teacher to the rest of humanity. Its first duty was to itself. The best it could ask of its international environment was to be left alone to develop its institutions in its own way and to prove, if possible, that a nation thus conceived and thus dedicated could, as Lincoln put it, "long endure."

In the opposite strain of perception, Americans saw themselves not as conducting and enacting a great experiment but as fulfilling a predetermined destiny. This view had its origins in the religious convictions of many early New England colonists. They saw in the very fact of their removal to this continent the influence of "a wonder-working Providence"—a "journey of the elect," as Schlesinger describes it, "to salvation beyond history." From this, it was only a step to the belief that Americans had inherited the Old Testamentary concept of the chosen race. Schlesinger cites several striking examples of the intensity of this feeling among prominent figures of the early decades of the republic. With time, of course, this view became secularized. Nationalistic fervor, that contagious hysteria of all nineteenth-century Western society, gave it a far wider currency than it had ever before enjoyed. Strength was lent by the nation's survival of the Civil War, which to many appeared as evidence that the experiment of American nationhood had been successfully completed. What remained, then, was a widespread impression, supported by patriotic emotion, that the Almighty, in Schlesinger's words, "had contrived a nation unique in its virtue and magnanimity, exempt from the motives that governed all other states."

Of central importance in this dichotomy of views was the relationship to a sense of history. The old concept of America as experiment was imbedded in profound historical consciousness. It was as part of history's endless web, partially inscrutable but still man's greatest aid to self-understanding, that the experiment was seen to have its existence. Not so for those who saw America as destiny. Essential to their outlook was "a narcissistic withdrawal from history"—a phenomenon that, as Schlesinger correctly observes, reached its apotheosis in the recent postwar decades. "For all the preservation of landmarks and the show biz of bicentennials," he writes, we have become, so far as interest and knowledge are concerned, an essentially historyless people. The young no longer study history. Academics turn their back on history in the enthusiasm for the historical behavioral "sciences." As American historical consciousness has thinned out, the messianic hope has flowed into the vacuum.

At this point, Schlesinger leans heavily on the brilliant insights of Reinhold Niebuhr's *Irony of American History* to challenge directly the validity of the messianic approach. He describes this as an illusion:

> No nation is sacred and unique. . . . All nations are immediate to God. America, like every country, has interests real and fictitious, concerns generous and selfish, motives honorable and squalid. Providence has not set Americans apart from lesser breeds. We too are part of history's seamless web.

In the essay "Foreign Policy and the American Character," Schlesinger traces the effect of this deep dichotomy on the recent and current conduct of American foreign policy. Here, the two poles have acquired, justifiably, a different semantic clothing: realism versus ideology. Admitting that in the mentality of most political leaders of this century the division between these two outlooks was never a complete one (so powerful were the two strains in mass opinion that the practical politician has had no choice but to try to appeal simultaneously to both), Schlesinger nevertheless sees the Reagan administration as representing "a mighty comeback of messianism in foreign policy." He draws attention, in particular, to the way this affects outlooks toward the Soviet Union. Realism sees in that political entity "a weary, dreary country filled with cynicism and corruption, beset by insuperable problems at home and abroad, lurching uncertainly from crisis to crisis." Ideology, on the other hand,

> withdraws problems from the turbulent stream of change and treats them in abstraction from the whirl and contingency of life. So ideology portrays the Soviet Union as an unalterable monolith, immune to historical vicissitude and permutation, its behavior determined by immutable logic, the same yesterday, today and tomorrow. . . . We are forever in 1950, with a dictator in the

Kremlin commanding an obedient network of communist parties and agents around the planet. In the light of ideology, the Soviet Union appears as a fanatic state carrying out with implacable zeal and cunning a master plan for world dominion.

These observations provide the point of departure for an attack on the Reagan foreign policy as forceful and eloquent as any I can recall having seen. Drawing attention to the contradictions even in the handling of the East-West confrontation ("a long twilight struggle between bark and bite"), this polemic runs the gamut from Central America to the arms race. It comes down hard on the irony of the simultaneous and symbiotic prospering of Pentagon and Soviet Defense Ministry: "There is no greater racket in the world today than generals claiming the other side is ahead in order to get bigger budgets for themselves. This tacit collusion, based on a common vested interest in crisis, remains a major obstacle in the search for peace." And the conclusions are uncompromising:

> Ideology is the curse of public affairs because it converts politics into a branch of theology and sacrifices human beings on the altar of dogma. In the end [it] is out of character for Americans. . . . They would do well to sober up from the ideological binge and return to the cold, gray realism of the Founding Fathers, men who lucidly understood the role of interest and force in a dangerous world and thought that saving America was enough without trying to save all humanity as well.

Similarly related to the choice between realism and ideology is the next of the essays, addressed to the respective roles of moral absolutes and national interest in foreign policy. The discussion gains in significance by virtue of the pervasive bewilderment that prevails today in academic, journalistic, and governmental circles on this particular question of political philosophy. Schlesinger takes as his point of departure the wholly sound observation, already recognized by thinkers as far apart in time as Alexander Hamilton and Reinhold Niebuhr, that morality is not the same thing for an individual, responsible only to himself, as it is for a government, trustee for the interests of others and bound to represent those interests as it sees them, rather than obeying its own moral impulses. But Schlesinger also recognizes that the concept of national interest, essential as it is as a foundation for national policy, is a poorly defined term, varying greatly with circumstances and vulnerable to serious error and distortion both in understanding and in application. A democracy, he notes, presents particularly ample possibilities for just this sort of confusion and error. The concept requires, for this reason, a certain sort of disciplinary restriction; and this he finds in the observance of the values of prudence, of proportionality (action should bear a reasonable relationship to its presumed consequences), and of international law.

With these modifications, Schlesinger finds national interest "an indispensable magnetic compass for policy," without which "there would be no order or predictability in international affairs." And he ends his discussion with a conclusion, firmly rooted in Federalist thinking, that could scarcely be better expressed. Moral values, he concludes, "do have a fundamental role in the conduct of foreign affairs." But this role is not to provide abstract and universal principles for foreign policy decisions. "It is rather to illuminate and control conceptions of national interest." The beginning of a true state morality lies, in his view, in "the assumption that other nations have legitimate traditions, interests, values and rights of their own." Thus:

> national interest, informed by prudence, by law, by scrupulous respect for the equal interests of other nations and above all by rigorous fidelity to one's own sense of honor and decency, seems more likely than the trumpeting of moral absolutes to bring about restraint, justice and peace among nations.

These considerations lead into the next of the essays, "Human Rights and the American Tradition." Here, perhaps inevitably, the sharpness of vision is somewhat dimmed—inevitably, for the problem at hand is one of great and baffling complexity. Schlesinger gives us as balanced an appraisal of this problem as any I have seen. He does full justice to the many sober voices out of the American past warning us that the influencing of political practices in other countries is best done by the power of example rather than by preaching and exhortation. He recognizes the disadvantages that rest on direct efforts by our government to bring pressure on other governments for the correction of human rights abuses. He feels that the greatest part of this burden should be assumed by nongovernmental professional associations and, to the extent we can persuade them to do it, by the United Nations and other international agencies. But he also recognizes, and approves, what he calls "the profound and admirably uncontrollable American impulse to exhibit sympathy for victims of despotism in other lands." He notes (and one supposes with agreement) that Franklin Roosevelt never doubted that foreign policy must be founded on national interest but considered ideals "an indispensable constituent of American power." He admits that the American pressure for the observance of human rights elsewhere will never make such rights forever secure; but it will, he thinks, "make tyranny insecure for a while to come."

Perhaps, perhaps. But even the most sober discussion of the human rights problem in this country fails, in my judgment, to probe the depths of this complex subject. There is the general failure to distinguish between personal and judicial rights (protection against the abuse of person and the invasion of property) on the one hand, and civil, largely electoral, rights on the other. The one can exist without the other, and has done so many times. But to demand the first, and less intrusive, of the two without demanding the other (as seems to be the case when we approach the Soviet Union) raises the unanswered question as to whether we are saying that we would be satisfied with a species of benevolent despotism. Beyond this, there is the common failure to take into consideration the possible or probable consequences of what we are demanding—a particularly weighty omission, since it is others, not we, who will have to live with those consequences. Nothing in the vast historical record justifies the common American assumption that anyone who opposes oppression would, if he were to succeed in overthrowing it, invariably govern more humanely himself. Too many past efforts to overthrow a given tyranny have been motivated not by a desire to do away with tyranny altogether but by a desperate determination to replace one such system with another system of one's own making.

What we are faced with here is, in many instances, the need for changing an entire political culture; and this is not accomplished simply by urging a given ruling group to behave more humanely. Demands that this or that regime should concede more in the way of "human rights" to its citizens raise, in other words, questions both of national custom and of political philosophy that we ourselves, at least in our collective capacity, are unlikely to have thought through, and without the answers to which our efforts are only too likely to be fumbling and confusing. I remain of the opinion that the best way we—and particularly our government—can influence the political practices of other governments is to apply our axe vigorously to some of the failures and evils of our own society, letting the chips fall where they may. This fallout, we may be sure, will not be ignored.

These observations will have sufficed only to give some idea of the general thrust of those of Schlesinger's essays that touch on foreign policy. The ones that deal with purely national affairs strike a different note. There are six of them, all richly informed by Schlesinger's familiarity with American political history, all interesting and deserving of a detailed critical comment that cannot be given within this space. But three of them—one on the questionable fate of American political parties, another on the past, present, and future of the presidency (and who could be better qualified to write on this subject than the author of great works on the age of Andrew Jackson and the life of Franklin Roosevelt?), and a third on the vice-presidential office—go to the heart of some of the country's greatest concerns.

By virtue of his party and organizational connections and his views on specific national questions, Arthur Schlesinger rates as a liberal. But what emerges from these highly interesting papers is a very conservative outlook. Despite all its faults and its declining fortunes, Schlesinger wants to see the party system preserved; this despite what he terms "the devastating and conceivably fatal impact" on that system of television and the computerized public opinion poll. "Without the stabilizing influence of parties," he says, "American politics would grow angrier, wilder and more irresponsible."

He rejects, similarly, all suggestions for the reform of the presidential office. He recognizes the multitudinous deficiencies of the existing system, but fears that to change it could produce even greater faults. He rejects the proposals for a single six-year presidential term. He disagrees with those who would introduce into our government the essential features of the British and Canadian parliamentary systems, centering on the establishment of a relationship of mutual responsibility between executive and legislative organs. He rejects, on balance, the proposals for abolition of the Electoral College in favor of direct presidential elections; though he favors the so-called National Bonus Plan, under which a pool of 102 electoral votes would be conceded, within the college, to the winner of the popular vote. He favors a further shortening of the interregnum between successive presidential administrations. But in general, he is against structural surgery. "If the political will exists in Congress and the citizenry," he thinks, such surgery "will not be necessary. If the will does not exist, it will make little difference."

With respect to the vice presidency, Schlesinger's view is less conservative. He joins many others in the conclusion that the vice-presidential office as we now know it is an anomaly, and sometimes even an absurd one. He deplores the Twenty-fifth Amendment, giving to a onetime vice president who has succeeded to the presidency the power to appoint his successor with the confirmation of both houses of Congress. He would prefer to see the vice presidency, as such, abolished and replaced by an arrangement under which succession to the presidency, in case of the death or disability of an incumbent, would be submitted to the will of the voters in a special election—an arrangement that would meet the principle that no one should come to occupy the highest office in the land other than by decision of the voters themselves.

These views, argued in the book with a comprehensiveness and historical authority to which this summary can do no justice, come before the public at a peculiarly appropriate moment. In less than a year, the two hundredth anniversary of the signing of the Constitution will be upon us.

One can well agree with Schlesinger that we should approach only with greatest skepticism and caution suggestions for the amendment of a document that for over two centuries has served its purpose as well as has the American Constitution. But the fact remains that our present federal system is simply not working well—not well enough, in any case—in a number of areas of decision where the entire future of the country may be at stake. These are, in the main, the areas that require the long view: environmental protection, immigration, drug control, public finance, and above all nuclear arms control. In all of these areas, the failures are evident; in some of them, the Congress even confesses its helplessness. It is idle to shrug these failures off with the comforting reflection that our institutions have worked well enough in the past. So great have been the changes in the physical and technological environment of our lives in this present century that there can be no assurance that what was adequate to the past will continue to be adequate to the future.

There are two thoughts to which, in my mind, these gloomy perceptions conduce. The first is the question whether, if the traditional political institutions of the country cannot be usefully altered, they might be usefully supplemented with something that does not now exist: namely, some sort of standing outside advisory body (advisory both to president and to Congress) made up of persons remote from participation in partisan political activity but qualified by training, experience, and temperament to look deeply into present trends and possible remedies and to tell both legislative and executive branches of the government the things they *must* do, whether they like it or not, to head off some of the worst eventualities that seem now to be, almost unhindered, in the making. The constitutionally created institutions of government would, of course, have to remain the seats of final decision; but the existence of a sober and deliberate outside voice of this nature might conceivably serve to remove from the bull pit of partisan contention questions to which, while the imperative need for solutions is everywhere evident, partisan politics can find no answers. In a body of this nature, scientific authority could be prominently represented, as could distinguished previous experience in public affairs; but the accent, in the determination of its composition, would have to be on character rather than on smartness, and on wisdom rather than on narrow expertise, on knowledge of the past as well as a sense of the future. Such a body might provide much of the answer to a demand that has recently been raised with growing insistence: the demand for a better use of our great fund of acquired experience in our public life— for a better use, that is, of the "elder statesmen" who are to be found in some abundance in our society but whose experience, as things now stand, goes largely wasted.

This leads to the second thought. If no more imaginative effort is undertaken, there is a danger that the celebration of the two hundredth anniversary of the Constitution may exhaust itself in what Schlesinger calls "show biz"—the sort of parades, costumes, replicas, and reenactments that characterized the anniversaries of the Declaration of Independence and the Statue of Liberty. A story in the *New York Times* (September 17, 1986) about plans for the occasion gave no grounds for the assumption that anything much more than this is now contemplated. Should not the president and Chief Justice Warren E. Burger (the latter as chairman of the National Committee on the Bicentennial) put their heads together and arrange for the convocation, by official invitation, of a small gathering of historians, authorities on constitutional law, and other qualified persons (no more in number than those who deliberated on the Constitution two hundred years ago) to examine the adequacy of that document at the distance of two centuries (as the authors hoped and expected would occasionally be done), with a view to confronting collectively not only the questions Arthur Schlesinger has raised in this book but also to assessing the soundness and suitability of the habits and traditions that have grown up in these past two centuries around the institutional framework the Constitution has provided? Again, the findings of such a body could, of course, be no more than advisory; but they might serve an educational purpose for the public at large; and they might point the way, as nothing else could, to the improvement of an institutional and traditional framework whose inadequacy to the challenges now before us threatens in many ways the continuity and intactness of our national life.

The Gorbachev Prospect
(1988)

————··◦◦◦··————

More than a month after the first advance publicity by the publishers, and half a month after the appearance of the Russian edition in Moscow, the English edition of Mr. Gorbachev's book has finally appeared in American bookshops and become available to the American reviewer. It is, as such books go, a handsome one, with an equally handsome photograph of Mikhail Sergeyevich's face on the back cover, with nothing to show, to be sure, that the book is a translation, or who was the translator; but for the most part, it is not badly translated.

The first question that will presumably be asked about this book is: did Gorbachev write it himself? The answer is: in all probability, yes, most of it at least. Aside from the fact that he is not known to be given to the use of ghostwriters, it is hard to think of anyone who could have written it on his behalf. The delicacy of some of the subjects treated, the boldness of statement, the relative freshness and directness of style, and the defensive undertone of portions of the argument: all these point to an extensive personal involvement on his part with the authorship of the work.

A second, and related, question is, then: to what extent do the contents of the book reflect his own unadulterated thinking, and to what extent did it require or reflect approval, if not formal clearance, by his

Review of *Perestroika: New Thinking for Our Country and the World*, by Mikhail Gorbachev (New York: Harper & Row, 1987); originally published in the *New York Review of Books*, January 21, 1988.

senior associates? Here, the answer is more complicated. He was writing in this instance in the first person, speaking only in his own name and committing only himself. In such circumstances, the rules of clearance were presumably quite different from what they were in the case of his numerous official speeches and reports, where he was speaking in the name of one or another of the senior Party bodies; and one may assume that he enjoyed a greater liberty to present things as he saw them.

On the other hand, he could not, in matters of established policy, go much beyond what had been agreed to and announced by those senior bodies in formal session, especially since a great deal of all that was the reflection of his own ideas and initiatives. Beyond which, it is not to be supposed that he could or would have produced a work of such importance without at least letting his senior associates know what he was doing and giving them an opportunity to register objections. One may surmise, therefore, that what appears in this book represents a body of material with which his associates were, for the most part, in agreement or to which they were unwilling to register objection. If the defensive undertones suggest that there were still many in the Soviet hierarchy opposed to Gorbachev's program, these were evidently people who had opposed it all along, on the basis of his previous statements and initiatives, and not just because of what is repeated in this book.

In both these questions, the answers depend partly on what portion of the book one is talking about. The work falls into two parts. The first deals with *perestroika* as an internal program of economic, social, and attitudinal change, and is apparently addressed primarily to the Soviet reader. It represents in effect a digest, in popular form, of the concepts of *perestroika* that were set forth in the two long and serious reports tendered by Gorbachev in January and June of 1987 to the respective plenary sessions of the Central Committee of the Party.

The second part, more personal and more vigorously presented, deals with the problems of the relations of the Soviet Union with its world environment, including prominently, as was inevitable, its relations with the United States. Here, too, most of the ideas brought forward were previously expressed by Gorbachev, but in less formal presentations: speeches in provincial Soviet centers, interviews with foreign personalities, appearances at international gatherings, etc.

While, then, little of the material presented will be new to the reader who has followed carefully many of Gorbachev's earlier statements for the internal Soviet readership, the book is a useful summary of that far greater body of material. It includes, of course, a small amount of the traditional ideological distortions about the early period of Soviet-American relations and about the "neo-colonialism" of the Western powers. But these passages are little more than perfunctory—a slight obeisance, perhaps, in the direction of the old Party *apparat*. Everywhere else, the focus is on contemporary problems; and here the work will be useful to the Western reader as evidence of the full scope and novelty of what this man is undertaking to do. He himself was not exaggerating in his several references to his program as "revolutionary." And this, in the Soviet Union, is a very strong term. In the view of Russian Communists, the events of November 1917 were *the* great revolution of all time. It is from this event, and from this alone, that the Soviet regime derives its claim to legitimacy. To suggest that the revolution had such imperfections, or that the political movement it inaugurated was guilty of such distortions, that another revolution is now necessary to put things to rights: this goes very far.

Perestroika is an elaborate and far-flung program affecting Soviet society at a host of points. For this reason, it is not easily described in a few words. It might be said to have taken its departure from the recognition of two great deficiencies that have hampered development of the Soviet economy. The first was the overcentralization of economic decision making. Gorbachev, and others by whom he has been inspired, has recognized that the myriad of decisions essential to the smooth working of a great modern economy cannot all flow from one center, and that a great proportion of them have to be delegated to people down the line, even if at the cost of a certain impairment of central governmental control.

The second deficiency has been that the Soviet economy cannot be made to function as it should (and indeed as it must, if it is to compete with the free-enterprise economies of the great powers) until there can be implanted in the breasts of a host of people at lower levels—workers, foremen, and administrators—a greater measure of what Gorbachev calls "inner stimuli." Hence: decentralization of the power of economic and in part political decision making, and the encouragement of what he thinks of as "democratization" all down the line. This last does not mean the dismantling of the authoritarian political system; but it means a greater measure of consultation, and of something a bit more than consultation: of the feelings and views of people at the bottom.

The forms this program takes, where they vary importantly from what existed before, are well summarized in the book itself. "Many things are unusual in our country now," Gorbachev writes:

> election of managers at enterprises and offices; multiple candidates for election to Soviets [i.e., local government organs] in some districts; joint ventures with foreign firms; self-financed factories and plants, state and collective farms; the lifting of restrictions on farms producing food products for enterprises and run by them; wider cooperative activities; encouragement of individual enterprise in small-scale production and trade; and closure of non-paying plants and factories operating at a loss; and of research institutes and higher educational establishments working inefficiently.

Anyone who has known Soviet Russia in earlier years will recognize at once how far-reaching are these intended reforms. In their application to agriculture, where they envisage measures as drastic as the restoration of the independent family farm, their chances for success, as Gorbachev himself notes, will probably be greater than in their application to industry. The peasant, used to local barter and exchange, takes more readily to private enterprise than does his city cousin. In industry, as in trade, many problems remain to be solved before any of Gorbachev's principles can be applied with full effectiveness; and some of them may prove not to be workable at all. But all of this he takes into account with characteristic boldness. "We realize," he writes, "that there is no guarantee against mistakes." But the worst of mistakes, he goes on to point out, would be "to do nothing out of fear of making one."

Even more far-reaching are the changes of approach in foreign relations. They include not only extensive reversals of established policy but actual revisions of basic Marxist postulates. Admitting that "the class-motivated approach to all phenomena of social life" was once "the ABC of Marxism," Gorbachev boldly asserts that the nuclear weapon has changed all that. Class confrontation, once the final determinant of all social-political development, now for the first time finds itself confronted with "an objective limit." Unable to advance beyond that limit, it is being supplanted by what Gorbachev calls "a real, not speculative and remote, common human interest"—the need, that is, to save all humanity from nuclear disaster. Traditional Marxist logic had it that imperialism inevitably engendered major arms confrontations, the ultimate outcome of which would be social upheavals; and these, in turn, would finish off the capitalist system for good and thus establish global peace. Still valid? No, says Gorbachev; the "cause and effect relationship between war and revolution" has itself fallen victim to the harsh realities of the nuclear age. Political and ideological competition between capitalist and socialist countries will, of course, continue; but "it can and must be kept within a framework of peaceful competition which necessarily envisages cooperation." Hence the necessity of "a new dialectic of the common human and class interests and principles in our modern age."

For the leader of a movement that takes its ideology seriously and regards Marx as the creator and inspirer of the revolution from which it derives its origin, these are not only strong words but words of great theoretical import. And the practical conclusions to which these conclusions relate, when it comes to the nuclear arms race and its implications for policy, are no less significant. The nuclear weapon is recognized as a suicidal device, capable of bringing nothing less than disaster to whoever might venture to use it. It can serve neither offensive nor defensive purposes. So long as it remains in national arsenals, and to the extent that it does, it is a menace to all of us. Nor is there any security to be gained from the effort to diminish the security of anybody else. The other fellow's security is in fact one's own. The striving for military superiority thus serves no purpose; it is only a means "of chasing one's own tail." Nor do these realities derive only from the existence of the nuclear weapon. "Even a conventional war," says Gorbachev, "would be disastrous for Europe today." What is required in both nuclear and conventional armaments is, in his view, only a defensive posture of "reasonable sufficiency"—a far cry from the once fashionable doctrine that a formidable offensive posture was the best deterrence.

To suggest, as some Western commentators seem to do, that words and insights of this nature are brought forward only to deceive people in the West and to lull them into a sense of false security while Soviet forces prepare to attack them reveals a lack of understanding for the realities of Gorbachev's position that borders on the bizarre. Such words cut to the heart of established beliefs and policy. They represent a serious responsibility on the part of the statesman who articulates them. To suppose that Gorbachev has all internal problems so beautifully solved that he can afford to play around irresponsibly, for the purpose of throwing sand in our eyes, with statements of this nature is to misjudge fundamentally the responsibilities he assumes in making them, and the priorities he has to bear in mind between the external and the internal effects of his words.

A wholly different matter is, of course, the question of the prospects for the success of Gorbachev's program, as summarized in this book. What he has taken upon himself with the launching of this program is truly a task of gargantuan dimensions. It is not certain that he himself realizes this; for the implications of what he is proposing far exceed the aims of the program as he has described them. Whether he realizes it or not, what he has set out to correct are not only the damages done to Russian society by Brezhnev's regime of social laxness and entrenched privilege, not only the effects of the fearful abuse and corruption inflicted on that society by Stalin's regime of terror, but also the costs of the cruelties and excesses of the initial years of revolution and civil war from 1917 to 1920. And then, beyond all these, and reaching back into the prerevolutionary period, lies much of the unfinished business of the old tsarist regime, whose not inconsiderable positive efforts—to introduce into Russian political life the elements of a proper parliamentary system, to restructure Russian agriculture, and to modernize Russian society generally—were so rudely put to an end by war and revolution in 1917. These great setbacks to Russia's development rise to confront Gorbachev today as he sets out not only to render the country reasonably competitive in the modern world of technological and electronic revolution but also to give to its life a quality more responsive to the hopes of the great social idealists whose figures have punctuated the dark pages of Russian history.

For no one who reads this book can doubt (or so it seems to me) that Gorbachev is at heart something of an idealist. He is a true believer—in a dream that he calls socialism. One may think as one likes about the realism of the dream. The faith itself is evident. His regime, in its treatment of dissidents and its restrictions on movement and thought, remains bound to many brutal practices of the past. But compared with what has gone before him—compared with the savagery, the cynicism, the ritualistic shallowness, and the heartlessness with which this same symbol has been manipulated by numbers of his predecessors—his vision of socialism, realistic or otherwise, is relatively humane. When he says, as he does in this book, that "whatever values you defend, what matters most is whether the people's destiny and future are of concern to you," he is not joking. Under any other view, he would be a fool or a martyr to take on what he has.

There can be no question of the formidableness of the forces of resistance now marshaled against Gorbachev's undertakings. Intentionally or otherwise, he has created opposition, formidable and unpitying, on every hand. A sullen, embittered industrial and agricultural labor force—a population whose inherited embitterment has sources reaching back over centuries rather than decades; a population wholly unfamiliar with the concepts, procedures, and responsibilities of democracy, schooled only in the arts of dependency on higher authority; a population that, to use Chekhov's phrase, wakes up from the bad dream of daily life only behind the vodka glass in the pub on Saturday nights—how can such a population be aroused out of its profound apathy and moved to accept the responsibilities of democratic initiative in the managing of large agricultural and industrial enterprises?

How are industrial laborers, accustomed to a total irresponsibility with respect to the successful functioning of the enterprises in which they serve; accustomed to doing only the minimal amount of work for the hours they put in, confident that they could not easily be fired or that even if they should be, other jobs would at once be waiting for them—how are such people to react to a leader who tells them that the day is upon them when they will work hard and well, or else? How are hordes of run-of-the-mill administrative bureaucrats, in many instances fully twice as many as were really needed for the function at hand, to react to a governmental policy that tells them they are redundant and must soon scrounge around for other occupations? And what of the public at large, accustomed to receiving staples of daily life—bread, meats, rent, and whatnot—at a fraction of the prices people in the West pay for these same things? How are they to react to the news that the prices of these staples are shortly to be greatly raised, and to the suggestion that they should accept this because at some dim future date their lives will be better for it?

What, again, of the senior bureaucrats, the members of the "nomenclatura," who are asked to give up many of their privileges— their special stores, schools, and dachas, their chauffeured cars, their attractive vacations—in the interests of a program the rigors of which are near at hand, the beneficial fruits of which are far away? What of the senior figures around Gorbachev, finding themselves impelled, at a pace they find both dangerous and uncomfortable, along a path plainly strewn with obstacles? And what, finally, must be the effect of all this upon the more reactionary leaders in the other Warsaw Pact countries, long accustomed to oppressing their peoples in the name of the Soviet example but now tripped up by Soviet pronouncements and policies that belie the very basis of their fidelity, and faced, in the bargain, with a rising generation of younger political rivals who quote Gorbachev against them?

Can Gorbachev hope, in the face of all this, to carry his entire program to successful completion? Of course not. No statesman ever does that, even in the face of lesser obstacles. Nor do the results of statesmanship ever bear anything other than an ironic relation to what the statesman in question intended to achieve and thought he was achieving. At some point, assuredly, the forces arrayed against Gorbachev will coalesce to unseat him; and there is no reason either to assume that this could not occur at an early date or to firmly predict that it will. But even if it were to happen tomorrow, it is safe to say that Russia would never again be the same as it was before his passage. If it may be said with reasonable assurance that not all of his program will be achieved, it may be said with equal assurance that some of it undoubtedly will be; and whatever portion will have been accomplished could hardly be other than for the better.

That Gorbachev's personal position at this juncture has elements of precariousness cannot be denied. The significance in this connection of the Yeltsin episode has, to be sure, been much exaggerated by the Western press. If important questions of principle were involved, no solid evidence of this has yet emerged. The Russian Communist Party, like closed social or political collectivities everywhere, has its traditional standards of comportment. These Yeltsin obviously violated. In doing so, he embarrassed his senior colleagues, Gorbachev included; he paid the price in a significant demotion. When he confessed publicly to at least a portion of his misdemeanors, he was following a Party tradition of self-abasement that seems to many outsiders more repellent than it seems to many of the Party members themselves. He presumably did so to save his status, perhaps even his membership, in the Party. But it certainly did not have to be done to save his life; and to compare his plight with that of Bukharin fifty years ago is to suggest a serious lack of understanding for what was going on in that terrible year of 1937.

To depreciate the significance of the Yeltsin episode is not, however, to underestimate the difficulty of Gorbachev's present position. The point at which he has arrived   where his program has advanced just far enough to create discomfort in many quarters and to bar any retreat, but not far enough to produce conspicuous positive results—is obviously the point of greatest strain and danger. And it is surely not without significance that the public advocacy of this program has been left almost exclusively to him. Not one of the major personalities in his immediate political entourage, unless it be his fellow Politburo member Alexander Yakovlev, has given him any significant political assistance in this task. He is on his own.

Yet his position, this ominous loneliness notwithstanding, is not without its aspects of strength. It is one thing to sit on one's hands and hedge one's bets—to grumble and murmur behind Gorbachev's back—to try to keep one's options open until one sees how things turn out. It would be another thing to overthrow him and face the question of who should succeed him. The other members of the senior bodies of the Party—the Politburo, the Secretariat, and the Central Committee—find themselves extensively and formally committed to his program by the decisions they have already made. And there could be no turning back. No one wants to revive—indeed there could be no revival of—the regime of Brezhnev. Gorbachev could be opposed, therefore, only by someone who could claim to be able to advance his program more successfully than he could. But who would want to try this? Who else has the stomach for it, the enthusiasm, the drive, the eloquence, and the courage—the courage, particularly, to take it on precisely at this most difficult of moments? Without those qualities, a successor would find himself in a position in which he could neither advance nor retreat. Nothing could be more dangerous.

A removal of Gorbachev, in the present situation, would also have incalculable ulterior consequences. It would come as a serious and unsettling shock to the Soviet intellectuals—his sole whole-hearted supporters. Could they again be tamed and cowed as they were under Stalin? It seems unlikely. This is another epoch. *Glasnost* is a genie that, once released from the bottle, will not easily be put back in again. And how about the non-Russian nationalities within the Soviet Union? These, if the private letters published in the book are any indication, have a much better understanding of what Gorbachev is trying to do than does the Russian center. And how about the reactions in the Eastern European "satellite" countries, where Moscow's political hold is already tenuous, and where, as noted above, a new generation, much more attuned to Gorbachev's music, is waiting in the wings?

And how about world opinion? Hundreds of millions of people the world over, electrified by Gorbachev's striking appearance at the Washington summit, have been moved to a new level of hope for real progress, at long last, in the overcoming of the nuclear nightmare. Are these hopes to be dashed and compelled to yield to a proportionate level of consternation and despair, with Moscow appearing as the party guilty of this spectacular setback?

For better or worse, this is an age of change; and Gorbachev has made himself its angel and its instrument. His disappearance, in present circumstances, would leave Russia with nothing ahead of it and nothing to return to. Could the system, without charismatic leadership, long endure the resulting aimlessness and paralysis?

For seven decades, people in this country have been basing their suspicions of the Soviet Union and their hostility to Soviet policies on a given pattern of Soviet life and outlook that they have found unacceptable. Whatever else Gorbachev has done, he has mounted the most strenuous effort to date to change some of the very conditions and policies to which people here have so negatively reacted. Beyond this, he is, as his book confirms, a man who would like to see Soviet-American relations develop in a peaceful, businesslike, and generally constructive direction—and this not just for reasons of state or of personal political advantage (although he has such reasons, too) but because he has realized, in advance of some of his Western confreres, that in the nuclear age such purposes cannot be usefully served by competitive military efforts.

All this being so, the prospects on the Soviet side for a significant improvement of Soviet-American relations will continue to be greater, so long as Gorbachev's preeminence endures, than they have been at any time since the revolution. These prospects will continue, however, to be endangered on the American side by two factors. One is the continuing existence of a substantial, politically influential, and aggressive body of American opinion for which the specter of a great and fearful external enemy, to be exorcised only by vast military preparations and much belligerent posturing, has become a political and psychological necessity. The other is the influence of the American commercial media of communication. The improvement of Soviet-American relations poses difficulties enough even when the attendant problems are viewed soberly and in life-size dimensions. When everything has to be oversimplified, sensationalized, and blown up to dimensions two or three times beyond reality to meet the commercial demands of the press and television, the entire process of constructive statesmanship becomes subject to a heightened level of precariousness.

Whether the process can successfully withstand these strains is a question I am able to answer optimistically only—one might say—on the brighter days. But in this political world, where artificially created images are considered more significant than realities, the unexpected is just as likely to assume favorable forms as unfavorable ones. It is always possible, then, that the irrational can provide hope where rationality perceives little reason for it.

The Buried Past
(1988)

———···⟨∞⟩···———

Before me, as I write these words, there lie the two handsome volumes of the official Russian-language version of the memoirs of Andrei Andreyevich Gromyko, chairman of the Presidium of the Supreme Soviet of the Soviet Union, as published in 1988 in Moscow by the Publishing Company for Political Literature. In their entirety, these memoirs run to nearly 900 pages, including some 180 illustrations, mostly snapshots of Andrei Andreyevich together with one or another of the many prominent world personalities with whom he was brought into contact in his long years as Soviet foreign minister.

Most of this material relates to the international scene of the post-Stalin period: its historical significance cannot be doubted, and I have no intention of disparaging it. To define that significance will have to be the task of someone more closely involved with the diplomacy of that period, either as a participant or as a historian, than myself. But there are certain aspects of Gromyko's view of Russia in the Stalin period that strike the eye of anyone who, although himself neither a Communist nor a fellow traveler, lived and worked either in Russia or in close contact with Russian affairs during those particular years. And these aspects, for reasons that have still not lost all their relevance, might merit a word or two of comment.

Most of us who had the experience just mentioned tended to marvel over the two planes of consciousness on which the situations and

Review of *Memoirs,* by Andrei Andreevich Gromyko (New York: Doubleday, 1988); originally published in the *New York Review of Books,* October 27, 1988.

events of that time could be, and were, perceived in Moscow. There
was what I myself then liked to think of as the plane of reality, as revealed to any reasonably disinterested observer. But there was also the
image of itself and its doings created by the Soviet regime and expos-
tulated daily in a thousand ways by the Soviet press and the other out-
lets of the Party's propaganda machine. So far removed from each other
were these two versions of reality—or, if you will, of perceived reality—that the images derived from them appeared to be those of two
wholly different countries. A considerable portion of the population,
perceiving both of these images, learned, for good reason, to think in
terms of the first of them but to speak in terms of the other. We foreigners, too, tried to hold both in mind and to identify the occasional
veiled connections between them. But upon all of us, Russians and
foreigners alike, this effort inflicted a species of double vision, in light
of which life had, somehow, to proceed.

In the years following Stalin's death, the sharpness of this disparity
between what was pretended and what was real declined, to the extent at least that much of the officially cultivated image, its preposter-
ousness now being evident to almost everyone, was no longer emphasized even when it could not be officially disowned; and now, in
the days of Mr. Gorbachev's *glasnost,* it is rapidly disappearing altogether. This being the case, it is a startling experience to be suddenly
thrust back into the atmosphere of the 1930s and 1940s and confronted
again with the view of itself taken at that time by the Stalin regime in
all its bland and brazen effrontery, as though nothing had ever occurred
to disprove it—and this from the memoirs of a man who, even in the
age of Gorbachev's *perestroika,* remains one of the two or three most
powerful figures of the Soviet Union. For here, in the confrontation
with this book, the two planes of consciousness with which one learned
to live in the time of Stalin are evoked again in all their weird and
painful irreconcilability.

My own view of the Russia of that day (and that of other foreigners,
I am sure) was evoked partly by memory: of what I knew of the earlier history of the Soviet Union, of the revolution, the civil war, and
the events of the early 1920s. But imposed on these memories were
the dramatic impressions of the first years of the 1930s: the famine of
1931–32; the deeply ravaged countryside, terribly—almost fatally—
damaged by the disaster of collectivization; the wasteful and costly ex-

periments of the First Five-Year Plan; the murder of Kirov and the sinister beginnings, in 1935, of the purges. And then the horrors that followed: the mass arrests; the great public purge trials; the decimation of the Party hierarchy and the military command; the disappearance into the limbo of death or penal servitude of millions of essentially innocent Party members and ordinary citizens. Superimposed very shortly upon all this, there were, then, the shattering events of the war and its aftermath: the cynicism of the attempt to buy off Hitler by sharing with him the booty of Eastern Europe; the overrunning of the Baltic countries and eastern Poland; the cruel deportations of hundreds of thousands of innocent people, from Poland in particular (but not only from Poland), into the interior of Siberia and Central Asia; then, as the war took its course, the unpitying reprisals against people who had perforce remained behind in the German-controlled areas or who had fallen into German hands as prisoners of war; then, as the war moved to a close, the behavior of the Soviet police authorities in the areas "liberated" from the Germans; and finally, in the immediate post-hostilities period, the fastening upon the Polish people, and in a more gradual and subtle form upon the other Eastern European peoples, of regimes that were mockeries of the principles of self-determination and self-rule.

This list could be continued; but it will suffice to support my statement that the Russia Mr. Gromyko saw around him in those years was a different Russia from the one that passed before my eyes.

At a later point (Chapter VI) of his memoirs, one will find, to be sure, tacked on to the account of a single instance where the author thought he was right and Stalin was wrong (having to do with the failure of the Soviet Union to use its veto in the Security Council in connection with the Korean War), a page of balanced judgment about Stalin as a statesman—a passage in which, together with a summary of Stalin's impressive achievements, there is a recognition that he was "a cruel person, taking no account of the number of those sacrificed for the achievement of his purposes, practicing a nightmarish arbitrariness of rule that led to the deaths of masses of Soviet people." The country and the people, Gromyko writes, "would never be able to forgive him these acts of illegality—the mass destruction of communists and non-party people, guilty of nothing at all—patriots, devoted to the cause of socialism."

Well enough. Let us assume—and hope—that this was Mr. Gromyko's ripe judgment of later years and not just something added, at the insistence of those around Gorbachev, to what was actually a rather irrelevent passage. One is left, nevertheless, with the fact that in Mr. Gromyko's account of his youth, of his experiences during the 1930s, and of his official activity down through the remainder of the Stalin era, nothing that he specifically records would substantiate, or even explain, this harsh judgment.

He was, he relates, as a young Communist, sent out on a number of occasions in the 1920s and 1930s on *kommandirovki* into the hard-pressed countryside—first, to extract from the peasants their last hoardings of grain; then, in the 1930s, to argue them into the acceptance of collectivization and sometimes even to help with what we know today to have been the brutal enforcement of it. In all of this, he saw no evil, heard no evil. In his life in Moscow from 1934 to 1939 as a Party propagandist and a doctoral candidate at a senior research institution, he could not have been oblivious of what was happening in the senior echelons of the Party to which he belonged. He could not have failed to note the ominous disappearance from the scene, one by one, of his Party superiors and academic associates. He could not have neglected to read in the papers the accounts of the great purge trials of 1936–37, with all their weird absurdities. And it cannot have failed to occur to him that if the accusations were false (as of course they were), then monstrous injustices were being perpetrated upon the accused and equally monstrous abuses upon the credulity and good faith of the Soviet public; whereas if they were true, then the immediate entourage of the revered Lenin consisted largely of a nest of traitors, and Lenin himself was the most naive and most easily imposed upon of men.

Gromyko must also have seen on all sides, even if he was lucky enough to avoid taking part himself, the massive wave of denunciations encouraged by the Party, participation in which became for many people the only way they could see of saving their own skins. And when, in 1939, he was suddenly and unexpectedly lifted out of his normal scholarly entourage, assigned to the Foreign Ministry, and placed (albeit wholly without diplomatic experience) in charge of the American desk there, he could scarcely have been ignorant of, or indifferent to, the fate of his predecessors in that position, or indeed of much of the remainder of Maxim Litvinov's staff at the ministry. And so on—and so on. But none of this is mentioned, nor is any of what was soon to follow. Gromyko, rapidly becoming a prominent and influential diplomat, knew nothing, we are asked to conclude, of the Molotov-Ribbentrop Nonaggression Pact, of the Winter War in Finland, of the intimidation and seizure of the Baltic countries, of the deportations from eastern Poland, of the Katyn massacre, etc.; or, if he did know of these things, they made insufficient impression upon him to warrant mention in his memoirs.

I raise these unpleasant memories not to revive the tensions and asperities of a terrible time. They have passed into history. There is no reason to doubt that many of them are as deeply regretted in the entourage of Mikhail Gorbachev as they were by some of us who were witnesses. Let us, by all means, permit the past to bury its dead. But I cannot concede the validity of a view of Russia and of her place in the life of the twentieth century that takes no account of any of these developments, or finds them unworthy of specific note in the memoirs of a great and honored Russian political figure.

I have often been struck, in discussions with some of the more sanguine Cold War enthusiasts in our own country, by the fact that not only did they see most senior Soviet political figures as men of great personal iniquity, but they assumed that these figures knew themselves to be just that, and that their only reaction to such charges from our side was annoyance and chagrin at having been found out. I could assure them that even if this was the way some Americans viewed the Soviet leaders, it was not at all the way the latter viewed themselves. Many foreigners would be amazed, I suspect, to learn with what self-satisfaction and complacency—an almost bourgeois complacency, in fact—a great many senior Soviet statesmen have come to look back upon their own part in the dramatic, and so often terrible, events of their own time.

Of no one, I am sure, could this be more true than of Andrei Andreyevich Gromyko. He was, according to his lights (and not without justification), a man of rock-bound fidelity to ideological principle, and of unlimited and unquestionable loyalty to the interests of the Party in which his life proceeded and to which it was devoted. It was in the mid-1920s that the Party first took him to its demanding but otherwise protecting breast. He was then scarcely more than a boy: a ragged country youth, the child of hardworking and struggling peasant parents, a youth longing for education, dreaming of escape from the dreariness of village life and of entry into a more interesting and promising one. All these things the Party gave him—gave him (let us recognize it) as no one else at that time could have done. And by so doing, the Party became, in the emotional sense, his mother, his father, his teacher, his conscience, and his Master. He was never to question its ideals, its authority, its moral purity. He was, as he himself writes at the end of his memoirs, "a communist to the marrow of his bones."

Taken in this context, he was, I have no doubt, in many ways what we would call "an exceptionally fine person": devoted, hardworking, loyal to the movement to which he had dedicated his life, a good comrade (within limits, of course, for you never knew when someone would fall from virtue) to those who shared his dedication, and—as one will see from the photograph of him seated at the center of a large and fine-looking family circle in his later years—a good husband, a good father, even a good grandfather and great-grandfather. Surely, few Soviet officials of his day could have looked back with a greater feeling of satisfaction, in the closing phases of an official career, on a long record of tasks loyally assumed and successfully completed.

But for this comfortable contentment (and how eloquently the memoirs reveal it!), something more was essential than just the normal working of memory. We all know (and we scarcely needed Sigmund Freud to point it out to us) the great role that the repression of memory *(Verdrängung)* plays in the effort of the individual to come to terms with himself and his conscience. We know that this repression, like Shakespeare's sleep, "knits up the ravel'd sleave of care." We know that it reconciles the errant, bewildered soul to the painful record of its own mistakes, stupidities, and cruelties, the active awareness of which, if allowed to accompany the person as a companion through life, would paralyze the will and destroy the enthusiasm for life itself.

What is not so often understood is that this capacity for repression of memory can be easily transferred from the individual's sense of responsibility for his own conduct to the behavior of a political collectivity into the hands of which he has committed his confidence and his loyalty. When this transference occurs, it is—in the personal, psychic sense—enormously health-giving, even more so than when it is one's own conscience that is at stake; for here the moral responsibility is shifted entirely to someone else. The individual in whom this change has occurred might reproach himself, on occasion, for behavior on his own part that did not contribute to the interests of the collectivity. *That* could undermine his confidence. *That* could keep him awake at night. *That* could cause him to run to the collectivity to confess, to be punished, to be corrected. But with that confession and retribution, the brand of shame would be removed.

For anything undertaken beyond that, and particularly for anything undertaken in response to the will of the collectivity (in this instance the Party), no matter how distasteful, no matter how unattractive from the standpoint of individual morality, there could be no guilt, no questioning, no remorse. And if it turned out that what the Party required to be done, whether by one's self or others, involved apparent injustice or cruelty—well, one might regret that it was found necessary, one might wish that it could have been otherwise; but it was not one's own responsibility. And one was justified in later years—was one not?—in pushing the memory of it back into those dim precincts of forgetfulness that already veiled so many other evidences of man's savagery and nastiness, so many other evidences of the triumph (momentary and unavoidable, of course) of the beast over his tragic cousin, the saint.

It is this that shines out, for me at least, from the account by Andrei Andreyevich Gromyko of his life and activities in the Stalin era. Perhaps he deserves our forgiveness and understanding. The Russian Revolution involved many mass bewilderments. Perhaps there was really no other way to go. He was and is, within his lights, an eminently loyal person; and it can be argued, after all, that loyalty is perhaps the only absolute virtue, in the sense that to be loyal to even the worst causes is better than being incapable of loyalty to any at all.

But it may reasonably be asked whether the national society can hope to cope successfully with the challenges of the present, any more than can the individual, unless it can come to terms with its own past. It is this, surely, that Mr. Gorbachev and others around him have perceived. Only this could explain the courage and resolution with which they are opening the pages on which the realities of the 1930s and 1940s are recorded, as distinct from the pretenses by which a great political movement endeavored over the decades to live. That this development is hard to accept for such a man as Gromyko, who gave so much so long, so faithfully, and so effectively to the movement in question, everyone can understand. But the necessity of it, from the standpoint of Russia's future as well as its present, few could now deny.

Letter to Robert Tucker
(1994)

———··◄∞►··———

Dear Bob:

When I wrote the small comment that appears on the jacket of your *Stalin in Power,* I did so only on the basis of a relatively brief perusal of the book, which was all that I could give it at the time. It is, as you will yourself admit, a lengthy, if solid, work. But I felt justified in offering my comment on this slender basis, because my knowledge both of the subject matter and of the author meant that it took only a relatively casual glance into the contents of the work to reveal to me that it was what I was sure it would be. But I never ceased to have in mind the prospect that as soon as circumstances permitted, I would give the book the more careful reading that it deserved. With this in mind, I took it to Norway with me; and although the summer has not been as free as I hoped it would be of other demands on my pen and my time, I have now been reading it, page after page and chapter after chapter, with close and, as you can imagine, rapt attention. I am now just on the final pages; but I hasten to write these words, because I can never be sure what the rest of the summer will bring.

The reading has aroused in me so many terrible and sometimes painful memories, so many thoughts, and so many questions that I could not possibly mention them all in a letter. But there are a few reactions that I would like to share with you at this time. The rest we can talk about when we meet personally.

Personal letter, August 11, 1994.

Let me say at once that this reading has not brought me to regret or to wish to change a single word of what I said for the book's jacket. What you have produced here (words come hard) is indeed a fine and impressive work, and one that fills a gap of high importance in the historical record of this century. It is hard to think of anyone else who could have brought to the task of writing it the experience, the insights, the sensitivity, and the quality of analytical scrutiny you have given to the subject. There have been and are many others, of course, who saw and experienced much of what you have written about; but few of these are still alive and capable of writing, and fewer still would have been able to bring to the subject the scholarly detachment, the breadth of judgment, the background, and the integrity that have gone into your work.

It has occurred to me, in writing these last sentences, that just as no American could have written the book about the America of the 1830s that Tocqueville wrote, so no Russian could have written this book about Stalin at the peak of his power. And there is more to that observation than just the possibility of being too close to what one is viewing. I cannot picture any Russian having the detachment and the perspective that mark your book. Few members of a national community are capable of looking at their own community from the outside as well as from the inside. And in this, the Russians are singularly untalented. Russia is their world; and along with their absorption with their own country goes their relative lack of serious curiosity about the world outside. I was amazed, years ago, by what seemed to me to be the superficiality and the provincialism of the reactions of even some of the greatest literary artists of nineteenth-century Russia—Dostoyevsky, Tolstoy, and even Chekhov—to the western Europe they visited. To be sure, they sometimes headed for the art museums, but more often (at least in the case of Dostoyevsky) the heading was for the gaming tables of Monte Carlo. And it seemed to me that the greater good order of western European life—the strength of the physical infrastructure, the tidiness and solidity of both urban and rural scene—made little impression on them. They tended to find all that, generally speaking, uninteresting and even boring. They only yearned back for the charms of Russian disorder, charms to which neither you nor I are totally immune, but which, I hope, we have learned to put in their place.

239

However, I am wandering. Back to Stalin.

Generally speaking, I find your analysis of Stalin's emotional makeup well-founded and convincing. The greater part of it I can only accept and applaud. I see the heroic self-image you have described. I see the extreme sensitivity to anything that appeared to challenge that image. Your diagnosis of the reason for this sensitivity (namely, that any challenges of this sort came too close to a subconscious, repressed, but immensely vulnerable self-hatred) strikes me as, in the main, a brilliant, profound, and original perception. If it is not the entire truth, it is so close to it as to represent a major advance in our understanding of this otherwise almost incredible personality. And my purpose in taking that diagnosis under critical scrutiny in this letter is not to impugn its value but rather to suggest that to leave the inquiry where you have left it may have been to give Stalin more credit or, better stated, less discredit, than he deserved.

My doubts center on the concept of self-hatred. Hatred of something implies, as I see it (or am I wrong?), if not a *love* for the opposite of what one hates, then at least an understanding and recognition of its merits. And the opposite, in the case at hand, could have been only such qualities as kindliness, charity, tolerance, humanity, understanding, loyalty, a reasonable personal modesty, and, above all, pity.

Now, we both recognize (and no one in the world has seen this more closely than you) that in Stalin's conduct there was no evidence of respect for any of these qualities. He himself never manifested any of them, nor did he seem to have any respect for them when they appeared in the behavior of others. He knew, to be sure, that they commanded general respect, and that to be caught out flagrantly disregarding them might have consequences adverse to his ambitions. Consummate actor that he was, he was quite capable of giving a good performance of respecting, and even extending, these qualities when he thought this might be useful to his purposes. But he was devoid of the emotional background out of which they could have found a real basis in his behavior. Take only, for example, the quality of pity. Not only does his record exhibit no plausible instance of the exercise of pity on his part, but one is constrained to doubt that he would have been capable (and this was a deficiency he shared with Hitler) of the emotional impulse to extend it. He never *felt* it, I am sure, toward anyone.

Whence, then, the extreme sensitivity with which he reacted to any hint of challenge, intended or unintended, to his self-image? If it was not that it came too close to his own self-hatred, what was it?

I would suggest, in reply to that question, that it was in essence the product of his awareness of the immense gap that existed between the very real limitations on his talent and ability on the one hand, and the enormity of his ambitions on the other—particularly his ambitions for the acquisition of power over others, ambitions so open-ended that they could never be, and never really were, entirely satisfied. Could it not have been an awareness of this incongruity, and of the dangers and vulnerabilities associated with it, that lay at the heart of the insane and clearly uncontrollable jealousy and resentment that took possession of him whenever he encountered the slightest evidence of superiority to himself on the part of any other person, and this in any field, and regardless of whether there was any reason why that person's superiority in the field in question should be seen as discreditable to him? He simply could not bear it that anyone else should be given credit for any significant virtues or competencies, particularly for those he knew himself not to possess.

It is with all this in mind that I have to question whether Stalin's abnormal reactions reflected any sort of Freudian repression of the awareness of his true deficiencies of character and ability, or any belief in the reality of the self-image he had fashioned for himself. The evidence seems to me to favor a contrary conclusion: namely, that he was only too well aware of his various insufficiencies and determined that they should not come to light if there was anything (and this meant literally anything, however cruel, unjust, or destructive) to prevent it.

I see the evidence for this in the fact that his most savage exactions upon others were linked to the points where his past record was most terrible and inadmissible; and his most absurd positive pretensions, to the areas in which he knew his lack of competence to be the greatest. Others, for example, had to be charged with the murders of Gorky and Kirov and required to confess falsely and in public their guilt for these murders, not because Stalin felt any pangs of conscience about them (I doubt that he ever felt such pangs over anything) but because he recognized these murders to be, in the eyes of other Marxists, particularly heinous, and the revelation of his part in them, should it occur, as bound to be particularly damaging to him. And similarly, his most absurd pretensions to eminence in cultural fields were advanced precisely where his incompetence was greatest. It was not by chance that he, knowing nothing about military matters and having even made dreadful mistakes in that area, insisted that he be recognized as the greatest military theorist since Clauswitz; or that he, who spoke no language with facility (unless it was his native Georgian), had to be accepted as the greatest authority of his age on linguistics. So obvious was the connection, in many instances, between his own anxieties about his past conduct and the cruelties and humiliations he inflicted on others, and so clearly were his pretensions to cultural eminence concentrated in fields where he knew his incompetence to be greatest, that the student of his life could find, in the demands he placed upon others, something like a perfect index of the crimes he really committed and of the weaknesses of which he was really conscious.

I mention all this because it seems to me to indicate that Stalin was by no means unaware either of the monstrosity of his previous crimes or of the weaknesses and limitations from which he suffered. Little of this, if any, was blanketed out of his consciousness, or thrust into the realm of the subconscious. But does this mean that he hated himself for these reasons? Was it not rather hatred of others that so often took possession of him in such instances—hatred of them, as a rule, not primarily for what they *did* but simply for what they *were?* Their very presence, as members of the same political and cultural world as his own, was intolerable to him, because it seemed implicitly to challenge not his own view of himself, but the view that he wanted others to take of him.

To see this as a form of self-hatred would imply, it seems to me, that there was in Stalin's makeup something that might be called a sense of shame. But I see no evidence that there was. My impression is that he was no more capable of feeling shame than he was of feeling pity. (I am not sure, in fact, that the two incapacities were not connected.) He was aware of his own criminality and of his limitations. But he could not endure awareness of them on the part of others, because that, more than anything else, seemed to him to threaten the realization of his most burning ambitions. These ambitions, unlimited in their scope and therefore in reality ultimately unrealizable, ran overwhelmingly to the achievement of power over other human beings, and particularly over those whose obedience was necessary to him for the achievement of his preeminence in the political realm that he conceived himself to inhabit.

But here, things were complicated. Great as were his crimes, ordinary as were his competencies in many aspects of life, and absurd as were his pretensions, Stalin did indeed have certain exceptional and highly remarkable talents. Outstanding among them were: (1) an almost diabolic ability to sense, and to see into, the innermost thoughts and motivations of persons near to him; (2) a truly impressive tactical skill in the manipulation of others, both as individuals and in groups; and (3) a capacity for dissimulation for which even the greatest of performing actors might have envied him. So formidable were these qualities that if greatness could be seen to rest upon them alone, he would fully have deserved the true greatness so often attributed to him.

But these qualities were not the only ones; and his historical figure (to whom am I saying this?) cannot be allowed to rest on them. His inadequacies in other respects were no less remarkable than his talents. To be born, as he was, without the capacity for either shame or pity (and we might add to that list: loyalty) was a very real deprivation (like his withered arm). It was a species of birth defect. He was in that sense born a moral cripple. And the effect of this, superimposed on the exceptional talents that he did have, was appalling. For only this combination of qualities could have made possible his advance to supreme power in Russia and the monstrosity of the ways in which he acquired that power and used it. Without the talents that he *did* possess, he could never have obtained the power he did obtain, or have misused it as he did. Politics, after all, is never a pleasant business; and a certain hardness and ruthlessness, alas, is essential to its acquisition and preservation even in the case of men far more humane than Stalin was. Had he not been deprived of the more positive capacities, particularly those for shame, pity, and loyalty to others, he would scarcely have progressed up the political ladder as he really did, or made such atrocious use of the power once he acquired it. These capacities would have retarded his advance and placed limits on his ambitions as well as his brutalities. This combination of the negative capacities he had and the positive ones he lacked was plainly a devil's brew, out of which arose some of the greatest disasters of the century now passing.

You may say: Stalin was not responsible for the negative qualities he possessed, or for the positive ones he was without. In either case, they were only birth defects; and therefore he is to be forgiven.

Perhaps, perhaps. But there is none of us born totally without the power of self-scrutiny. We all have to accept some measure of responsibility for the use we make of our lives. Seen in this way, Stalin appears to me as a man to whom the application of the term "scoundrel" would be an egregious understatement. Envy, suspicion, a very real tendency to sadism, and a truly unlimited and insane jealousy were, in addition to an equally unlimited ambition, his driving qualities. And, lacking the restraint that would normally have been imposed by the positive qualities he lacked, he indulged the negative ones without stint or hesitation. The result was an almost immeasurable tragedy for all who came under his rule. It is this that your book reveals; and you have, as I see it, done a truly great service in bringing it all out.

Now, one more thing that I want to tell you: you *must* write the third volume, covering the remaining twelve years of Stalin's life. If you feel that for one reason or another you really cannot write it, then you must see to it that someone else does. Without it, the story is not complete. The picture you have given is essentially unshakable; but without the account of the remaining twelve years, it does not achieve its full impact. This further account would present a powerful substantiation of all that you have written. So please, don't let this remaining task go uncompleted. See what you can do.

With affectionate greetings to Zhenya,

Very sincerely,

Foreword to Before the Storm, *by Marion Gräfin Dönhoff*
(1990)

⸺◦⸺

The geographic entity known historically as East Prussia, a territory somewhat larger than the state of Maryland, was at one time a province of the Kingdom of Prussia; later, from 1871 to 1919, of the German Reich; then finally, from 1919 to 1939, of Weimar Germany. Its northeastern reaches contained a large, heavily forested and beautiful lake district. Much of the remainder of the province consisting of rich and well-cultivated farming country, including a considerable number of large and highly productive estates. Some idea of the extent of its agriculture may be gained from the fact that it was supporting, on the eve of the Second World War, some 1,380,000 head of cattle and nearly 2 million pigs, not to mention half a million horses, among them many of Europe's finest.

The Second World War brought with it, of course, no end of sufferings and disasters: immense loss of human life, great displacements of innocent civilian populations, massive destruction of material values. One did not have to go to East Prussia to look for that sort of thing. But it is hard to think of any other region of this size, anywhere, that suffered so sweeping, indeed almost total, a disaster—any that had so much to lose and lost so much of it—as this ill-fated territory. When the tide of war had swept over it in the terrible winter of 1944–45, the region was, to anyone who had known it before, scarcely recognizable—a single great field of devastation, parts of it almost devoid of human inhabitants. Its few cities had been terribly destroyed.

New York: Knopf, 1990.

245

Its agricultural infrastructure was in ruins. Most of the people, some 1,750,000 of them in fact, and 95 percent of them Germans, had been killed or had fled to the west—fled under conditions of danger and hardship that would be difficult today to imagine. And when, shortly thereafter, the war came to an end, this ravaged and nearly deserted territory was cheerfully abandoned, so far as the Western allies were concerned, to the Communist conquerors—left to be divided between the Russians and the Poles and to disappear for years and decades to come behind the Iron Curtain, remote from the attention, the thoughts, even the curiosity, of the Western peoples. One is told that it has been largely resettled by Russians and Poles. Beyond that, one knows little of what has happened to it. There is no evidence that anything even resembling its former civilizational infrastructure and prosperity has ever been restored.

Among the victims of this tragedy, there were none for whom the disaster was more extensive, more heartrending, and more final than the inhabitants of the great landed estates. Almost all of the manor houses, some of them structures of great historical and aesthetic value, appear to have been, whether by deliberate intent or otherwise, burned to the ground, carrying with them to destruction all of the rare works of art, antiquities, and libraries that a number of them housed. Think as one may about the sociological and economic qualities of this particular form of land tenure—judge as one may the qualities of the societies and the persons that supported it—what occurred to such places during the war, in East Prussia and elsewhere, represented a grievous impairment of the historical and cultural heritage of European civilization.

It was on one of these East Prussian estates and in just such a manor house (one of the greatest and finest of them, in fact) that the childhood and early youth of Marion Dönhoff were passed. She was destined, after long absence, to return during the war to these familiar places and there, in the absence of almost all of the male family members and relatives who could have taken over this responsibility (they were, nearly to a man, killed in battle or executed by the Nazi authorities), to administer the agricultural operations of two of these great estates. She bore this responsibility to the very end, to the point where the advancing Soviet forces were only hours away and no choice remained for her but to do what she actually did: to mount a horse, to join the endless road-clogging columns of fugitives, and to ride her horse over hundreds of miles, in zero-degree weather, to the relative safety of the defeated and semi-destroyed non-Communist Germany of the west.

So sweeping, so definitive, was the expunging of the civilization Marion Dönhoff left behind her in East Prussia that there was a problem, in the years after the war, in the preserving of the very historical memory of it. Of the visible ruins and other relics that normally serve to remind us of past civilizations, less would seem to have survived in the case of East Prussia than in the case of civilizations that reached their high points centuries in the past. The only bonds that could now link the earlier life of that East Prussian region with the consciousness of people of later generations were the memories of those who had participated in that life and were capable of recording for posterity what they remembered of it.

This, we may be sure, was one of the factors Marion Dönhoff had in mind as she set out to commit her own reminiscences to paper, thus making them available to the German- and English-speaking publics of later generations. In doing so, she has made a significant contribution to the history of this troubled century, and has rendered a notable service to those who have an interest in that history and the ability to discern the lessons it holds for the peoples of the present age.

Witness
(1990)

———◦∞◦———

In the course of the 1980s, the small coterie of Anglo-American writers who had been addressing themselves to the movement of life in
Eastern Europe in the years since 1948 found itself somewhat abruptly
enhanced by the accession to its ranks of a remarkable young English
scholar, Mr. Timothy Garton Ash. Issuing, in the late 1970s, from that
formidable stronghold of interest and sympathy for all things "dissident" in the Communist world, St. Antony's College at Oxford, Mr.
Garton Ash traveled extensively in East Germany, lived for some
months as a humble post-graduate scholar in East Berlin, and capped
these experiences by writing, in the German language, a book about
the German Democratic Republic, which he published in West Germany.[1] This last seems to have deprived him, not surprisingly, of the
privilege of access to East Germany for some time into the future. It
did not, however, put an end to his intense interest in Eastern Europe
generally, and particularly in Poland, Czechoslovakia, and Hungary.
In the first two of those countries, he evidently formed close personal
connections; he learned enough of the respective languages to allow
him to communicate effectively with those who particularly engaged

Review of *The Uses of Adversity: Essays on the Fate of Central Europe,* by Timothy
Garton Ash (New York: Random House, 1989); originally published in the *New York
Review of Books,* March 1, 1990
[1] *Und willst Du nicht mein Bruder sein? Die DDR Heute* (Rowohlt Taschenbuch,
1981). (This book has not, to my knowledge, appeared in English translation, and I
do not at this time have access to the German original.)

his interest and attention; and he cultivated to good effect the attendant associations.

The literary results of this preoccupation have been considerable.
First, there was a book of nearly four hundred pages, published in 1984,
about the struggle of the Solidarity movement in Poland in the period
immediately preceding the imposition of martial law upon that country in 1981—a book that, for a number of its qualities, deserved a much
more prominent and enduring circulation than it received.[2] Then, from
1983 down to the sensational events of late 1989 in all of Eastern Europe, there appeared a series of articles, written mostly for the London
Spectator and *The New York Review,* fourteen of which were gathered
together and republished in 1989 in the book here under review. And
finally, it would not be fair to the author to omit, in this listing, the
further articles written too recently to be included in the book but dealing with the *crescendo* of events that marked the final two months of
1989 in the region in question.[3]

The bulk of this output could be said to have lain in that small and
rarely visited field of literary effort where journalism, history, and literature (in the sense of belles-lettres) come together. Garton Ash is, in
the most literal sense of the term, a *contemporary* historian. He writes
primarily as a witness to the events he is treating, and not just as an
outside witness but often as an inside one as well; for his own involvement in these events, intellectual and emotional, is of such intensity that he can speak, in a sense, from the inside as well as from the
outside. Yet the sense of the historic dimension of the events in question is never lost. And the quality of the writing places it clearly in the
category of good literature. If indeed there is any reason to mention
journalism in connection with this work, it lies solely in the high con-
temporaneousness of the material.

That there are dangers as well as glories in this form of writing is
obvious; and Garton Ash is well aware of them. One lies in the relative narrowness of perspective that inevitably attends the description

---

[2] *The Polish Revolution: Solidarity* (New York: Scribner's, 1984).

[3] See "Revolution in Hungary and Poland," in *The New York Review of Books* (August 17, 1989); "The German Revolution" (December 21, 1989); "The Revolution
of the Magic Lantern" (January 19, 1990); and "Eastern Europe: The Year of Truth"
(February 15, 1990).

of very recent events. Garton Ash cited, in his book about the Polish events of 1980–81, the apt warning of Sir Walter Raleigh that "who-so-euer in writing a modern Historie, shall follow truth too neare the heels, it may happily strike out his teeth."

The other danger relates, of course, to what Garton Ash himself called the "crippling incompleteness of sources." Here he excused himself, in the book just mentioned, by pointing to what then appeared the extreme improbability that the official records would become available in our time.

The works in question are not exclusively eyewitness accounts. Such passages are accompanied here and there by analytical and re-flective material. But what lends vitality to the entire effort is the vividness and the high literary quality of the description of many of the scenes observed—small scenes, for the most part, but viewed with a keen eye to their significance for wider judgments, and with a liter-ary touch that loses none of their color. There are so many examples of this, scattered throughout this literature, that it is hard to know how to select them. Sometimes the events described are momentous, some-times ostensibly trivial. Here, for example, is the opening of the first tense discussions, in August 1980, between the Communist Polish government, represented by a deputy prime minister, Mieczyslaw Jagielski, and striking workers in Gdansk:

> At eight o'clock Jagielski and his team arrive in a coach. As it nudges its way through the crowd before the gate, people drum furiously on the sides and windows. Then the Deputy Prime Min-ister, pale and tight-lipped, runs the gauntlet of two thousand hos-tile eyes. On the platform in the main hall he shakes hands punc-tiliously with all the Presidium, before walking back between the long tables and across a small lobby into the room which will be used for the talks. Here, the two sides will have to sit in low lounge chairs, facing each other across Formica tables. The whole wall be-tween this room and the lobby is made of glass, and throughout the proceedings a succession of strikers, supporters and photogra-phers will peer and leer and let off their flashbulbs through the glass wall, like a never-ending crowd of schoolchildren at an aquarium.

Or this, the description of a visit paid by Garton Ash in Prague, in the mid-1980s, to a onetime student of philosophy, an oppositionist, now reduced by the Husák regime to making his living by stoking the furnace boiler in the basement of the Ministry of Culture. The room in which Garton Ash was received, in the basement adjoining the boiler, contained, among the usual bric-a-brac consigned to such premises, a battered and discarded piano. The host, after a two-hour discussion of the philosophy of Hayek, proceeded to play the piano for him. Garton Ash noted

> how, against the white keys, his fingernails are broken and black from shoveling coal. He's not really a good player—but . . . his playing, here, is somehow electric. It has a kind of defiant ferocity. I see the music leap out of the basement skylight, like an escaping genie, force its way up through the pouring rain, giving a two-finger salute to the ministry of culture as it passes, and then up, up, high above the sodden city, above the smoke from his boiler's chimney, above the rain clouds, the two fingers turn the other way now, proclaiming *V* for Victory.

This is a kind of writing—it could be called the history of the present—for which it is not easy to find examples in earlier literature. The two most apt ones, in my memory, are Tocqueville's brilliant account of the crucial revolutionary days of February 1848 in Paris, and N. N. Sukhanov's classic volumes of day-to-day observations on the revolutionary events of the year 1917 in Petersburg.[4] Whether such writing rates the term "history" is debatable; but it may be said without hesitation that serious historians will someday find themselves greatly indebted to Garton Ash, as they are to his predecessors in the other cases cited, for a species of evidence about historical events they will not be apt to find preserved in many other places.

The focus of Garton Ash's work over the years of the 1980s was on the leading members of what might be called the literary-philosophical opposition in the countries in Eastern Europe, such personalities as Adam Michnik in Poland, Václav Havel in Czechoslovakia, and Györgi Konrád in Hungary. He was obviously enthralled (and not without good reason) by the spectacle of the efforts of these people to come to terms, intellectually and emotionally, with the repression and

---

[4]Alexis de Tocqueville, *Souvenirs* (1850); N. N. Sukhanov, *The Russian Revolution, 1917* (New York: Oxford University Press, 1955).

frustration to which they, as independent-minded writers and thinkers, had all been subjected under their respective Communist regimes. He clearly admired them, extended to them his understanding and sympathy, and made himself in a sense their spokesman and interpreter in the English-speaking world. They appreciated all this, respected the honesty of his accounts, gained confidence in him from his understanding of their situations, and apparently came in some instances even to regard him as one of their own.

That this, too, had its dangers is again obvious. There are times when Garton Ash's admiration for these people gives the impression of a modern version of *Lives of the Saints*. Yet his judgment was not uncritical; nor could one say that the admiration was unjustified. These were indeed, for the most part, sorely tried people: writers who were accustomed to living by that calling but found themselves pressed by the exactions of their respective regimes into either a helpless silence or a desperate recourse to *samizdat,* "writing for the drawer," or both. Their moral indignation over the arbitrariness and the hypocrisies of their oppressors was understandable. They regarded themselves everywhere as being in the vanguard of the opposition. Many spent time in prison or undergoing other forms of repression; and most showed great courage in the face of this treatment.

Since these people were given by temperament to thinking and writing rather than doing, condemned now in any case to a species of exclusion from active and overt participation in the life of their respective societies, it is not surprising that, having nothing else to do, they leaned heavily in the direction of philosophical-political speculation. Nor is it surprising to discover, in their pronouncements and reactions, heavy doses of that curious species of intellectual snobbery that seems to affect the victims of oppression everywhere: the belief that they are unique in their suffering, and that they derive from it a kind of superior wisdom to which others could never hope to aspire.

Yet there is in these writers, all their admirable qualities notwithstanding, an otherworldliness that strikes one with double force in this remarkable age when the structure of oppression, under the shadow of which they then lived, is now disintegrating, and when their views about human political affairs must soon face the test of responsibility for the creation and management of new and presumably democratic political systems. Those who believe, as do I, that freedom is defin-

able only in terms of the restraints that it accepts will bridle, occasionally, at the constant use of the term "freedom" without mention
of responsibility, and will find themselves wondering, as they confront
the reactions and statements of Garton Ash's heroes, whether there is
not, here, a certain naïveté about politics generally, a certain anarchic
leaning, and an obliviousness to the fact that politics is by its very nature, everywhere, even in the democratic setting, a sordid and messy
affair, replete with disturbing moral dilemmas, painful compromises,
departures of every sort from the ideal—yet necessary. To say this, of
course, is not to vindicate those against whom these cultural "dissidents" have been for so long rebelling. There is, after all, a point
where relative distinctions become essential ones; and the Communist regimes, in their departures from truth and humanity, had passed
that point. But the oppositionists will find, as they now come to meet
the realities of political responsibility, that many of the idealistic moral
standards they have been inclined to apply to their Communist tor-
mentors will not be easy to meet in the everyday realm of democratic government.

Be that as it may, Garton Ash remains their outstanding interpreter
and spokesman for the Western world. They deserved to have one.
And none could say that he did not fulfill this function with talent,
with imagination, and with scrupulous respect for the truth as he saw
it.

It might be argued, I suppose, that the fourteen articles that form
this book, all written before the dramatic events of the final weeks of
1989, became outdated—overtaken in their significance—by the ultimate explosion in which so many of the tensions they described found
their denouement. Actually, this is not the case. This final explosion
did not arise out of nothing at all. It had a historical background, without which these final events could never have occurred. Some of this
background is still mysterious, not fully clarified even by Garton Ash's
book. But for much of it, the answers will be found, for whoever
wishes to look for them, in his description of what was going on in
the earlier years of the 1980s.

Of particular significance in this respect is his striking depiction of
the curious connivance, in this final period, of the ruled with the rulers
in the maintenance of the fictions clung to and treasured by the Communist regimes. Garton Ash describes this situation as "the split be-

tween the public and the private self, official and unofficial language, outward conformity and inward dissent—in short, the double life . . . a phenomenon common to all Soviet-bloc countries." What was significant here was not the participation of the helpless peoples in the outward observation of these semantic rituals. The latter were the shield—the only one they had—behind which they led whatever real lives they were capable of living. What was significant was the complacency of the regimes in the face of what they knew perfectly well to be the underlying pretense. The pretense, after all, was universal. The officials of the regime, not believing a word of it themselves, said what they thought was necessary for them to say. The people, also not believing a word of it, said the things they thought the regime wanted to hear. And the regime, knowing that they were pretending, pretended to be satisfied. "We don't ask you," Garton Ash has the regime saying, by implication, to the people at one point, "to believe in us or our fatuous ideology. By all means listen to the Voice of America and watch Austrian television (*sotto voce:* So do we). All we ask is that you will outwardly and publicly conform: join in the ritual 'elections,' vote the prescribed way in the 'trade union' meetings, enroll your children in the 'socialist' youth organization. Keep your mind to yourself."

Whether Garton Ash saw in this complacency on the part of the regime the definitive evidence that it had lost what the Chinese call the "mandate of Heaven," that it was on the slippery and irresistible decline into final failure and disaster, seems unclear. But we are permitted to wonder, with the benefit of hindsight, whether this was not indeed the case. The regimes, after all, did not accept this situation by preference. They would surely have preferred to be able to say what they themselves believed, and to feel that the people believed it, too. And one might well ask, on the strength of this book, whether it should not be considered a firm law of political life that when a given regime is no longer able to carry on without accommodating itself to a wide-ranging pretense that it shares with its subject people, the artificiality of that pretense being perfectly evident to both sides, then its ultimate fall must be considered as inevitable and probably imminent, even if no one can tell when and how it will occur.

Whether Garton Ash, in these years of the curious agony of the mid-1980s, foresaw the imminence of what was to occur in late 1989 is, I repeat, uncertain. No one else did, and there is no reason why he should have done so. But that he had premonitions is clear; for he, writing in 1984, attributed to the Czechoslovak opposition group, the Chartists, the "knowledge" of "how suddenly a society that seems atomized, apathetic, and broken can be transformed into an articulate, united civil society. How private opinion can become public opinion. How a nation can stand on its feet again." And there could scarcely have been a better description of what was to happen in that very country in the final weeks of 1989.

There is, among the fourteen articles comprising this collection, one that differs considerably from most of the others. There is no eye-witnessing in it (from the absence of which it suffers a bit, for it is in the eyewitnessing that Garton Ash excels). It is entitled "Does Central Europe Exist?"; and it consists mostly of a rather critical examination of some of the published views of Michnik, Havel, and Milan Kundera, with the tendency of the last two to attach a special significance to their Central European, as distinct from purely Eastern European, origin.

The article is inconclusive and not of great importance. But it is interesting insofar as it points to a dim spot in the conceptual world of Garton Ash himself and, one suspects, in that of the Eastern and Central European oppositionists about whom he writes. This dim spot relates to the frame of close international associations into which the peoples of this region might, once liberated, be accepted, to replace the Communist one in which they had so long been held against their will.

The problems of these peoples are examined here primarily within a frame of regional isolation. Their great neighbors—Russia and West Germany—scarcely figure in the vision that emerges. While there is, here and there, a grudging admission that Gorbachev might have had something to do with the trend of events in this region, one gains the impression that Gorbachev's policies, to the extent that they were of positive effect, were extorted from him by the necessities of his position, and did not in any case reflect any particularly generous motives or convictions on his part. West Germany, too, finds only dim mention: it is the seat of a distasteful materialistic Western civilization, philosophically shallow, uninteresting, devoid of ideals, superior only when measured against the Soviet alternative. Little attention is given to the manner in which the "East Central" peoples, their liberation once achieved, might relate to the remainder of the European family.

This dim spot was perhaps a natural one. Liberation, under the perspective of Garton Ash's articles, was still far off. The main thing was to achieve it; and no one knew when that would come to pass. If and when it did come, there would be time enough to think about all these other things.

Reasonable enough. But one sees, in the views and preoccupations of Garton Ash's heroes, little to suggest an interest in the future relationship of their countries to the European community as a whole. Nationalism is there in abundance, its significance heightened by the fact that it has been for so long the natural rallying point for resistance to foreign domination. But there is no suggestion of an appreciation that a total national independence might, in the liberated dream world of the future, not be enough, might not even be a feasible solution; that the day was at hand when the old romantic ideals of self-realization within the national system would have to yield to a wider sense of community; that in this rapidly emerging world of the future, where intra-European wars would make no sense at all, the danger would be not what nations might do to one another but rather what all of them together were doing to their environment and to themselves. These realities were ones in which the peoples of the poorly regarded, non-suffering, materialistic, and "capitalistic" West were perhaps better schooled than their cousins in the East, preoccupied as these latter had so long been with their own sufferings and problems.

Garton Ash was evidently intrigued by the views of those writers, particularly the Hungarian, who thought they saw in a common Central European heritage a form of unity, cultural and spiritual, in which some day, in that happier, hoped-for future, they could find the wider sense of community of which they felt the need. Garton Ash himself, in the years following the writing of the article referred to above, began to use the term "East Central Europe" in place of the "Eastern Europe" that had previously engaged his attention. The idea is not wholly without historical justification; and one can understand its appeal to people searching for an orientation wider than the national one but anxious to avoid a relationship with the East that had given them such bitter unpleasantness, or with a Western Europe that, as many of them felt, had evinced so little understanding for all they had been through.

But "Central Europe," for the purposes Garton Ash had in mind, is a vague and uncertain concept, particularly when one faces the question whether it is to include all of Germany (with relation to which, again, not all Eastern European memories were pleasant). And the logical conclusion of all such speculations is that the peoples of "East Central Europe," whatever their relations with Central Europe itself, will eventually have to come to terms with the remainder of the continent as well, and perhaps, swallowing many unhappy memories, even with the "European house" that figured so recently in the imagination of Mikhail Gorbachev and also had a place at an earlier date (if one reads the record correctly) in the mind of Charles de Gaulle.

Keeping the Faith
(1992)

———⸰⟨∞⟩⸰———

Václav Havel, courageous and outstanding dissident in the years of Communist control of Czechoslovakia, and more recently president of that country, needs no further introduction to the readers of the *New York Review*. His name has appeared on the pages of the *Review* in a number of capacities. Himself always a prolific and engaging writer, known originally primarily as a playwright, Havel's literary output of later years has taken almost exclusively the form of essays, letters, and published interviews. After his release from prison in 1983, several volumes of English translations of such materials saw publication prior to the appearance of the volume here under review.[1]

With minor exceptions, the pieces contained in those volumes were written during the Communist period of Czechoslovak history and reflected Havel's preoccupation with the tremendous strains that rested upon his life and those of so many others in those tragic years. The volume to which this present discussion is devoted was the first to be written after the liberation of the country in the years 1989–1990. It consists of essays written in the summer of 1991 and edited by the author in early 1992—in the period, that is, of his second presidency of that country, now terminated by his recent withdrawal from that po-

Review of *Summer Meditations,* by Vaclav Havel (New York: Knopf, 1992); originally published in the *New York Review of Books,* September 24, 1992.

[1]*Living in Truth* (1987), *Letters to Olga* (1988), *Disturbing the Peace* (1990), and *Open Letters* (1992). The dates shown here are only those of the major English translations. Most of the materials had seen earlier publication in one form or another, in Czech or in languages other than English, but none prior to 1983.

sition. It is the first such volume, therefore, to reflect the author's re-actions to the tremendous events, including so prominently his own experiences, of the period of liberation. It speaks, however, for the depth and solidity of his own thinking that this fundamental change in the political environment occasioned, and required, no significant revision of the convictions and principles that had inspired his earlier writings. These works were simply applied to the new situation; and they seem to have lost none of their relevance or their force in the process.

Leaving aside the first section of the book, entitled "Political Moral-ity and Civility" (which was placed last in the original Czech edition and will be given similar place here), the first material to meet the reader's eye is the long section (the longest in the book) that deals, under the title "In a Time of Transition," with the internal political problems of the Czechoslovak state as they presented themselves to Havel during the period of his second presidency. Much of the con-tent of this section was devoted to constitutional problems. The ex-isting constitution, inherited from the Communist period, being plainly unsuitable for the present era, Havel, a strong opponent of proportional representation and advocate of the strengthening of the presidency, pressed hard while president for the early preparation of a new one; but this question soon became entangled in the Slovak problem (among others); and pending a resolution of that problem, no serious progress in the constitutional question was possible.

This being the case, it was not surprising that a large portion of this first section of Havel's book was addressed to the future of the Czech–Slovak relationship. And an agonizing matter this was for a man of Havel's generous impulses—torn, as he appears to have been, between a broad-minded sympathy and understanding for Slovak national feel-ing on the one hand, and exasperation with the erratic and irrespon-sible behavior of Slovak politicians (and some of the Czech ones as well) in the official discussions over this bitter problem on the other. Throughout this entire ordeal, it remained his conviction, and one for which he offered a number of serious arguments, that a complete sep-aration of the two peoples would be nothing but "a grave misfortune" for all concerned. His reluctance to preside over a breakup of the coun-try was apparently one of the principal reasons for his withdrawal from the presidential office.

There is a particularly tragic aspect to Havel's helplessness in the face of this problem, for it is hard to believe that the Slovaks, whether independent or otherwise, could ever have had a fairer, more tolerant, or more understanding chief of state than would have been a Václav Havel at the head of a continuing Czechoslovakia. And indeed, I know of no evidence that the majority of the Slovaks, if challenged by the sort of referendum Havel urged, would have favored a complete separation. But here is where the professional politicians came in. The drift toward separation appears to have been largely the product of their narrowness of concept and their tendency to play light-heartedly with politically arresting words and slogans. Things will no doubt continue to be this way.

Among Havel's comments in this connection were a few observations about politicians and politics that were clearly part of his general political philosophy and had a much wider relevance than to Czechoslovak problems alone. He did not challenge the usefulness or the necessity of the political party as such. He saw it as "an integral part of modern democracy and an expression of its plurality of opinion." But he minced no words in expressing his impatience with what he called "the dictatorship of partisanship," which he defined as "the excessive influence of parties in the system of political power." Political parties, he wrote, could become "a shadow state within a state." The loyalties they demanded could "count for more than the will of the electorate." Their pre-electoral maneuvering had a tendency to supersede society's interests. Electors came to be governed by people they never elected. Political decisions came to be determined by the tactics and strategies of partisan competition. "A few months before the election," he noted,

> electoral politics are already dominating political life. . . . There are articles about partisan bickering, bragging and intrigue, predictions about who will join with whom and against whom, who is beholden to whom or falling out with whom. Politicians seem to be devoting more time to party politics than to their jobs. Not a single law is passed without a debate about how a particular stand might serve a party's popularity. Ideas, no matter how absurd, are touted to gain favour with the electorate. . . . All this displaces a responsible interest in the prosperity and success of the broader community.

These views were written, of course, about conditions in Czechoslovakia; and this being a country in which, according to Havel's translator, Paul Wilson, "forty parties, coalitions, and movements" were competing in the most recent election," they are not surprising.[2]

But no one who has been following pre-election developments in the United States could fail to note the wider connotations of Havel's remarks. It is not hard to detect in them not only echoes of eighteenth-century Federalist anxieties about "factionalism" in the emerging American political system, but also something of the impatience with rampant partisanship that caused so many Americans to greet with sympathy and satisfaction Mr. Ross Perot's strictures on the American party–political establishment of this day.

It is in fact a question whether Havel, in these observations, did not strike a chord that resonated with the publics of a number of modern democracies. It would be hard, of course, to deny the vulnerability of modern democracy generally to domination by party machines and personalities in whose motivation for political involvement a devotion to the public interest is diluted, to put it mildly, by considerations of another and less admirable nature. It has been customary in the past for most Western peoples to accept this situation with a resigned shrug of the shoulders, as one of the prices of political freedom. But the years immediately ahead mark the passage not only of a century but of an age in Western civilization, and the advent of an age that is bound to place many new and unprecedented strains on the resources of modern democracy. What Havel has done, intentionally or otherwise, is to raise the question of whether these developments do not call for adaptive changes in democratic systems, and whether, in particular, the democracies can continue to afford the luxury of leaving the great affairs of state so extensively dependent upon the outcome of struggles among political factions more immediately concerned with their own competitive fortunes than with the major problems of national interest. This comes out particularly clearly in his opposition to proportional representation, and in his feeling that the choices the common citizen should be permitted to make in the election booth should be ones among individuals, not among parties.

[2]Paul Wilson, "The End of the Velvet Revolution," in the *New York Review of Books,* August 13, 1992.

The next section of Havel's book, entitled "What I Believe," is devoted primarily to questions of ideology, doctrine, dogma—whatever one wishes to call it. Its principal thrust is to emphasize his skepticism and aversion with relation to all schematic thinking of this nature. He firmly rejects what he describes as the Communist effort "to unite all economic entities under the authority of a single monstrous owner— one central voice of reason that deems itself more clever than life itself"; and he accepts without stint the basic necessity of a market economy. But he warns against making a dogma out of attachment to the free market. The state, too, has its part to play in the economic process; but this, he feels, consists only of establishing by legislation the rules of the game, making the usual "macroeconomic decisions," and formulating clear policies for all those situations in which government finds itself compelled to accept involvement. All this admittedly requires some sort of a master plan, or strategy; but the aim of this plan, he considers, should be the maximum gradual reduction of precisely this involvement, recognizing, of course, that its total elimination will never be possible.

The following chapter ("The Task of Independence") is devoted to the foreign policy of the Czechoslovak state as it existed at the time of Havel's writing (although there is no reason why most of it should not be applicable to the rump "Czech" state by which that older one will now presumably have to be replaced). Not surprisingly, it is a moderate and thoroughly peaceable policy that Havel envisages. It is marked by an eagerness for association with the remainder of Europe through whatever international bodies—whether the European community, or the Council of Europe, or the C.S.C.E., or even NATO—lend themselves to such a relationship, and this in whatever ways seem possible and promising. Of Havel's policy it can only be said, and this with assurance, that a Europe concerned for its own peace and prosperity will encounter no obstacles in any Czechoslovak or rump Czech state dominated, as either of these is likely to be, whether or not Havel holds the presidential office, by his ideas and personality.

In his observations on this subject, Havel could not avoid the effort to come to terms with one of the great overarching problems of international life in the emerging age, which is the tension, everywhere, between the forces of integration and disintegration. This is a problem that embraces not only the restlessness of national minorities within the framework of larger states but also the struggles of new and small states to find a middle ground between their overpowering longing for the trappings of sovereignty on the one hand, and the existence on the other of a degree of real dependence on outside forces that makes a mockery of all pretenses of total independence. Underlying this entire problem is, of course, the lack of any suitable intermediary status between complete formal subservience as a minority within a larger state and a theoretically total (but unreal) independence and equality with all other states as a member of the universal U.N. community. What Havel has to say about Czechoslovakia's relationship to these problems is thoughtful and sensible; but no more than anyone else is he in a position to come up with sweeping and universally applicable answers to this most baffling and recalcitrant of contemporary world problems.

The chapter entitled "Beyond the Shock of Freedom" sets forth Havel's vision—a dream, he calls it—of Czechoslovakia as he would hope to see it one or two decades hence. The text of this chapter having appeared in somewhat different form in the *New York Review* of June 25, 1992, under the title "My Dream for Czechoslovakia," there is no need for a recounting of its many features at this point. Suffice it to note that Havel would be the first to deny that what he is presenting is a plausible utopia. He is well aware that his dream could never be realized in its totality.

> A heaven on earth in which people all love each other and everyone is hard-working, well-mannered, and virtuous, in which the land flourishes and everything is sweetness and light, working harmoniously to the satisfaction of God: this will never be. On the contrary, the world has had the worst experiences with utopian thinkers who promised all that. Evil will remain with us, no one will ever eliminate human suffering, the political arena will always attract irresponsible and ambitious adventurers and charlatans. And man will not stop destroying the world. In this regard, I have no illusions.

But all great statesmanship, as Martin Luther King suggested, must begin with some sort of a dream; and the one Havel describes—the dream of a small people with limited resources that has nevertheless come to terms with its international entourage, its natural environment, and itself—is so far ahead of most of the dreams that have inspired statesmanship in this brutal century that the reader can only acknowledge his respect for the dreamer, while sharing the wistfulness that inspired the dream.

In the first chapter of this book, Havel sets forth and defends his effort to move his country, despite the many obstacles that lie across the path, in the direction of his dream. Of the difficulty of the task he has no illusions. He is aware, as few others could be, of the damage done to the moral fabric of Czechoslovak society by the decades of Communist abuse. He made this clear in his earlier writings. But the reality, as became evident in the years following the liberation, exceeded his worst fears. What followed upon the removal of the heavy Communist hand was, in his words, "an enormous and dazzling explosion of every imaginable human vice." Society had indeed freed itself; but in some ways, it was behaving "worse than when it was in chains." It would take years to develop and cultivate a new moral order.

This, however, in Havel's view, was no cause for despair: "The only lost cause is the one we give up on before we enter the struggle." And he had no doubt that the people at large would be responsive to his effort to create that new order. There was among them a dormant good will that needed only to be touched—longed, in fact, to be recognized and cultivated. Nor was there any need for cynicism or deception in its recognition and cultivation. Politics was *not* essentially a disreputable business. There *was* no ultimate conflict between morality and successful political leadership. Politics as the practice of morality was not easy; but it *was possible.*

In this moving affirmation of confidence in the decency, the good will, and the latent responsiveness of the common man to responsible leadership, there was bound to be, one might suppose, even in a man as little given to outward piety as Havel, a touch of something very close to a religious faith—guarded and undemonstrative, if you will, but none the less sincere. "Our death," he wrote,

> ends nothing, because everything is forever being recorded and evaluated somewhere else, somewhere "above us," in what I have called "the memory of Being"—an integral aspect of the secret order of the cosmos, of nature, and of life, which believers call God and to whose judgment everything is subject. Genuine conscience

and genuine responsibility are always, in the end, explicable only as an expression of the silent assumption that we are observed "from above," that everything is visible, nothing is forgotten, and so earthly time has no power to wipe away the sharp disappointments of earthly failure: our spirit knows that it is not the only entity aware of these failures.

Havel denies being a philosopher. He describes himself, instead, as "only an occasional essayist or a philosophically inclined literary man." But what emerges from these pages is a remarkably integral view, and a strongly held one, of many things. And it is surely a rare thing for the president of a modern country, while still in office, to offer to the public so unsparing an exposure of what one can only call his political and personal philosophy. What is even more striking still is the elevated quality, morally and intellectually, of the philosophy that emerges from this effort. If we look for its origins, we find that they were forged and tempered primarily in the grueling experience of his long personal conflict with a Communist regime (an experience that included some four years in prison) and in his persistent effort to understand both that regime and his own people's reaction to it.

Is there not, one wonders, a lesson in this? How much more comfortable and easy it was, by comparison, for the leaders of Western societies never touched by the Communist hand to concentrate their heavy-lidded gaze exclusively on the material aspects of modern life—such as economic growth, unemployment, budgetary problems—and to leave the moral condition of society to the public schools, the churches, and the commercially dominated mass media. But can this, one asks, go on? Will there not have to be a more serious and structured effort to confront young people with the seriousness of life and its problems, and with the full measure of their responsibility for responding to it, if they are to meet the coming age head-on? These, in any case, are the questions with which at least one reader puts down Havel's book; and they suggest that in the writing of it, he was serving purposes wider than those of which he was aware.

Part Five

MISCELLANEOUS

Morality and Foreign Policy
(1985)

————····⋘⊗⋙····————

1

In a small volume of lectures published nearly thirty-five years ago, I had the temerity to suggest that the American statesmen of the turn of the twentieth century were unduly legalistic and moralistic in their judgment of the actions of other governments.[1] This seemed to be an approach that carried them away from the sterner requirements of political realism and caused their statements and actions, however impressive to the domestic political audience, to lose effectiveness in the international arena.

These observations were doubtless expressed too cryptically and thus invited a wide variety of interpretations, not excluding the thesis that I had advocated an amoral, or even immoral, foreign policy for this country. There have since been demands, particularly from the younger generation, that I should make clearer my views on the relationship of moral considerations to American foreign policy. The challenge is a fair one and deserves a response.

2

Certain distinctions should be made before one wanders further into this thicket of problems.

First of all, the conduct of diplomacy is the responsibility of gov-

Originally published in *Foreign Affairs* (Winter 1985–86).
[1]*American Diplomacy, 1900–1950* (Chicago: University of Chicago Press, 1951).

ernments. For purely practical reasons, this is unavoidable and inalterable. This responsibility is not diminished by the fact that government, in formulating foreign policy, may choose to be influenced by private opinion. What we are talking about, therefore, when we attempt to relate moral considerations to foreign policy, is the behavior of governments, not of individuals or entire peoples.

Second, let us recognize that the functions, commitments, and moral obligations of governments are not the same as those of the individual. Government is an agent, not a principal. Its primary obligation is to the *interests* of the national society it represents, not to the moral impulses that elements of that society may experience. No more than the attorney vis-à-vis the client, nor the doctor vis-à-vis the patient, can government attempt to insert itself into the consciences of those whose interests it represents.

Let me explain. The interests of the national society for which government must concern itself are basically those of its military security, the integrity of its political life, and the well-being of its people. These needs have no moral quality. They arise from the very existence of the national state and from the status of national sovereignty it enjoys. They are the unavoidable necessities of a national existence and therefore not subject to classification as either "good" or "bad." They may be questioned from a detached philosophic point of view. But the government of the sovereign state cannot make such judgments. When it accepts the responsibilities of governing, implicit in that acceptance is the assumption that it is right that the state should be sovereign, that the integrity of its political life should be assured, that its people should enjoy the blessings of military security, material prosperity, and a reasonable opportunity for, as the Declaration of Independence put it, the pursuit of happiness. For these assumptions the government needs no moral justification, nor need it accept any moral reproach for acting on the basis of them.

This assertion assumes, however, that the concept of national security taken as the basis for governmental concern is one reasonably, not extravagantly, conceived. In an age of nuclear striking power, national security can never be more than relative; and to the extent that it can be assured at all, it must find its sanction in the intentions of rival powers as well as in their capabilities. A concept of national security that ignores this reality, and, above all, one that fails to concede the same legitimacy to the security needs of others that it claims for its own, lays itself open to the same moral reproach from which, in normal circumstances, it would be immune.

Whoever looks thoughtfully at the present situation of the United States in particular will have to agree that to assure these blessings to the American people is a task of such dimensions that the government attempting to meet it successfully will have very little, if any, energy and attention left to devote to other undertakings, including those suggested by the moral impulses of these or those of its citizens.

Finally, let us note that there are no internationally accepted standards of morality to which the U.S. government could appeal if it wished to act in the name of moral principles. It is true that there are certain words and phrases sufficiently high-sounding the world over that most governments, when asked to declare themselves for or against, will cheerfully subscribe to them, considering that such is their vagueness that the mere act of subscribing carries with it no danger of having one's freedom of action significantly impaired. To this category of pronouncements belong such documents as the Kellogg-Briand Pact, the Atlantic Charter, the Yalta Declaration on Liberated Europe, and the prologues of innumerable other international agreements.

Ever since Secretary of State John Hay staged a political coup in 1899 by summoning the supposedly wicked European powers to sign up to the lofty principles of his Open Door notes (principles that neither they nor we had any awkward intention of observing), American statesmen have had a fondness for hurling just such semantic challenges at their foreign counterparts, thereby placing themselves in a graceful posture before domestic American opinion and reaping whatever political fruits are to be derived from the somewhat grudging and embarrassed responses these challenges evoke.

To say these things, I know, is to invite the question: how about the Helsinki accords of 1975? These, of course, were numerous and varied. There is no disposition here to question the value of many of them as refinements of the norms of international intercourse. But there were some, particularly those related to human rights, that it is hard to relegate to any category other than that of the high-minded but innocuous professions just referred to. These accords were declaratory in nature, not contractual. The very general terms in which they were drawn up, involving the use of words and phrases that had different meanings for different people, deprived them of the character of specific obligations to which signatory governments could usefully be held. The Western statesmen who pressed for Soviet adherence to these pronouncements must have been aware that some of them could not be implemented on the Soviet side, within the meanings we would normally attach to their workings, without fundamental changes in the Soviet system of power—changes we had no reason to expect would, or could, be introduced by the men then in power. Whether it is morally commendable to induce others to sign on to declarations, however high-minded in resonance, one knows will not and cannot be implemented is a reasonable question. The Western negotiators, in any case, had no reason to plead naïveté as their excuse for doing so.

When we talk about the application of moral standards to foreign policy, therefore, we are not talking about compliance with some clear and generally accepted international code of behavior. If the policies and actions of the U.S. government are to be made to conform to moral standards, those standards are going to have to be America's own, founded on traditional American principles of justice and propriety. When others fail to conform to those principles, and when their failure to conform has an adverse effect on American *interests,* as distinct from political tastes, we have every right to complain and, if necessary, to take retaliatory action. What we cannot do is to assume that our moral standards are theirs as well, and to appeal to those standards as the source of our grievances.

3

So much for basic principles. Let us now consider some categories of action that the U.S. government is frequently asked to take, and sometimes does take, in the name of moral principle. These actions fall into two broad general categories: those that relate to the behavior of other governments that we find morally unacceptable, and those that relate to the behavior of our own government. We will take them in that order.

There have been many instances, particularly in recent years, when the U.S. government has taken umbrage at the behavior of other governments on grounds that at least implied moral criteria for judgment, and in some of these instances the verbal protests have been reinforced by more tangible means of pressure. These interventions have marched, so to speak, under a number of banners: democracy, human rights, majority rule, fidelity to treaties, fidelity to the U.N. Charter, and so on. Their targets have sometimes been the external policies and actions of the offending states, more often the internal practices. The interventions have served, in the eyes of their American inspirers, as demonstrations not only of the moral deficiencies of others but of the positive morality of ourselves; for it was seen as our moral duty to detect these lapses on the part of others, to denounce them before the world, and to assure as far as we could with measures short of military action—that they were corrected. Those who have inspired or initiated efforts of this nature would certainly have claimed to be acting in the name of moral principle, and in many instances they would no doubt have been sincere in doing so. But whether the results of this inspiration, like those of so many other good intentions, would justify this claim is questionable from a number of standpoints.

Let us consider first those of our interventions that relate to internal practices of the offending governments. Let us reflect for a moment on how these interventions appear in the eyes of the governments in question and of many outsiders.

The situations that arouse our discontent exist, as a rule, far from our own shores. Few of us can profess to be perfect judges of their rights and wrongs. These are, for their governments, matters of internal affairs. It is customary for governments to resent interference by outside powers in affairs of this nature, and if our diplomatic history is any indication, we ourselves are not above resenting and resisting it when we find ourselves its object.

Interventions on moral principle can be formally defensible only if the practices against which they are directed are seriously injurious to our interests, rather than just our sensibilities. There will, of course, be those readers who will argue that the encouragement and promotion of democracy elsewhere is always in the interests of the security, political integrity, and prosperity of the United States. If this can be demonstrated in a given instance, well and good. But it is not invariably the case. "Democracy" is a loose term. Many varieties of folly and injustice contrive to masquerade under this designation. The mere fact that a country acquires the trappings of self-government does not automatically mean that the interests of the United States are thereby furthered. There are forms of plebiscitary "democracy" that may well prove less favorable to American interests than a wise and benevolent authoritarianism. There can be tyrannies of a majority as well as tyrannies of a minority, with the one hardly less odious than the other. Hitler came into power (albeit under highly unusual circumstances) with an electoral mandate, and there is scarcely a dictatorship of this age that would not claim the legitimacy of mass support.

In some parts of the world, the main requirement of American security is not an unnatural imitation of the American model but sheer stability, and this is not always assured by a government of what appears to be popular acclaim. In approaching this question, Americans must overcome their tendency toward generalization and learn to examine each case on its own merits. The best measure of these merits is not the attractiveness of certain general semantic symbols but the effect of the given situation on the tangible and demonstrable interests of the United States.

Furthermore, while we are quick to allege that this or that practice in a foreign country is bad and deserves correction, seldom if ever do we seem to occupy ourselves seriously or realistically with the conceivable alternatives. It seems seldom to occur to us that even if a given situation is bad, the alternatives might be worse—even though history provides plenty of examples of just this phenomenon. In the eyes of many Americans, it is enough for us to indicate the changes that ought, as we see it, to be made. We assume, of course, that the consequences will be benign and happy ones. But this is not always assured. It is, in any case, not we who are going to have to live with those consequences: it is the offending government and its people. We are demanding, in effect, a species of veto power over those of their practices that we dislike, while denying responsibility for whatever may flow from the acceptance of our demands.

Finally, we might note that our government, in raising such demands, is frequently responding not to its own moral impulses or to any wide general movements of American opinion but rather to pressures generated by politically influential minority elements among us that have some special interest—ethnic, racial, religious, ideological, or several of these together—in the foreign situation in question. Sometimes it is the sympathies of these minorities that are most prominently aroused, sometimes their antipathies. But in view of this diversity of motive, the U.S. government, in responding to such pressures and making itself their spokesman, seldom acts consistently. Practices or policies that arouse our official displeasure in one country are cheerfully condoned or ignored in another. What is bad in the behavior of our opponents is good, or at least acceptable, in the case of our friends. What is unobjectionable to us at one period of our history is offensive in another.

This is unfortunate, for a lack of consistency implies a lack of principle in the eyes of much of the world; whereas morality, if not principled, is not really morality. Foreigners, observing these anomalies, may be forgiven for suspecting that what passes as the product of moral inspiration in the rhetoric of our government is more likely to be a fair reflection of the mosaic of residual ethnic loyalties and passions that make themselves felt in the rough and tumble of our political life.

Similar things could be said when it is not the internal practices of the offending government but its actions on the international scene that are at issue. There is, here, the same reluctance to occupy oneself with the conceivable alternatives to the procedures one complains about or with the consequences likely to flow from the acceptance of one's demands. And there is frequently the same lack of consistency in the reaction. The Soviet action in Afghanistan, for example, is condemned, resented, and responded to with sanctions. One recalls little of such reaction in the case of the somewhat similar, and apparently no less drastic, action taken by China in Tibet some years ago. The question inevitably arises: is it principle that determines our reaction? Or are there other motives?

Where measures taken by foreign governments affect adversely American interests rather than just American moral sensibilities, protests and retaliation are obviously in order; but then they should be carried forward frankly for what they are, and not allowed to masquerade under the mantle of moral principle.

There will be a tendency, I know, on the part of some readers to see in these observations an apology for the various situations, both domestic and international, against which we have protested and acted in the past. They are not meant to have any such connotations. These words are being written—for whatever this is worth—by one who regards the action in Afghanistan as a grievous and reprehensible mistake of Soviet policy, a mistake that could and should certainly have been avoided. Certain of the procedures of the South African police have been no less odious to me than to many others.

What is being said here does not relate to the reactions of individual Americans, of private organizations in this country, or of the media to the situations in question. All these may think and say what they like. It relates to the reactions of the U.S. government, as a government among governments, and to the motivation cited for those reactions. Democracy, as Americans understand it, is not necessarily the future of all mankind, nor is it the duty of the U.S. government to assure that it becomes that. Despite frequent assertions to the contrary, not everyone in this world is responsible, after all, for the actions of everyone else, everywhere. Without the power to compel change, there is no responsibility for its absence. In the case of governments, it is important for purely practical reasons that the lines of responsibility be kept straight, and that there be, in particular, a clear association of the power to act with the consequences of action or inaction.

4

If, then, the criticism and reproof of perceived moral lapses in the conduct of others are at best a dubious way of expressing our moral commitment, how about our own policies and actions? Here, at least, the connection between power and responsibility—between the sowing and the reaping—is integral. Can it be true that here, too, there is no room for the application of moral principle and that all must be left to the workings of expediency, national egoism, and cynicism?

The answer, of course, is no, but the possibilities that exist are only too often ones that run against the grain of powerful tendencies and reflexes in our political establishment. In a less than perfect world, where the ideal so obviously lies beyond human reach, it is natural that the avoidance of the worst should often be a more practical undertaking than the achievement of the best, and that some of the strongest imperatives of moral conduct should be of a negative rather than a positive nature. The strictures of the Ten Commandments are perhaps the best illustration of this state of affairs. This being the case, it is not surprising that some of the most significant possibilities for the observance of moral considerations in American foreign policy relate to the avoidance of actions that have a negative moral significance.

Many of these possibilities lie in the intuitive qualities of diplomacy—such things as the methodology, manners, style, restraint, and elevation of diplomatic discourse—and they can be illustrated only on the basis of a multitude of minor practical examples, for which this article is not the place. There are, however, two negative considerations that deserve mention here.

The first of these relates to the avoidance of what might be called the histrionics of moralism at the expense of its substance. By that I mean the projection of attitudes, poses, and rhetoric that cause us to appear noble and altruistic in the mirror of our own vanity but lack substance when related to the realities of international life. It is a sad feature of the human predicament, in personal as in public life, that whenever one has the agreeable sensation of being impressively moral, one probably is not. What one does without self-consciousness or self-admiration, as a matter of duty or common decency, is apt to be closer to the real thing.

The second of these negative considerations pertains to something commonly called secret operations—a branch of governmental activity closely connected with, but not to be confused with, secret intelligence. Earlier in this century, the great secular despotisms headed by Hitler and Stalin introduced into the pattern of their interaction with other governments clandestine methods of operation that can only be described as ones of unbridled cynicism, audacity, and brutality. These methods were expressed not only by a total lack of scruple but also by a boundless contempt for the countries against which these efforts were directed (and, one feels, a certain contempt for themselves as well). This was in essence not new, of course; the relations among the nation-states of earlier centuries abounded in examples of clandestine iniquities of every conceivable variety. But these were usually moderated in practice by a greater underlying sense of humanity and a greater respect for at least the outward decencies of national power. Seldom was their intent so cynically destructive, and never was their scale remotely so great, as some of the efforts we have witnessed in this century.

In recent years, these undertakings have been supplemented, in their effects on the Western public, by a wholly different phenomenon arising in a wholly different quarter: namely, the unrestrained personal terrorism that has been employed by certain governments or political movements on the fringes of Europe as well as by radical-criminal elements within Western society itself. These phenomena have represented, at different times, serious challenges to the security of nearly all Western countries. It is not surprising, therefore, that among the reactions evoked has been a demand that fire should be fought with fire, that the countries threatened by efforts of this nature should respond with similar efforts.

No one will deny that resistance to these attacks requires secret intelligence of a superior quality and a severe ruthlessness of punishment wherever they fall afoul of the judicial systems of the countries against which they are directed. I do not intend here to comment in any way on the means by which they might or should be opposed by countries other than the United States. Nor do I intend to suggest that any of these activities that carry into this country should not be met by anything less than the full rigor of the law. On the contrary, one could wish the laws were even more rigorous in this respect. But when it comes to governmental operations—or disguised operations—beyond our borders, we Americans have a problem.

In the years immediately following the Second World War, the practices of the Stalin regime were so far-reaching, and presented so great an apparent danger to a Western Europe still weakened by the vicissitudes of war, that our government felt itself justified in setting up facilities for clandestine defensive operations of its own; all available evidence suggests that it has since conducted a number of activities under this heading. As one of those who, at the time, favored the decision to set up such facilities, I regret today, in light of the experience of the intervening years, that the decision was made. Operations of this nature are not in character for this country. They do not accord with its traditions or with its established procedures of government. The effort to conduct them involves dilemmas and situations of moral ambiguity in which the American statesman is deprived of principled guidance and loses a sense of what is fitting and what is not. Excessive secrecy, duplicity, and clandestine skulduggery are simply not our dish—not only because we are incapable of keeping a secret anyway (our commercial media of communication see to that), but, more important, because such operations conflict with our own traditional standards and compromise our diplomacy in other areas.

One must not be dogmatic about such matters, of course. Foreign policy is too intricate a topic to suffer any total taboos. There may be rare moments when a secret operation appears indispensable. A striking example of this was the action of the United States in apprehending the kidnappers of the *Achille Lauro*. But such operations should not be allowed to become a regular and routine feature of the governmental process, cast in the concrete of unquestioned habit and institutionalized bureaucracy. It is there that the dangers lie.

One may say that to deny ourselves this species of capability is to accept a serious limitation on our ability to contend with forces now directed against us. Perhaps; but if so, it is a limitation with which we shall have to live. The success of our diplomacy has always depended, and will continue to depend, on its inherent honesty and openness of purpose and on the forthrightness with which it is carried out. Deprive us of that, and we are deprived of our strongest armor and our most effective weapon. If this is a limitation, it is one that reflects no discredit on us. We may accept it in good conscience, for in national as in personal affairs the acceptance of one's limitations is surely one of the first marks of a true morality.

5

So much, then, for the negative imperatives. When we turn to the positive ones, there are, again, two that stand out.

The first is closely connected with what has just been observed about the acceptance of one's limitations. It relates to the duty of bringing one's commitments and undertakings into a reasonable relationship with one's real possibilities for acting upon the international environment. This is not by any means just a question of military strength, and particularly not of the purely destructive and ultimately self-destructive sort of strength to be found in the nuclear weapon. It is not entirely, or even mainly, a question of foreign policy. It is a duty that requires the shaping of one's society in such a manner that one has maximum control over one's own resources and maximum ability to employ them effectively when they are needed for the advancement of the national interest and the interests of world peace.

A country that has a budgetary deficit and an adverse trade balance both so fantastically high that it is rapidly changing from a major creditor to a major debtor on the world's exchanges, a country whose own enormous internal indebtedness has been permitted to double in less than six years, a country that has permitted its military expenditures to grow so badly out of relationship to the other needs of its economy and so extensively out of reach of political control that the annual spending of hundreds of billions of dollars on "defense" has developed into a national addiction—a country that, in short, has allowed its financial and material affairs to drift into such disorder, that is so obviously living beyond its means and confesses itself unable to live otherwise—is simply not in a position to make the most effective use of its own resources on the international scene, because they are so largely out of its control.

This situation must be understood in relation to the exorbitant dreams and aspirations of world influence, if not world hegemony—the feeling that we must have the solution to everyone's problems and a finger in every pie—that continue to figure in the assumptions underlying so many American reactions in matters of foreign policy. It must also be understood that in world affairs, as in personal life, example exerts a greater power than precept. A first step along the path of morality would be the frank recognition of the immense gap between what we dream of doing and what we really have to offer, and a resolve, conceived in all humility, to take ourselves under control and to establish a better relationship between our undertakings and our real capabilities.

The second major positive imperative is one that also involves the husbanding and effective use of resources, but it is essentially one of purpose and policy. Except perhaps in some sectors of American government and opinion, there are few thoughtful people who would not agree that our world is at present faced with two unprecedented and supreme dangers. One is the danger not just of nuclear war but of any major war at all among great industrial powers—an exercise that modern technology has now made suicidal all around. The other is the devastating effect of modern industrialization and overpopulation on the world's natural environment. The one threatens the destruction of civilization through the recklessness and selfishness of its military rivalries, the other through the massive abuse of its natural habitat. Both are relatively new problems, for the solution of which past experience affords little guidance. Both are urgent.

The problems of political misgovernment, to which so much of our thinking about moral values has recently related, is as old as the human species itself. It is a problem that will not be solved in our time, and need not be. But the environmental and nuclear crises will brook no delay. The need for giving priority to the averting of these two overriding dangers has a purely rational basis—a basis in national interest—quite aside from morality. For short of a nuclear war, the worst that our Soviet rivals could do to us, even in our wildest worst-case imaginings, would be a far smaller tragedy than that which would assuredly confront us (and if not us, then our children) if we failed to face up to these two apocalyptic dangers in good time. But is there not also a moral component to this necessity?

Of all the multitudinous celestial bodies of which we have knowledge, our own earth seems to be the only one even remotely so richly endowed with the resources that make possible human life—not only make it possible but surround it with so much natural beauty and healthfulness and magnificence. And to the degree that man has distanced himself from the other animals in such things as self-knowledge, historical awareness, and the capacity for creating great beauty (along, alas, with great ugliness), we have to recognize a further mystery, similar to that of the unique endowment of the planet—a mystery that seems to surpass the possibilities of the purely accidental. Is there not, whatever the nature of one's particular God, an element of sacrilege involved in the placing of all this at stake just for the sake of the comforts, the fears, and the national rivalries of a single generation? Is there not a moral obligation to recognize in this very uniqueness of the habitat and nature of man the greatest of our moral responsibilities, and to make of ourselves, in our national personification, its guardians and protectors rather than its destroyers?

This, it may be objected, is a religious question, not a moral-political one. True enough, if one will. But the objection invites the further question as to whether there is any such thing as morality that does not rest, consciously or otherwise, on some foundation of religious faith; for the renunciation of self-interest, which is what all morality implies, can never be rationalized by purely secular and materialistic considerations.

6

The above are only a few random reflections on the great question to which this paper is addressed. But they would seem to suggest, in their entirety, the outlines of an American foreign policy to which moral standards could be more suitably and naturally applied than to the policy we are conducting today. This would be a policy founded on recognition of the national interest, reasonably conceived, as the legitimate motivation for a large portion of the nation's behavior, and prepared to pursue that interest without either moral pretension or apology. It would be a policy that would seek the possibilities for service to morality primarily in our own behavior, not in our judgment of others. It would restrict our undertakings to the limits established by our own traditions and resources. It would see virtue in our minding our own business wherever there is not some overwhelming reason for minding the business of others. Priority would be given, here, not to the reforming of others but to the averting of the two apocalyptic catastrophes that now hover over the horizons of mankind.

But at the heart of this policy would lie the effort to distinguish at all times between the true substance and the mere appearance of moral behavior. In an age when a number of influences, including the limitations of the electronic media, the widespread substitution of pictorial representation for verbal communication, and the ubiquitous devices of "public relations" and electoral politics, all tend to exalt the image over the essential reality to which that image is taken to relate— in such an age, there is a real danger that we may lose altogether our ability to distinguish between the real and the unreal, and, in doing so, lose both the credibility of true moral behavior and the great force such behavior is, admittedly, capable of exerting. To do this would be foolish, unnecessary, and self-defeating. There may have been times when the United States could afford such frivolity. This present age, unfortunately, is not one of them.

Security and the Moscow Embassy
(1987)

———⌁———

The public discussion of the problems of security at the Moscow embassy has revealed a wide measure of confusion in both media and Congress as to what a diplomatic mission really is or is supposed to be, what purposes it is supposed to serve, and what part secrecy plays or should play in its proper functions. Perhaps a few observations on these subjects may serve to dispel some of this confusion and to suggest easier ways of escape from the problems at hand than those that re now being so widely urged.

The institution of diplomatic representation by one state at the capital of another is one that has grown up, in response to certain clear and prevailing needs, with the development of the modern national state. Its modalities were largely codified at the Congress of Vienna in 1815. They have subsequently been further developed by experience, by necessity, and by common consent.

Central to this institution is, of course, what is called the diplomatic mission—normally, in this present age, an embassy. It is the permanent office of one government stationed and maintained in the capital of another. This mission has three basic functions. One is to constitute a useful channel of official communication between the two governments involved. The second is to keep its own government reasonably well informed of the situation prevailing in the country where it is stationed. A third is to give guidance to its own government in the shaping of its policy toward the other.

Originally published (in a different version) in *Newsweek,* July 13, 1987.

The performance of these functions has not normally required a large staff. Never, in particular, has it required anything like the hundreds of people who now populate so many of the missions maintained by major powers in foreign capitals. Traditionally, the staff of an embassy was expected to consist only of an ambassador, who figured as the personal representative of his own sovereign (in our case, the president); a deputy chief of mission, called the Counselor, who ran the mission's staff and assumed charge of it in the ambassador's absence; three or four subordinate diplomatic secretaries, having the quality of accredited officials (and not to be confused with the clerical personnel); and two or three military, naval, or other attachés, representing the armed forces of the mission's country and expected to transmit to their own government such military information as it was proper for them to receive. All these, supported by the necessary clerical and secretarial staffs, numbered, as a rule, something in the range of thirty to fifty people.

The operation of such a mission, addressing itself simply to the functions named above, did not pose serious problems of security and did not require elaborate arrangements for its protection in this respect. The ambassador had a right to the privacy of his office and of confidential communication with his own government. Certain considerations of prudence had to be observed in the handling of the mission's files and premises. There were times, too, when effective diplomacy involved playing one's cards close to one's chest. But a large part of the mission's work did not involve or require elaborate secrecy. Diplomacy, after all, was not a conspiracy. The best diplomacy (as was often recognized by great statesmen) was the one that involved the fewest, not the most, secrets—the one that could be most frankly and freely exposed to the host government. And the best assurance of the mission's security, beyond those elementary arrangements mentioned above, lay in the trained discretion and the mature good sense of its responsible officials.

The diplomatic mission, above all, was not supposed to be, and had no need to become, a center for espionage. Its task was to promote good relations with the government to which it was accredited, not to approach it as an enemy, not to snoop on it and arouse its suspicions. To do these things would have been to damage the mission's potential for usefulness in the exercise of its principal established functions. The host government, after all, had its own right to privacy in matters where its national interest was at stake; and it was the duty of the diplomatic representative to respect that right, just as he asked others to respect his own.

Charged with the task of informing his own government about what was going on around him in the host country, the diplomatic representative was naturally curious and naturally concerned to obtain whatever information would be useful to his government in the designing of its policy. This was normally understood by the government to which he was accredited; and the information gathering that went under this heading was not resented, provided only that it remained within the boundaries of propriety. Its procurement was not to involve, for example, violation of the laws of the country. It was not to take the form of intrusive snooping around in places where the foreign eye was known to be unwelcome. It was certainly not to involve efforts to subvert the loyalty of local citizens. But wherever these and other proprieties were observed, the reporting activities of the diplomatic representative were accepted as a normal exercise of his diplomatic function. Indeed, the diplomat who was scrupulous in the observance of these restraints could often expect the help of the host government in providing him with such information as he might legitimately wish to acquire.

All this applied, generally speaking, to the military and naval attachés as well as to the others. Their position was a particularly delicate one, because their responsibilities involved the gathering of information about military matters, where the requirements for secrecy were wider and more sensitive. For this reason, it was especially important for them to acquire and maintain a relationship of confidence with their opposite numbers in the armed forces of the host country and to avoid damaging this relationship by actions that could only draw down upon them suspicion and hostility. In saying these things, I must avoid gilding the lily. In the periods of sharp military rivalry and of chauvinist hysteria of earlier decades, particularly in the half-century just preceding the First World War, these rules were frequently violated by the military attachés of the various powers, especially when political tensions and suspicions were at their highest (one has only to think of the Dreyfus case of the late 1890s). Seldom, however, were the respective foreign offices and their civilian-diplomatic representatives engaged in this sort of mischief. And the American diplomatic missions abroad were singularly free of it.

Such, then, was the situation prevailing with respect to the traditional diplomatic mission in which I and others of my generation had the good fortune to serve in the early years of this century; and perhaps the reader will understand why some of us look back to it today with such nostalgia. But there have been, beginning in 1917 and achieving their full flowering only after the Second World War, extensive and highly unfortunate changes, to which we must now turn.

For these changes, particularly in their initial stages, the Russian Communists (not those we have before us today but their predecessors of the immediate post-revolutionary period) bore a heavy responsibility. Their ideological convictions had taught them to see in every "capitalist" government a dangerous and unreconcilable enemy. Experience, however, soon taught them the need, in their own interests, of diplomatic intercourse with other countries. They were unable to reconcile this contradiction. So while they sought diplomatic recognition by the major non-Communist governments, sent diplomatic missions to other capitals, and encouraged other governments to respond in kind, they tended to treat the foreign diplomatic representative, once he got to Moscow, as a dangerous personal enemy. They did what they could to isolate him socially. They were concerned to deprive him of what would have been considered elsewhere as normal sources of information. Worse still, they did not hesitate to use their own diplomatic missions abroad as centers for activities that went far beyond the bounds of propriety, including intensive efforts at political intrigue and subversion.

It would probably have been better had the non-Communist governments, recognizing that they had an important stake in preserving the integrity of diplomatic institutions, declined to put up with this sort of thing—had they declined, that is, either to tolerate in their own capitals or to dispatch to others missions that did not conform in their purposes and methods of operation to the established principles of diplomatic intercourse. This, unfortunately, is not the way they generally behaved. Having, in most instances, their own reasons for wanting to maintain missions in Moscow, they tended to wink at the cynicism involved in these ambiguities and excesses and came eventually to share them and in part to imitate them. Some of them proved to be apt pupils.

And with the emergence, in the late 1940s, of what has come to be called the Cold War, there began in earnest a general deterioration of the amenities, the decencies, the prevailing tone of international diplomacy. Legitimate forms of information gathering came to be supplemented, and in some instances almost crowded out and replaced, by intrusive and clandestine ones. The very personality of the diplomatic mission, as perceived by the host government, began to change. It became difficult to tell whether the mission was friend or enemy whether it was to be considered and treated as the welcome outpost of a friendly foreign government, devoted to the cultivation of peaceful and mutually beneficial relations between the two countries, or as a dangerous foreign presence, tolerated only for the privilege of sending a similar mission to the adversary's capital, but held in most baleful suspicion and kept under the most elaborate hostile surveillance.

And this was only one source of the deterioration. Another, closely connected with it, lay in the inordinate numerical growth of the staffs of the missions themselves. The fact of the matter is that the average great-power mission has grown, in the period since World War II, to dimensions exceeding by several hundred percent what was once considered essential and suitable for basic diplomatic purposes—a sure sign, when one stops to think of it, that the purposes for which it is now maintained go far beyond those that the diplomatic institution was originally designed to serve.

Although most of the major governments bear some measure of responsibility for this unfortunate development, I think it may fairly be said that the U.S. government, if it did not actually lead the rest, was highly prominent among the leaders. I would not like to speculate on the motives that have caused other governments to participate in this drastic bloating of their diplomatic missions. Perhaps these varied greatly in the individual instance. In the case of the United States, the motives and causes were multiple. To trace them all would require an article longer than this one. Prominent among them were the insistent pressures from departments and agencies of the government other than the Department of State for the privilege of placing some of their own personnel in the missions. Here, too, a variety of motives were involved: bureaucratic jealousies, considerations of prestige, the desire to have representatives in Russia protected by the traditional immunities and privileges of diplomatic personnel, etc. The fact that these pressures were not more stoutly resisted probably had something to do with the fact that whereas the Department of State has no significant domestic constituency to defend its interests, most of the other departments and agencies do have them. The State Department, in any case, has proved relatively helpless in the face of such intrusions. And the result is that some 70 percent of the personnel now stationed at the embassy in Moscow have been sent there by other departments and agencies; and in very few instances, if any, have their functions and duties anything to do with the traditional and legitimate tasks of traditional diplomacy.

Another cause and consequence of the bureaucratic bloating in the American missions abroad has been the gradual turning over of administrative and financial services to professional hierarchies of administrators, accountants, and security personnel whose duties are unrelated to the substantive work of the mission, and who are in effect subordinate not to the ambassador but rather to unseen and unknown superior bureaucrats far away in Washington. The reason offered for this practice, when it was introduced, was that the help of these people would relieve the regular diplomatic personnel of duties not strictly related to their own function. In theory, that sounds fine. In practice, as organizations everywhere have discovered, what happens is that such services, after starting with the best of will, end up as the masters rather than the servants of those they were supposed to help, themselves adding to the bloating of personnel and tending, in the long run, to crowd out the others. By virtue of all these tendencies, the foreign service personnel charged with real diplomatic functions in our embassies abroad have often been pushed helplessly into a small and insignificant corner of what was once supposed to have been their own embassy building, the greater part of the premises being occupied by people who bear little or no relation to these central traditional functions.

Now, it should not be hard to understand that the problem of providing security for a mission in another country increases drastically—perhaps by the square of the total—with the size of the mission. In the small, compact mission of earlier years, there were far fewer people who were privy to any secrets, fewer whose discretion had to be assured, smaller premises and fewer files that had to be protected, and actually, for various reasons, fewer secrets to be preserved. Our present problems have arisen largely from the various nondiplomatic uses to which we have permitted our missions to be put.

Even as it is, we have greatly magnified the dimensions of the situation by presenting exaggerated images of the problem of electronic surveillance in those missions, and exaggerated ideas of what would have to be done to assure their security. We should remember that 95 percent of the audible chitchat that goes on in any large American mission has nothing to do with governmental secrets and could well be listened to by a foreign government without the slightest effect on our national security. Particularly is this true of the residential premises; but it is true of a great deal of the office space as well. In fact, it may be regarded as highly doubtful whether any foreign government would find it an economical use of its own personnel to attempt to record and transcribe the vast flood of trivial discourse that flows from the mouths of people in large embassy staffs, most of whom are not privy to any official secrets, and who, if they were properly selected and trained, would know better than to discuss such secrets in insecure premises anyway.

To assure that *all* residential and office premises in a foreign capital are 100 percent immune to electronic eavesdropping is probably not possible and in any case impractical; nor, if suitable precautions are observed, would it be necessary. For at least fifty years, to my personal knowledge, our official personnel in Moscow have acted on the assumption that the walls and the telephones of the premises they inhabited were wired for sound, even if it was improbable that they were being monitored every minute of the day. The possibility of bugging was not viewed, over all these years, as an intolerable danger; nor, actually, did the heavens fall because it took place. The fact that the girders of a new building might be wired therefore changes nothing over the situation that had existed for many decades.

What were and are important from the standpoint of the security of such a mission are only three principles. First, that there should be at least one place, if only a small one, where private discussion could be held without danger of surveillance. Second, that facilities for private communication with one's own government should be maintained. And third, that all personnel should be selected and trained in

289

such a way that they could be relied upon to use mature judgment and discretion in any talking they might do in endangered premises. In so large a mission as we maintain in Moscow today, these requirements may not be easy to satisfy, but it is not impossible to meet them in adequate degree. And it might be well to bear in mind that this problem, like so many other problems in life, is one where the fussy pursuit of perfection may hold more dangers than a sensible coming to terms with life's inevitable uncertainties.

Thus the fact that certain of the Marine guards (as the rarest of exceptions to the thousands who for decades have served in similar positions with magnificent loyalty and discipline) would appear to have done certain inexcusably foolish things in a single instance, and the fact that the new building in Moscow is likely to have been wired for eavesdropping purposes: these are not of themselves any cause for panic or for extreme reactions, such as tearing down the new building in Moscow or doing other wild things in the name of official security. The situation we confront is difficult, more difficult, indeed, than it would be if our missions were smaller, more compact, and more directly focused on strictly diplomatic tasks; but it is not intolerable.

Yet a far better, less burdensome and more hopeful attack on this problem would surely lie in the effort to reduce this bloated mission in Moscow and others elsewhere to more easily controllable dimensions, endeavoring, at the same time, to assure that the smaller staff addressed itself exclusively to its essential diplomatic and consular functions and allowed the rest to go by the board. Security precautions could be concentrated on those functions that truly require them, leaving the needs of peripheral functions, such as the consular and informational services, to be handled in less onerous ways. Less use could be made of coded telegraphic communication, and greater use of courier service. If personnel are more carefully selected and trained (which is easier to assure in a smaller mission), there is no need to bar them mechanically from all personal association with Soviet citizens; for wherever our people know how to handle themselves, we should have more to gain than to lose by such contacts. To assume that no American could hold his own in association with a Soviet citizen—to assume that all our people are so hopelessly naive, and the Russians they might meet so diabolically clever and dangerous, that all fraternization between our embassy personnel and Russians must be, if not totally forbidden, at least subject to the closest and most anxious control—to make this assumption would be to imitate the worst habits of the Soviet security agencies and to sacrifice our true political and diplomatic interests to the extreme demands of security people who know nothing about questions of political policy and have no responsibility for its successful promulgation. In a mission of 150 people, most of whom serve other masters than the secretary of state, to assure such maturity and such discretion is admittedly a harder task. In a small compact mission, under the secretary of state's direct control, there is no reason why it could not, with proper personnel handling, be accomplished in satisfactory measure.

Security officers tend to be perfectionists and to concentrate exclusively on their own concerns to the detriment of those that are not their immediate responsibility. To subordinate our entire diplomacy at the Moscow end to their most extreme demands would require such extensive restrictions that one would have to question the desirability of maintaining any sort of an official mission in Moscow in the first place. But there is, especially if we could act to reduce the dimensions of the problem, no reason to damage ourselves, our relations with the Soviet Union, and the prospects for world peace in this foolish and unnecessary way.

Unquestionably, any effort to streamline our Moscow embassy and our missions in other Communist capitals in the directions just suggested would encounter frantic and stubborn opposition all over Washington. Furthermore, it could not, and should not, be made without reciprocal reductions in the Soviet diplomatic mission in Washington—reductions that would doubtless materially simplify the task of our security authorities in assuring the propriety of activities carried out by members of its accredited personnel. It would have to be expected that this, too, would be fiercely opposed by those official services in Moscow that have become accustomed, over several decades, to abusing and exploiting the Soviet diplomatic missions for purposes other than purely diplomatic functions. But on their side, too, and certainly in a measure no smaller than on our own, these abuses should stop.

This suggests, to me at least, that rather than indulging ourselves in spasms of indignation over Soviet efforts of surveillance over our Moscow mission and giving to the effort to achieve the impossible in the way of security priority over every other consideration of diplomatic intercourse, we might find it useful to sit down and discuss this whole problem quietly and peaceably with the Russians at the proper level. They also have a stake in seeing whether we could not, both of us, reduce the level of silly and dangerous misuse of our missions for purposes of espionage and counterespionage and restore them to a greater concentration on forms of activity from which both of us, not to mention the cause of world peace, have more to gain than to lose.

Actually, this question of security at the Moscow embassy is only a part of the difficulty the U.S. government seems to have in deciding whether we are primarily at war or at peace with the Soviet Union. It is not an easy problem. There are entire governmental services, and not a few individuals, in Washington who appear to assume (perhaps in many instances their professional dedications are seen to require them to do so) that some sort of an ultimate military showdown between ourselves and the Russians is inevitable, and that because it is inevitable, priority ought to be given to the effort to prepare for it rather than to the effort to avert it. To these people, the problems of security at the Moscow embassy deserve a clear priority over any value that mission might have for the purpose of improving our political relations with the Soviet government.

Certainly, these considerations of military precaution and of official security have their proper place and must, so long as the political tension continues, be given their due. But this "due" need not be, and must not be, an absolute one. The Soviet leaders have no reason to desire a war with us, and no incentive to initiate or provoke one. There is no political difference dividing the two of us that would be remotely worth the disasters that an armed conflict would unleash for both, whoever was ostensibly the military victor. Policies based, therefore, only on our fears, requiring us to subordinate all our actions to the demands of those fears, are purely negative and can, by causing us to neglect the more hopeful prospects, very well end by assuring the very disaster against which they are supposed to protect. In a situation where there can be nothing to be gained from the pursuit of our fears, we have no choice but to give maximum play to the pursuit of our hopes.

Let us, then, in handling the problems of security at the Moscow embassy, see first what we can do about reducing the dimensions of those problems, thus liberating the diplomatic staff for the full and concentrated development of its potential as an agency for a better understanding, and for more reassuring relations, with the government to which it is accredited. Let us recognize that the two governments, in this delicate time, react—and often overreact—to each other. Recognizing this, let us see to it that what we offer to the Soviet authorities for their reaction is something that diminishes, not heightens, the sterile and overwrought military tensions that have come to constitute so dark a cloud over the hopes and prospects of both worlds, ours and theirs.

Somalia, Through a Glass Darkly
(1993)

————··❦··————

The following is an item, dated December 9, 1992, in my personal diary, which I have kept intermittently for most of my life. I have left it unedited, exactly as then written.

PRINCETON, N.J.

When I woke up this morning, I found the television screen showing live pictures of the Marines going ashore, in the gray dawn of another African day, in Somalia. It is clear that with a very large part of the American public, but particularly with that part of the public that speaks or writes on public affairs, and—not last—with the political establishment, there is general support for this venture.

There was no proper public discussion, not even a congressional discussion, of this undertaking before the president, only a few days ago, announced his intention to launch it. It would be idle for me or for anyone else to come out publicly at this point with a questioning of the wisdom of this intervention. The action is already in progress.

Anything that might be said in criticism of its rationale would have no practical effect in any case, and, to the extent that it attracted any public attention, would be received as something tending to demoralize the forces now in action by sowing doubt as to the worthiness of the effort in which they are now involved. I see, therefore, no advantage to be gained by trying to say anything publicly about what is going on.

Originally published in the *New York Times*, September 30, 1993.

On the other hand, I regard this move as a dreadful error of American policy; and I think that in justice to myself, I should set down at this point, if only for the diary, my reasons for this view.

The purpose of this exercise is, we are told, to take charge of the channels of transportation and to assure the movement of food to certain aggregations of starving people. The reasons why we must do this are, in the official and widely accepted view, that the people are starving; that this is outrageous and intolerable; but that food cannot be brought to them in adequate amounts because the supply lines by which it would have to be delivered are subject to harassment on the part of armed bands and individuals along the way, as a result of which much of the food is plundered and lost before it can reach its destination. How many of these congregations of starving people there are, and where they are situated, seems not to have been clearly explained; perhaps our people do not even know.

Why, then, is our action undesirable? First, because it treats only a limited and short-term aspect of what is really a much wider and deeper problem. The idea seems to be that when we have made possible the original delivery to the collection points of the food that has already been shipped or is being shipped to Somalia, our forces will be withdrawn, and the United Nations, using other forces, will assure the further supplying of these people.

This last seems to me highly uncertain, and even doubtful. The situation we are trying to correct has its roots in the fact that the people of Somalia are wholly unable to govern themselves and that the entire territory is simply without a government. The starvation that we are seeing on television is partly the result of drought (or so we are told), partly of overpopulation, and partly of the chaotic conditions flowing from the absence of any governmental authority.

What we are doing holds out no hope of coming to terms with any of those situations. If we are to withdraw at any early date (and the President has spoken about the possibility of withdrawal before the end of January), these determining conditions will remain exactly as they were before. The marauding bands and individuals will resume their activity, and in the absence of any strong foreign military force, there will be no stopping them.

Beyond that, the problem of starvation is one that reaches much further than the aggregations of people we have seen on television. As one of the nurses pointed out, these wretched people are among the more fortunate, as is shown by the fact that they were able to walk to the camps. There are presumably, farther afield, even greater numbers of people who never showed up because they were too weak to walk at all. They, of course, are not touched by our actions.

The fact is that this dreadful situation cannot possibly be put to rights other than by the establishment of a governing power for the entire territory, and a very ruthless, determined one at that. It could not be a democratic one, because the very prerequisites for a democratic political system do not exist among the people in question. Our action holds no promise of correcting this situation.

The upshot of all this is that what we are undertaking will assure at best a temporary relief for those people who are gathered together in the camps, and probably a relief that will not be completed before our own departure, unless we propose to keep our forces there for many months, if not years, in the future. Second, this is an immensely expensive effort. What we are pouring into it must run into hundreds of millions, if not billions, of dollars. This comes at a time when our country is very deeply indebted and not even able to meet its own budget without further borrowing. This entire costly venture is, then, like so many other things we are doing, to be paid for by our children— the coming generation. Meanwhile, there are many needs at home, particularly in the condition of our cities and of the physical infrastructure of our society, that are not being met, ostensibly for lack of money.

All this being the case, one is moved to inquire into the inspiration and rationale of this enterprise. On Mr. Bush's part, one must assume that the reasons lay largely in his memories of the political success of the move into the Persian Gulf, and in the hope that another venture of this nature would arouse a similar public enthusiasm, permitting him to leave his presidential office with a certain halo of glory as a military leader using our forces to correct deplorable situations outside our country. The action, taken during the interregnum between two administrations, obviously saddles his successor with the task of completing it, albeit without responsibility for its origin.

The dispatch of American armed forces to a seat of operations in a place far from our own shores, and this for what is actually a major police action in another country and in a situation where no defensible American interest is involved—this, obviously, is something that the Founding Fathers of this country never envisaged or would ever have approved. If this is in the American tradition, then it is a very recent tradition, and one quite out of accord with the general assumptions that have governed American public life for most of the last two hundred years.

I have already pointed to the absence of any prior discussion in Congress of this undertaking. This raises the question, why, then, so suddenly and without any preparation in public or political opinion? If the President thought it wise to use our armed forces for this purpose, why did he not say so weeks or months ago and lay the question squarely before Congress and public opinion? The answer is obvious: the paralysis of government that has existed for the last six months—before and after the election. This is in itself significant.

But an even more significant question is that of the reason for the general acceptance by Congress and the public about what is being done. There can be no question that the reason for this acceptance lies primarily with the exposure of the Somalia situation by the American media; above all, television. The reaction would have been unthinkable without this exposure. The reaction was an emotional one, occasioned by the sight of the suffering of the starving people in question.

That this should be felt as adequate reason for our military action does credit, no doubt, to the idealism of the American people and to their ready sympathy for people suffering in another part of the world. But this is an emotional reaction, not a thoughtful or deliberate one. It is one that was not under any deliberate and thoughtful control— one that was not really under our control at all.

But if American policy from here on out, particularly policy involving the uses of our armed forces abroad, is to be controlled by popular emotional impulses, and especially ones provoked by the commercial television industry, then there is no place not only for myself, but for the responsible deliberative organs of our government, in both executive and legislative branches.

Remarks Delivered at a Birthday Party for the Slavic Division of the New York Public Library
(1987)

⸻⟨∽⟩⸻

This is a very special day in the life of the remarkable and unique entity that goes by the name of the Slavic Division of the New York Public Library, and there is a lot that I would like to say about it. I would like to talk about its curious origins, about its nearly three hundred thousand volumes of holdings just in the languages of the cultures to which it devotes its attention, and about the composition of the million and a half persons who have made use of its riches and its facilities over the eighty-eight years of its existence. I would also like to talk about the contribution it has made to the powerful but relatively recent development of Russian and other Slavic studies in this country—a development that has been roughly coterminous with my own life as well as with that of the Slavic Division itself.

But others, I expect, will be talking about all these things; and our time is short. So I will confine myself to a word or two about what this division has meant to me—and, I suspect, to many of those others who have not only patronized it and used its treasures but have sought sanctuary in its impartial embrace. I have not had occasion to work here recently; so I shall have to describe it as I saw it and as I remember it from the years when I did work here. My apologies if it should all be changed today.

I recall the Slavic and Baltic Division as an agreeably dim sort of place, with a faintly reverential, almost cathedral-like ambience. The windows, which looked out on the courtyard of the Public Library

The New York Public Library, March 11, 1987.

and seldom saw the sun except on long, hot summer afternoons, had what I may charitably describe as a certain venerable patina, like those of an ancient AMTRAK railway car. Many of the books had that peculiar dustiness that was the mark of a dignified old age; and if the paper of some of them tended to come apart in one's hands, that only added to the excitement of reading them.

The late Victorian countenance of my great-uncle the elder George Kennan, whose name and date of birth I share, used to look down upon me from a likeness that hung on the wall of the closed-off portion of the reading room but was visible through the high glass. He was a man who was a Russian expert—this country's leading Russian expert, in fact—a hundred years ago, before anyone ever went by that designation. Many of his papers still reside in the marvelous manuscript collections of this library. And I sometimes had the impression that he was saying to me as he looked down from his lofty perch: "You little pip-squeak, they tell me you pass as what they call a Russian expert; but what do *you* know about Russia? Have you, too, traveled five thousand miles through Siberia in the days before the railway, on sleds and springless wagons? If not, shut up and listen to me."

Back, however, to the public part of the reading room. The call numbers of the books were like nothing ever seen elsewhere: only two or three mysterious capital letters at the corner of each card, accompanied by a darkly cabalistic asterisk. But it put the most sophisticated computer system to shame: five minutes after you ordered a book, it appeared, silently and mysteriously, on your table. The librarians had the unerring hallmarks of great librarians the world over, which means that they obviously saw a great deal and said very little. The public they served was often racked by profound and violently conflicting political passions. Tales were still abundant of the former Russian Mensheviks and Social Revolutionaries glaring defiantly at each other from their separate tables in the reading room and indignantly snatching copies of *Pravda* from each other's table whenever they got a chance. But the librarians kept their own counsel and delivered to all of them, with sovereign dignity and impartiality, the items they requested. And the patrons kept on coming. They were even aware, I suspect, of sharing with their adversaries certain secret sympathies behind all their political animosities.

Because the love of Russian culture is something very powerful and, I think, quite unique. It united in those days, as it still unites today, people of the most varied and often conflicting ideological and political commitments. It united, too, the many Russian-born visitors with the relatively small but steadily increasing number of us born Americans who came to share their dedication. For all of us, the Slavic Division of the library provided, and has continued to provide, a curious sort of haven—a haven of quiet and decorum, of unspoken understanding, sympathy, and support, a haven of shared reverence for the great and tragic and immensely dramatic and moving history of the Russian people and of the other Slavic and Baltic peoples whose history is represented and preserved in these premises.

My friend Vartan Gregorian is unfortunately not with us today. He is, as you know, a man who has done many remarkable things. Perhaps he has already had the windows of the Slavic and Baltic Division washed and the books dusted, or is about to do so. But if he were here, I would have to say to him: all right, if you please; I understand that you can't stop progress; but please don't wash the windows *too* assiduously; leave just *enough* dust on the books so that our reverence for their antiquity is not disturbed; and, for the sake of everything that true scholarship holds dear, never, never, however wonderful computers may be, change the classification and call number of the system!

History, Literature, and the
Road to Peterhof
(1986)

Some twenty-seven years ago, it fell to me to address a meeting of the PEN Club in this city on the subject of "History and Literature." What I said that evening was published in the *New York Times Book Review* and several other publications under the title "It's History—but Is It Literature?" Well, is it?

I tried, on that occasion, to give an answer to just that question. The answer was essentially this: history doesn't necessarily have to be literature, and indeed much of it is not; but there is nothing in the book that says it cannot or may not be, and some of it obviously is. I scarcely need demonstrate this. Some of the classic works of history have long been regarded as great literary achievements as well. I think of the Gibbons and the Macaulays, the Parkmans, the Rankes, and any number of others who could be mentioned. I think, too, of the great biographers, from Boswell down to our own Leon Edel; because biography is essentially a form of history. And I find substantiation for my view in the long-standing practice of this academy, which places history and biography on a plane with such genres as poetry and the novel when it extends membership and when it confers its gold medals and other awards.

But I am aware that there are today, and have been in the past, people who would challenge the justification for including even a portion of history in the category of "letters." There are people who would

Blashfield Address delivered at the Annual Ceremonial of the American Academy of Arts and Letters, New York City, May 21, 1986.

object, that is, to seeing history lumped together with these great works of the creative imagination in poetry, drama, and fiction. Their argument would run, I suppose, something like this.

Of course, one finds occasionally, in the works of individual historians, a certain grace and distinction of expression that make these works pleasing, even sometimes entertaining reading. But this is purely a matter of style, not of content. And style alone does not make literature. What is it, after all, that the historian has done? He has poked around among the written or visual debris the past has bequeathed to us. He has unearthed some of it, put it into some sort of order, made it available to us with a few of his comments. He has purveyed to us, in other words, a certain amount of evidence, yes—but evidence outside of himself, not the product of his own creative imagination. He unearthed it—yes. But he was no more than an intermediary between the ascertainable fact and the reader. Let him be honored, then, if he must be, by the scholarly community, but not by the literary one. Let him be honored for his industry, for his patience, for the fortitude he has shown in burrowing around among all these dusty reliquiae and making some of them available to us with his critical commentary. And if, in doing this, he happens to have written here and there a few elegant or even amusing sentences, let us give a gracious nod of recognition in his direction. He no doubt needs encouragement. But let us not confuse things by putting his achievements on a plane with the great works of independent creative genius to which we give the name of literature.

You might, I repeat, say all this, and you might on the face of it make a plausible case in doing so. You could find plenty of distinguished authority to support your thesis. You could cite Aristotle's statement about the historian Herodotus: that you could put Herodotus into verse and he would still remain a historian. Or you could even profess to view the historian as did the sixteenth-century English poet Sir Philip Sidney (and I quote him) as a man "laden with old mouse-eaten records, authorizing himself for the most part on other histories, whose greatest authorities are built upon the notable foundation of hearsay, better acquainted with a thousand years ago than with the present age . . . curious for antiquities, . . . inquisitive of novelties, a wonder to young folks, and a tyrant in table-talk." And you would not be entirely wrong. There are still some like that.

But I am here today, as one who himself plies this uninspiring trade, to plead the case that things are not quite that simple. The truth is that the historian is not a mere purveyor. He does not stand entirely outside the historical evidence he brings to your attention. He stands in many ways inside of it. He is himself in many ways a part of it.

True, he describes historical events. And if he is a true historian, he describes them as accurately as they can be described on the strength of the available record. But he was not there. He did not see these events with his own eyes; or if he was there and did see them, then what we are talking about is journalism or autobiography but not history. And not having been there and not having seen them, what does he have to start with when he envisages these events and portrays them for us? He has, as a rule, only the hieroglyphics of the written word as preserved in crumbling old documents, and sometimes a few artifacts that have survived the ravages of time and neglect—perhaps even a portrait or a drawing or, if he works in recent history, a photograph or two. But these evidences only hint at the real story—they don't tell it. It is up to the historian to examine them critically and imaginatively, to select among them (for they are often multitudinous in number), to try to penetrate the reality behind them, and to try to depict them in a way that reveals their meaning. And to accomplish this task, what does he have to draw upon? Only what he already has within him: his knowledge, of course, of the historical background, his level of cultural sensitivity, his ability to put the isolated bit of evidence into the larger context, and, above all, his capacity for insight and empathy, his ability to identify with the historical figures he describes, his educated instinct for what is significant and what is not—in other words, his creative imagination.

What emerges from this scrutiny is something that is, of necessity, highly subjective. It is not, and cannot be, the absolute and total truth. It is, if the writer is a conscientious historian, as close to the truth as he can possibly make it. But it remains a vision of the past—not the past in its pure form (no one could ever recreate that) but the past as one man, and one man alone, is capable of envisaging it, of depicting it. It is perceived reality—reality in the eyes of the beholder—the only kind of reality that can have meaning for us other human beings and be useful to us. This is why every work of history—at least of narrative or explanatory history—is at least as revealing of the man who wrote it and the period in which it was written as it is of the people it portrays and the epoque in which they lived.

I can recall experiencing upon the completion of my first work of history (it was a work on the initial months of the Soviet-American relationship in 1917–18) a moment of panic when the question suddenly presented itself to me: what is it I have done here? Perhaps what I have written is not really history but rather some sort of a novel, the product of my own imagination—an imagination stimulated, inspired, and informed, let us hope, by the documents I have been reading, but imagination nevertheless.

In retrospect, I think the panic was exaggerated and unnecessary. I had, after all, obeyed to the best of my ability the rules of my trade as a historian—the first of which was to respect the evidence and not to go beyond it. And this, the question of the restrictions and limitations one accepts, is the point at which historical writing does indeed differ from other forms of literature. The historian may not give his imagination free reign. He is bound to respect the chronology of events as the documents reveal it, even when that chronology is contradictory and confusing. He cannot arrange the facts for dramatic or aesthetic effect, as can the novelist. He has to take his characters as he finds them; he may not invent them, or make them up as an amalgam of people he has known. The historical truth he pursues (even though he never fully achieves it) is not the same sort of truth as that pursued by the novelist or the poet. These latter also pursue truth, and they also have restraints and limitations they must respect—sometimes even historical truth—but what they are after is truth of a deeper and more intimate nature. It is primarily truth sensed, felt, and molded for effect, only secondarily truth observed; whereas in the case of the historian, it is just the other way around.

Sometimes the historian—one historian, at least—is carried away with the obvious elements of drama or tragedy in what he is describing, and is tempted to reach beyond his prescribed field and to encroach upon the liberties of the novelist in order to make his point more emphatically. In the last work of history I published, I had occasion to describe the rather pathetic funeral—the funeral of a Russian statesman, Nikolai Karlovich Giers, foreign minister of Tsar Alexander III, a modest man for whose strivings I had much sympathy but one who had outlived his time and become forgotten almost before he was dead. And I described the funeral in these words:

> Giers' body was laid to rest, with a few family members and officials in attendance, at the so-called Sergiyevskaya Pustyn—a monastery retreat on the shores of the Gulf of Finland, along the road to Peterhof, on January 31, 1895. It was a clear, bleak wintry day. It had snowed during the night. A chill wind swept in from across the partially frozen waters of the gulf. The little band of mourners were no doubt glad to get home after the ceremony, and to inaugurate, with a warming glass of vodka, the process of oblivion that so soon overtakes the memory of statesmen who have labored too modestly and lived too long.

Now I must confess that I cannot swear that a cold wind was sweeping in across the waters of the Gulf of Finland on that wintry day. I was not totally without reason for supposing that this was the case. I had once lived for six months on the shores of that same gulf. I had memories of the winds that could blow across it. I had taken the trouble to consult the weather reports in the Petersburg papers of that time. The day was indeed a cold one. It had indeed snowed. But I have no binding evidence that the wind was actually blowing; and I must admit that in suggesting that it was, I exceeded my true competence as a historian.

This was, however, a small transgression, a rare and isolated lapse, I hope, from the rules of the trade. I cite it only as an example of the temptations to which the historian is sometimes subject. Generally speaking, I was supported, as all historians must be, by the discipline of my profession—the stricture, that is, against venturing beyond what the evidence reveals. And if there were odd moments when this discipline hampered me, in general I found it a source of strength. It is not everyone who can safely and effectively give full reign to his feelings and his imagination, as does the poet, the playwright, or the writer of fiction. That is heady stuff, and not for everyone. Some of us need the protection of an external discipline—in this case, the commitment to demonstrable historical fact—to keep us in touch with reality. And this is not a bad thing. It was, after all, a poet, Goethe, who observed that it was precisely in the restraints the artist consents to accept that the true artistic mastery reveals itself.

Let us go on, then, hand in hand, as we do in this academy—the poet, the novelist, the dramaturgist in his own stratosphere of the inspired imagination and the commitment to sheer beauty; the historian crawling, earthbound, among his dusty records, like a bird without wings, but also a searcher for the truth, and sometimes the discoverer of it. Both are committed to the task of helping contemporary man to see himself, the one through the searching prism of personal emotional experience, the other through the revealing footprints that his ancestors—men, after all, like himself—can be shown to have left on the sands of time. Each of these literary efforts serves in its own way the cause of self-knowledge. And in this bewildering and dangerous age, when the very preservation of civilization has been placed, as though by some angry and impatient Deity, in the weak and trembling human hands that have so long abused it, what greater cause, what nobler commitment, could there be than to help people to see themselves as they really are? And what generation could ever have been more in need of that self-scrutiny, that self-awareness, and that self-judgment than the one to which we, poor denizens of this twentieth century, have the fortune, and the misfortune, to belong?

Acceptance Speech,
Gold Medal for History
(1984)

————⋅⋅⟨∞⟩⋅⋅————

I have, for my sins, written a respectable amount of history. I have also, especially in recent years, spoken and written a good deal on contemporary affairs; and it is these contributions to the public discussion of nuclear weaponry and Soviet-American relations that have received by far the most public attention, and at times approval.

Now, Anton Chekhov, who was a doctor as well as a writer, once said that medicine was his wife, whereas literature was his mistress. Well, for me, history has been my professional wife; whereas disagreeing publicly with my own government about foreign policy has been my professional mistress. And I must say that I am pleased and touched to be recognized, for once, for the modest degree of marital fidelity I have been able to muster toward this professional wife, toward this field of study—history, in other words—that has, after all, been my true professional dedication for some thirty-five years.

But beyond that, there is something less personal and far more important that is implied by this gesture on the part of the Academy. We live today, as I think all of us recognize, in a seriously endangered world—a world endangered in the first instance by nuclear weaponry, but also by the reckless way in which we are wasting and exhausting the finite, unreplaceable natural resources on which the continuation of civilized life is dependent. And not everyone realizes that it is not just our own generation, and not just our children's generation, that

On receiving the Gold Medal for History from the American Academy of Arts and Letters, New York, May 16, 1984.

we are placing at risk by these apocalyptic possibilities, but history itself as well. The very concept of history implies the scholar and the reader. Without a generation of civilized people to study history, to preserve its records, to absorb its lessons and relate them to their own problems, history, too, would lose its meaning. And whoever places at risk the existence of that scholar and that reader jeopardizes not just the present of our civilization but its past as well.

For this reason, not only the studying and writing of history but also the honoring of it represent affirmations of a certain defiant faith—a desperate, unreasoning faith, if you will—but faith nevertheless in the endurance of this threatened world, faith in the total essentiality of historical continuity. These efforts are the expressions of a determination not to permit this marvelous civilization of ours, without which nothing that we value, including this academy and all it stands for, could have existed or could have any meaning at all—not to permit all this to be put to an end by the various grotesque forms of civilizational suicide that our behavior, and that of our governments, is now inviting. Only people who had forgotten their historical roots could have created, or could be tolerating and ignoring, these tremendous risks—risks not just to themselves but, more important, to all that they are a part of.

It is all this that a medal for history, to my mind, implies; and if the Academy honors me by what it is doing here this afternoon, the very conferring of such a medal, whether I deserve it or not, honors the Academy.

Upon Receiving the Toynbee Prize
(1988)

———··◦◦◦◦··———

I am naturally pleased and flattered to be receiving a prize in the name of Arnold Toynbee. I knew him only slightly, many years ago, when he was a visiting scholar at the Institute for Advanced Study; but I then knew very little about his work. I had just finished twenty-six years in the American Foreign Service, where one read a great many other things but very little, I am afraid, about the history of ancient civilizations.

When we today speak of this man, we have first to make it clear which of two things we are talking about. One is the popular image that was at one time formed of him in this country. The other is what he really was and did. Living now in an age when, and in a country where, the image is valued so much more highly than the reality, we are all, I am sure, well aware of the distinction between these two things.

As a curious illustration of what the image was, as distinct from the reality, I might begin by quoting the first introductory sentences of an elaborate eleven-page article about Toynbee that appeared in one issue of *Life* magazine just forty years ago, in 1948. "A spare, blue-eyed Englishman named Arnold J. Toynbee was scheduled to arrive in the U.S. this week. He was headed for the Institute for Advanced Study . . . at Princeton, where he will resume work on one of the most ambitious chores the human brain has ever undertaken, his monumental *A Study of History.*"

Princeton, New Jersey, November 13, 1988.

309

Actually the work of the *Time-Life* concern in vulgarizing Toynbee's image in this country had been undertaken more than a year earlier, in March 1947, when Toynbee's picture appeared on the cover of *Time* magazine, followed by the usual explanatory article on the pages of the same issue. And to explain *Time-Life*'s interest, one has to note the coming together of several apparently quite disparate factors.

Nearly a decade earlier, just before the Second World War, Toynbee had completed the first six volumes of what was to become, many years later, his twelve-volume work *The Study of History*. In these volumes, Toynbee analyzed the dynamics of growth and decay in some twenty-one civilizations, ancient and modern; and he believed himself to have discovered in these phenomena certain patterns of development common to all civilizations, including, albeit with certain reservations, our own.

In 1947, when the *Time* article appeared, there could have been very few people in this country who had read anything of Toynbee's six volumes. These were not exactly light summer reading. The war had intervened. But there was appearing on the American market at this time a six-hundred-page condensation of their contents, done quite faithfully on independent initiative by another scholar. An advance copy of this condensation (or so, at least, it would appear) had, in 1947, just fallen into the hands of *Time*'s editors. Beyond that, Toynbee had just then been lecturing extensively around the eastern part of the United States. This activity had included a series of six lectures delivered at Bryn Mawr College, and these evidently had been attended by someone very close to the publisher of *Time,* Henry Luce, or possibly by that redoubtable gentleman himself.

Now, to explain some of the things Toynbee was saying in his Bryn Mawr lectures, I have to remind you that this, the late winter of 1947, was the very time when the British were confessing to our government their inability to lend further support to the government of Greece in its struggle against Communist guerrilla enemies, and when President Harry Truman, in his response to this British approach, was not only offering to relieve the British of this burden and to assume it in their place, but was also extending, in his so-called Truman doctrine message, what was in effect an open-ended assurance of support to any and every other government across the globe that could show itself to be faced with opposition of this nature.

It is clear that Toynbee was deeply affected by these events. He saw in the shifting of this and other burdens from Europe's shoulders to those of the United States what he called the "dwarfing of Europe" and the beginning of a great struggle between the United States and Russia for world supremacy. He was a man who believed (as I must say I have never done) that world government from a single center was indeed a real possibility. He was quoted as saying in the Bryn Mawr lectures that the early political unification of the world was "a foregone conclusion." But it was still a question, of course, which of the two superpowers would come out ahead. The behavior of all civilizations, he thought, had been determined by a process of challenge and response; and so it would be with the rivalry between the United States and Russia. The Soviet aspirations were the challenge; America's reaction would be the response. America, he thought, had the better chances of winning this contest, but it would not be the material or even military aspects of America's reaction that would be decisive: it would be the spiritual ones—Christianity, to be specific. The relationship of Christianity to the other spiritual forces of our time would be, he said, the only effective response to aggression, and would be decisive in creating the future of our civilization.

Now, it was, of course, from the standpoint of any detached observer, a long leap from these rather vague philosophical speculations to a recommendation that America should mount a new Christian crusade with a view to destroying Communism everywhere and achieving unification of the world under the benevolent shadows of the American flag. But this was not too long a leap to excite the imagination and the enthusiasm of the publisher of *Time* and *Life* magazines, Henry Luce. Luce was born the son of a Protestant-American missionary in China. He seems to have inherited a strong infusion of the missionary spirit; and this he combined with a vibrant and militant American nationalism. I am not sure that it was he to whom the motto "For God, for country, and for Yale" was attributed; but leaving Yale out of it (for I really do not know to what extent his enthusiasm was aroused by that estimable institution), the two concepts "God and country" described very well his most passionate commitments. So closely associated were these two concepts in his view of things that he even suggested, in one public utterance, that the churchmen and the military strategists should occupy the same room and that the churchmen should dictate the strategy. He was, not unsurprisingly, a sanguine supporter of Chiang Kai-shek and the China lobby. He was actually more interested in fighting Communism in China than in Russia. But his belief in the capacity of the United States for world leadership was unshakable; and it was, if I am not mistaken, in the journals of his publishing empire that the concepts of the "American Century" and the "American Empire" found their greatest currency and their strongest support. On today's terms, Henry Luce would have stood, I should think, considerably to the right of most of those around George Bush.

In light of this background, let me turn back now to the *Time* article of 1947. The article began by mentioning the great world responsibilities allegedly now falling to the United States, and went on to note the striking success of Toynbee's recent Bryn Mawr lectures. Then it launched into a summary of Toynbee's first six volumes. And it ended by describing these volumes as "the most provocative work of historical theory written in England since Karl Marx's *Capital.*" From the skillful juxtaposition of the various components of this article, the casual reader was left with the impression that the prediction of America's coming world supremacy was supported by the authority of the greatest work of historical analysis produced in the English-speaking world over the past century. This sufficed, as you can imagine, to assure to the somewhat bewildered Toynbee a notoriety he had never expected, had surely never sought, probably only partially welcomed, and would never be able to shake.

So much for the popular image created by *Time* and *Life*. I suspect you could find traces of it today. But now, how about the reality?

I must begin by making it clear that I regard Toynbee, as have so many others, as a truly remarkable and great scholar. His erudition was immense, his dedication unquestionable, his industriousness legendary, and his historical-literary output simply prodigious. In substantiation of this, let me just cite some words used by the man who was, I believe, the most serious and severe of Toynbee's contemporary critics. This was the well-known and highly respected Dutch historian Pieter Geyl. In 1949, there was published a book comprised in large part just of Geyl's magisterial criticism of the *Study of History*. Geyl could scarcely be charged, therefore, with an uncritical acceptance of Toynbee's work. Yet he began this fine critical essay by describing the *Study of History* as "an imposing achievement." And he went on to say:

> The reading, the learning, are almost without precedent. Toynbee moves confidently in the histories of the old civilizations of Asia, the Chinese, and the Indian, of Egypt, of America as well. He is thoroughly acquainted with Roman and especially Hellenic history. Classical literature he also knows, and . . . is able to draw upon it freely to evoke a deeper background for his arguments and his reflections. He knows how to use for his arguments ethnological, sociological, philosophical, psychological concepts. At the same time he . . . writes in a splendid, full and supple style, which retains command over a wealth of quotations by a constant flow of images and with an intensive and untiring vividness of argument. And, what is more important still, this rich and variegated abundance serves a majestic vision. He is . . . profoundly aware of the unity of the architectural pattern into which he fits. [His is] a remarkable mind, unusual in our everyday world of historians.

All this, I reiterate, is only the introduction to what was probably the most severe and searching criticism of Toynbee's work that has ever been written. And Geyl, in 1949, did not know the whole story. He could not then know of the immense outpouring of historical writing that would mark the remaining twenty-six years of Toynbee's life. For Toynbee would go on, in those final years, to write another six volumes of the *Study of History,* one major work of research on the effects of the Hanniballic Wars on the Roman Empire, another on the career of late-Byzantine emperor Constantine Porphyrogenitus, and smaller studies, lectures, and comments on a host of other subjects. The volume of his life's work, as I have said, was simply prodigious. The subject cards of works by Toynbee in book form in the Firestone Library catalogue lists something upward of seventy titles. The three works I have just mentioned must alone embrace nearly ten thousand pages.

So enormous were the dimensions of Toynbee's historical-literary offerings that they came in the end to pose an ironic and almost insoluble dilemma for the would-be critic. One could see how an industrious scholar might, over the course of a number of years, have personally gone over the entire vast expanse of historical source material cited in Toynbee's works. One could also see how another scholar might, but also only at the cost of years of effort, have read carefully and critically the entirety of Toynbee's oeuvre itself. But it is hard to see how any one scholar could, within the span of a single active scholarly lifetime, do both those things. The one undertaking seemed, if only for the dimensions of the time and energy involved, to preclude the other. Small wonder, then, that the totality of Toynbee's work had, since his death in 1969, few fully qualified scholarly critics.

It was, of course, for the effort to identify consistent patterns in the development of all known civilizations that Toynbee was most widely known. The patterns were composed of what he believed to be uniformities in the rise, the development, and the decline of civilizations, and also of the ways in which each of these civilizations transmitted something of itself to those that came after it. He saw in these uniformities, if I am not mistaken, the key to the understanding of the entire history of civilized man; and I have no doubt that he regarded this as the greatest of his contributions to the study of history. But it seems to be a feature of the lives of prominent people that what they see as their greatest contributions to the life of their times is not always what posterity sees in that way; and this seems to me to be the case here.

Toynbee's patterns rest, of course, on the foundations of a vast and impressive edifice of learning; and I have no intention of questioning its value. But the arguments used to demonstrate these uniformities and their significance strike me as forced, artificial, and unconvincing; and I know I am not alone in this impression. The very vocabulary used in this argumentation—the claim for the recurrence in all civilizations of elements described as "the dominant minority," "the internal proletariat," and "the external proletariat"—arouse my suspicions and set my teeth on end. It is my impression that the life of every society is marked by thousands of unique circumstances; and to attempt to press this multitude of variables into the procrustean bed of a great general system embracing all societies seems to me an unnatural and unpromising undertaking. I can only echo what Pieter Geyl described as his own impulse to exclaim as he made his way through this material: "C'est magnifique, mais ce n'est pas l'histoire!"

How does one explain the fact that Toynbee gave so much of his life to the erection of an edifice that many of us see as so implausible? There are no doubt several explanations; I cannot attempt to list them all. But I find myself wondering whether one of them was not perhaps Toynbee's failure to take full account of the element of the fortuitous—of pure chance—in the unfolding of human affairs, and his consequent assumption that everything that happened in those affairs had to have a reason visible and intelligible to the human eye.

I cannot help but recall, in this connection, the observation made somewhere in Goethe's *Faust* to the effect that the ways in which deliberate design and pure luck were connected in the products of human action was something fools would never understand. Well, Goethe, I am sure, would never have placed Toynbee among the fools; but he would surely have agreed that the element of pure chance played a greater role in history than that assigned to it by Toynbee in the development of entire civilizations.

The Harvard biologist Stephen Jay Gould, in reviewing a recent book by our faculty colleague at this institute Freeman Dyson, observed that "our empirical world is a temporal sequence of complex events, so unrepeatable by the laws of probability and so irreversible by principles of thermodynamics, that everything interesting happens only once in its meaningful details." If this is true of the natural sciences, how could it be otherwise in the social and political ones? There are, of course, a great many events in the historical records that are, or would appear to be, in large part the products of deliberate human design. They were certainly influenced and partly determined by human decision. But I can think of no such events for which, depending on how far back one wants to go, an equal number of apparently fortuitous contributing causes could not also be demonstrated. Here, in history, as elsewhere in our empirical world, "everything interesting happens only once in its meaningful details." And if that is true of each of the myriad of small events out of which the patterns of history are woven, how could it not be true of the great and strange tapestries that present themselves to our vision when entire civilizations are put under scrutiny?

And there is something else that I would like to note about Toynbee's work—not in the way of a criticism but as a feature that helps to explain it; and that is its extraordinary impersonality. No one could leaf through the volumes of his principal works without being struck by the rareness with which individuals make their appearance in this material. Toynbee was the historian of the behavior of masses of men—of civilizations, societies, tribes, castes, what you will—and sometimes of the institutions under which their lives were organized, but not of men as individuals. He saw the historical process as though from a great distance, as you might see a large mass of very small insects; and what interested him was not what any one of them did but what the entire mass of them did.

He would, I suppose, have been astonished that I should find this in any way remarkable. How else, he would probably have asked, could you possibly write a history of civilization? Billions of people walked across the scene. How could anyone trying to write such a history give attention to any one of those people? It was the great sweep of the behavior of masses of men which, he would have said, was the proper stuff of such a historian's scrutiny.

True enough, no doubt, from his standpoint. Yet at the bottom of all human experience, there lies, after all, the mystery of the individual personality—its ultimate autonomy of decision, its interaction with the mass. And I wonder whether the inconspicuousness of the individual figure in Toynbee's pageant of history is not the source of what I might call the pallor—the grayness—of so much of his work. There sweep across the pages the names of hundreds—I dare say thousands—of historical collectivities: peoples, tribes, religious groupings, cultures, what you will. To a person of his erudition, the designations no doubt meant something. But to the mass of his readers, these names could have been (as they were to me) only algebraic symbols with the values not filled in. And thus the book presented for many of us a vast kaleidoscope of semi-abstractions, oppressive in their very voluminousness, wearisome in their remoteness from the individual human predicament. Without the drama of the individual personality and the individual fate, Toynbee's history lost much of its immediacy, its color, and its bite.

Now, behind all these features of Toynbee the historian, there stood, of course, the figure of Toynbee the person. He himself was never unaware of this. He actually wrote a good deal about himself, about his education, his views, likes and dislikes, his loves and his hatreds. He wrote more about himself, in fact, over the course of the years than he ever wrote, so far as I can ascertain, about any other individual. What he wrote was devoid of vanity or boasting. It was also devoid of any exaggerated modesty; it appeared to assume a tacit understanding between him and the reader that he was an exceptional and interesting person, which of course he was.

In the twelfth and final volume of his *Study of History,* Toynbee included an annex entitled "Ad Hominem," the "Hominem" being himself. Some of it was by way of reply, always gentle and without rancor, to his numerous critics. But much of it was indeed about himself. And how characteristic this monograph was of all his other writings. For it dealt more with his education and his philosophy than with the other aspects of his person. It was heartily loaded with footnotes. It ran to what would be some 150 pages in one of our modern books. And in light of all of this, it tended, so help me God, to weary at least one reader.

Like most efforts of self-scrutiny, this treatise seemed to me to be more revealing for the things it did not say, and was not meant to say, than for what was actually set forth. Yet out of this, and out of his many other writings, there does emerge an image of the man inside.

Toynbee was born in 1889, out of the great final glow, that is, of the Victorian epoch. This was the glow, of course, that was about to be so precipitately extinguished by the tragic events of the first years of this present century. And Toynbee himself observed that he had caught the Victorian age, so to speak, by the tail, only to see it slip out of his hands. But it had warmed and colored his childhood and his youth. He would remain marked by it to some extent throughout the rest of his career: through Winchester School and Oxford, through Chatham House and the Paris Peace Conference and all the other sources of tension between a demanding past and an exciting present. It would continue to mark him in the further years through grievous personal tragedies, through the ferocious academic squabbles that dramatized his first professorship at Kings College in London, and through his sudden elevation to notoriety at the hands of the American journalistic media.

Through all these ups and downs of an unusual academic career, he would move with a curious personal detachment and imperturbability—very English, very Victorian—the familiar figure of the genteel English scholar, right out of *Sherlock Holmes* or *My Fair Lady,* the gentleman intellectual, wandering and browsing absentmindedly among the relics and incunabula of ancient civilizations, sloughing off with mild amusement the many criticisms of his own work, seemingly as unengaged emotionally with the individuals of his time as he was with the historical personalities who found occasional mention in his writings. His person seemed to reflect the polish but also the curious pallor of his writings. He had his hatreds, the principal of these being war. He had at least one love, which might be described as a deep but highly philosophical religiosity, centering around Christianity but not restricted to it. And it is characteristic that both the hatreds and the loves were directed to great impersonal intellectual phenomena, seldom, if ever, to individual fellow human beings.

Still, when all is said and done, Toynbee was essentially, and with all the passion of which he was capable, a scholar—a historian. And it is primarily as such that we who share or understand that dedication should remember him. He was, of course, on anybody's terms, an exceptional scholar; and for that he deserves our respect. He had his peculiarities, as which of us does not?—and for those he deserves our indulgence. But he was driven by the same fascination that drives so many of us. Like us, he struggled manfully with the tensions between the demands of a professional preoccupation with the past and those of an unavoidable involvement with the present. Like us, he had to weave his way between the physical and social demands of a personal life and the lonely and rarified atmosphere of academic research. He, too, had to seek the middle ground between the unattainable ideal of complete objectivity and involuntary subjectivity, which also has its merits and which no one ought fully to deny or to avoid. And he, too, had to come to terms with that quality of all cognitive pursuits that dictates that however dispassionately one tries to describe an external phenomenon, what one ends up doing is to reveal and express a portion of one's self.

Let us, then, as historians and as lovers of history, hold Toynbee in memory not primarily for the distorted image conferred upon him by the American media, and not for our own judgment of the value of his quest for uniformities among the mysteries of world history. Let us think of him, rather, fraternally, as one who labored long and mightily in the same vineyard that has claimed so much of our own devotion, as one who gave to that effort all that he could from the powers that God had bestowed upon him, and as one who deserves for that effort the same respect that we would all like to think would some day, regardless of the character of the product, be given to our own.

The New Russia as
a Neighbor

The thoughts that the ensuing discussion is designed to bring forward might best be introduced by asking the reader to recognize that there is, in these final years of the twentieth century, no country anywhere in the world whose inhabitants, including what the Communists used to call its "ruling circles," have less to gain and more to fear from new military involvements than do those of the Russian Republic. Not only is this the state of affairs now prevailing but it is one that may be expected to prevail for many years into the future.

It would require more than a single article, probably more than a single book, to cite all the reasons for this observation. Suffice it, for the purpose at hand, to note that the seven decades of Communist power so recently ended inflicted massive and appalling injuries—social, economic, genetic, and moral—on Russian society. They left a people profoundly weakened by the loss of at least 30 million of its citizens, in many instances the cream of its youth, on the battlefields of the Second World War, through civil strife, or through the veritably genocidal exactions of the Stalinist regime. They left a people suddenly confronted with the task of creating, almost at once, an entirely new political, social, and economic system—something for which its own history provided no models or guidelines. They left a successor regime forced to find means of dismantling a huge and unhealthy military industry and of restoring order to the semidisorganized and demoralized remnants of what was only recently one of the greatest of the world's military establishments. They left what was still a predominantly agrarian society confronted with the necessity of designing entirely new systems of agricultural ownership and technology—a challenge for which, again, the country's history provided no helpful models. The new, non-Communist, and supposedly democratic Russia was saddled, in short, with a series of immensely difficult but pressing tasks—tasks to which further military involvements could not conceivably offer any hopeful answers and could not fail to increase dangerously the heavy burden these tasks already imposed. If those who in the final years of this century are to bear the responsibilities of leadership of Russia should try to establish the principles by which they might most helpfully be guided in light of this situation, the first of these principles would have to be: avoid, if in any way possible, and even, if need be, at the cost of international prestige, military involvements of any sort, external or internal.

All this being so, it is distressing to note the many expressions of anxiety and suspicion of the new Russia, precisely as a supposed military power, that have marked the treatment of that country in a good portion of the Western press since the final breakdown of the Soviet Union in 1991. The number and variety of examples of this tendency are so great that any single brief statement along these lines could hardly be other than inadequate, if not misleading. A number of the apprehensions voiced there and elsewhere place particular emphasis on the relationship between Moscow and the fourteen countries the Russians themselves refer to as the "near-abroad"—namely, those fourteen entities, situated on the borders of the present Russian Republic, that were once included in the Soviet Union but have now struck out as independent states. Other suspicions and apprehensions have to do with supposed Russian imperialistic designs on countries farther afield, particularly Poland. But all appear to assume a Russian political leadership determined to achieve, if necessary ultimately by force of arms, not only its control over the recently released border countries but also its earlier predominance throughout Eastern and Central Europe.

Obviously, these two situations—a country having nothing to gain, only much to lose, by further military involvements and a Russian leadership and people dominated by imperialistic lusts of one sort or another—are mutually inconsistent. How are they to be reconciled?

In a number of instances, these alarmist views of likely Russian policy are based, at least by inference, on assumptions of a historical nature. "The Russians," one is given to understand, have always been an aggressive and imperialistically inclined people; hence, it would be naive to assume them to be any different today. But this thesis, when applied to the problems of this age, rests on two basic faults. First, it lumps all the major Russian regimes of past and present—the monarchical regime of the several centuries preceding 1917, the Communist (largely Stalinist) regime of recent memory, and the government of the present Russia—under a common heading, ignoring the enormous differences among them. Second, it implies wide enthusiasm on the part of the Russian populace at large for the past imperialistic exploits, real or fancied, of the regimes in question.

Departing from the so-called Time of Troubles at the outset of the seventeenth century, when the borders of Russia were closely coterminous with the area of residence of a purely Russian population, there have been in modern times two great phases of Russian expansion into neighboring regions of Eastern and (in part) Central Europe. The first began at the outset of the eighteenth century, endured for two centuries, and was brought to a complete end by the disaster of the First World War and the Russian Revolution of 1917. It took the form largely of dynastic rearrangements that had little effect on the situation of the lower orders of the affected societies. Only in the final decades of the tsarist period did emergent nationalistic tendencies begin to make themselves more widely and painfully felt on both sides, among the peoples as well as the governments involved.

The second of these incursions of Russia into Eastern and Central Europe began in the form of the pursuit by the Russians of the retiring Hitlerian forces in the final phases of World War II—a pursuit that carried the Russian forces all the way to Berlin and other advanced positions of Central Europe. This in itself was a natural concomitant of the military operations then in progress; and there is no more reason why it should be seen today in Western countries as something reprehensible than there was at the time. What subsequently occurred, of course, in the retention and development of Soviet power over the peoples of the regions thus overrun constituted one of the most terrible and inexcusable injustices of the modern age.

Yet it is worth noting that both of these great phases of Russian expansion—the dynastic one and the Communist one—were launched and conducted by wholly nondemocratic regimes that neither consulted the broad masses of the Russian population nor took much account of their feelings. While there was in fact, in the second of these instances, a wide and determined commitment on the part of these Russian masses to the total defeat of the armed forces of Nazi Germany, even if this should necessitate the movement of the Soviet armies into large parts of Eastern and Central Europe, I know of no similar popular enthusiasm for the various forms of oppression subsequently inflicted by Soviet authorities on the peoples of the affected areas. Indeed, very few Russians, if any, outside the tiny conspiratorial center of power in the Kremlin and the secret police establishment that served as its agency, had any idea of the appalling anti-Polish atrocities by which this hegemony was inaugurated in 1939–1940 or of the terrible and inexcusable procedures by which it continued to be exercised over most of the region in question over the entire Cold War period; nor is it to be supposed that most Russians would have approved of these procedures had they known of them.

Leaving aside these eighteenth- and nineteenth-century incursions of Russia into Eastern and Central Europe, which were really parts of what Gibbon referred to as "the contagion of the times," and also leaving aside the wholly abnormal situations of what we might call the terrible Hitlerian-Stalinist period, the worst that can be said about earlier Russian foreign policies is that they reflected an undue sensitivity to the proximity or threatened proximity to the Russian borders of any other strong power and a tendency either to push these borders farther from the Russian heartland or to create protective zones just beyond them. But this oversensitivity, deplorable as it may have been, was the reflection of precisely the nondemocratic character of the Russian regimes in question and their fear that rival power, unless held at a distance, might inflame the otherwise passive Russian masses. Unless one has given up all hope for a healthy degree of self-government in the Russia of the future, there is no reason to assume that these abnormalities of earlier governmental behavior will automatically find reflection in the policies of the present regime—a regime that still represents, with whatever ups and downs of failure and success, a bold effort to detach itself from earlier Russian patterns of government and to create a more normal relationship to the international community of its day.

As noted above, a number of the anxieties about future Russian behavior entertained in Western circles relate to the attitudes of the Russian government to the fourteen entities, once border regions of the Soviet Union, that have now broken off and are undertaking to lead an independent existence. To what extent are these anxieties justified?

This is not the place to trace the development of those centrifugal forces, longings and demands for independence, on the part of the non-Russian peoples of the Russian-Soviet Empire that made themselves felt in the final decades of tsarist power. They continued to lie, suppressed but latent, through the decades of Communist control, only to be released and stirred into frantic activity by the breakdown of Communist power in the late 1980s and early 1990s. They came to play a not insignificant part in the internal political agonies of the emerging new Russia. And they were, as we all know, finally given total release upon the termination of the existence of the Soviet Union at the end of 1991. Breaking away from the Russian center, these fourteen peoples claimed and were conceded, without serious remonstrance from any quarter, unrestricted sovereignty and independence.

Suffice it to note here that this transition from dependence to independence, complete as it was at the political level, was extremely abrupt. It could not carry with it an equally abrupt severance of the innumerable nonpolitical ties—personal, cultural, commercial, technological, and in certain respects even military—that had been formed in the decades, sometimes centuries, of association of these peoples with the Russian center. Had the transition to independence been preceded by careful and orderly negotiation about the forms it might take and the order in which its various phases should proceed, the political change might have been eased and have led to fewer misunderstandings. But this was not the case; and many of those who were inclined from the start to question Russian good faith in this entire process of transition were inclined to see, in the persistence of these nonpolitical ties into the present period, evidence in support of precisely this suspicion. All this may well be borne in mind as one glances as the realities of the present state of affairs.

Let it first be noted that there is very little unity in the situations of the various regions and countries concerned. There are a number of countries, including some of the most important ones, where not only are there no longer any Russian forces remaining, but their independence has been accepted by the Russian center in ways that permit of no ambiguity or withdrawal. Of these, the most prominent are Ukraine, Kazakhstan, and the three Baltic countries. Not only are these countries all of outstanding political importance, their territories comprise by far the greater part of the entire near-abroad area.

The situation of one of the other countries, namely Belarus, is unique. Here is a region whose connections with the Russian center, political, cultural, and otherwise, have always been particularly close, so much so that many have questioned whether it should ever have been considered a non-Russian territory in the first place. Something upward of half its people have continued to express themselves, in various recent tests of opinion, in favor not only of the retention of close ties with Russia but even of their further extension. The two governments are now linked by a vertical military alliance that covers and sanctions the stationing of large bodies of Russian military forces on Belarussian territory.

Of the remaining border countries, all would appear to have Russian military units of one sort or another on their territories. In several instances, particularly along the southern Central Asian frontiers, border-guard units, stationed there even before the countries became independent, have simply not yet been withdrawn; the reason for this being, in most cases, that these countries are not prepared either to replace the units or to do without them.

These countries, situated along the Central Asian borders of the former Soviet Union, confront Iran, Afghanistan, and China. These were sensitive borders even in the Soviet days, both from the political-military standpoint and from that of contraband operations and other minor but disturbing incursions. Constituting now, as they do, the southern borders of the new countries, they retain this quality. And were the respective governments to demand the withdrawal of the present Russian border-guard units, the Russian government might well see itself obliged to replace them by erecting similarly elaborate defenses along the northern borders of the countries in question, an alternative that, while leaving these countries extensively vulnerable to harassment from the south, would deprive them of all possibility of Russian protection and would cut them off from Russia in ways that they themselves would find undesirable.

Eventually, these Russian border–guard units will presumably have to be replaced by locally recruited ones. This is, I understand, already occurring in Kirghizstan and in Tadzhikistan, in the replacement of Russian noncommissioned personnel by local recruits. For the moment, in any case, the presence of these units in the positions they occupy seems to be the least undesirable solution; and it is not one that should give rise to any great fears for the security of the new countries. In no case, so far as I have been able to discern, have these units been used to press the respective local regimes into acceptance of a renewed political domination by the Russian Republic.

The remaining Russian forces stationed in several of the new countries, particularly Moldava, Georgia, and Tadzhikistan, are formally charged with peacekeeping functions. And where the life of the respective countries is marred by civil wars or other domestic conflicts (which is the case in Tadzhikistan and Georgia), involvement of the Russian peacekeeping units with the political fortunes of the regime now formally in power can hardly be avoided. Their functioning, in these circumstances, has sometimes been referred to by Western critics as a form of sinister "meddling" in the internal affairs of the countries in question. Whatever one wishes to call it, the security of the respective governments is certainly dependent at this stage of the game on Russian military support. But this would seem to be support precisely for the maintenance of their political survival and certainly not for any suppression of the independence of the countries in question.

The situation in Moldava is not only unique but highly complicated and defies any brief description. Suffice it to note that the Russian peacekeeping units there are not acting independently but are part of a joint force that functions under the benign observation of the Conference on Security and Cooperation in Europe. I know of no evidence that the presence of these units in Moldava at this time is anything other than welcome to the Moldavan government. Indeed, when the Russian government recently suggested the removal (for reasons of economy) of a good part of this force, the first to oppose the suggestion was the Moldavan government itself

This sketchy *tour d'horizon* of the relations between the Russian center and the near-abroad would not be complete without a special word about Ukraine—large portions of which were for centuries regarded as integral parts of Russia. Under contemporary concepts of qualification for independent statehood, as revealed in the practices of the United Nations, no one could deny to the Ukrainians (nor did, in 1991, the leaders of the Russian Republic) the status of an independent state. But the relationship of this state to the Russian center is in many respects a heavily burdened one. The borders within which it was established embraced several regions, containing millions of people who had never been Ukrainian at all but had for centuries been largely, and usually exclusively, Russian in speech, tradition, and character. One of these regions—the Crimean peninsula—contained the great former Soviet naval base at Sevastopol, together with all the ships and supporting institutions appertaining thereto. For the further manning and operation of these ships and facilities Ukraine alone had neither the human nor other requisite resources. These burdens on the new Russian-Ukrainian relationship played, of course, into the feelings and fears of those in the West who doubted the reality of the breakup of the traditional Russian state and who were quick with predictions that Moscow would take advantage of this situation as an excuse for obstructing the consolidation of Ukrainian statehood and eventually reasserting Russian control over the entire area.

These fears have shown themselves, to date, misplaced. There has been no visible wavering in the Russian commitment to an independent Ukraine. The fate of the naval base, which had the potential of becoming a very serious bone of contention between the two governments, has instead become the object of difficult and lingering but, after all, peaceful negotiations, the ships themselves in the meantime rusting away in various stages of inactivity and obsolescence and becoming of dwindling conceivable use for either party. And the Russian government, instead of identifying itself with the demands of many of the Crimean Russians for detachment from Ukraine, appears to have encouraged the latter to seek accommodation to their new position on the best terms they can obtain from the Ukrainian government. (A similar attitude has been taken by Moscow in the case of Moldava, which also has a sizable Russian minority.)

Seen as a whole, the relationship of Moscow to this band of new surrounding states has had, unavoidably in the circumstances, many abnormal aspects. There is admittedly little love lost among the various parties to the relationship. There can be no doubt that the leaders of the new states would like to normalize the present relationship as soon as possible, eliminating those aspects of it, particularly the presence of Russian military units on their territories, that involve or lend themselves to excessive dependence on the Russian center. If they have not been able to do this sooner, this is primarily a result of the extreme abruptness of their separation from Russia in 1991, and of their lack of preparation for any early assumption of the responsibilities of independent statehood. As things now stand, there is no reason to doubt that these abnormalities will be overcome with the passage of time, and the relationship regularized on a long-term basis acceptable to both parties.

This prospect is supported by a glance at the obvious interests of the new Russian government. There could in any case be little incentive for the latter to seek the reincorporation of any of these countries into the Russian Republic. Even if there were a possibility that this could be realized without military complications (and in several cases this would be most doubtful), any country thus reincorporated would only become another potential Chechnya; and this would be the last thing any Russian government in its right senses would like to invite. But beyond that, there seems to be a growing awareness in Moscow that Russia is better off without such colonial appendages than with them. Even a superficial glance at the economic aspects of the relationship suffices to show that while the metropolitan center may have profited here and there from individual aspects of the former relationship, these were overweighed by the many ways in which that relationship also proved to be a burden on Moscow. Examples of this can be seen not only in the considerable portions of the local budgets that were at one time assumed by the Soviet state but also in the obligation the latter seems to have felt to provide these non-Russian regions with various forms of energy at prices considerably lower than those prevailing on the world market. Of these burdens, too, the breakup of the empire has relieved them.

All these factors considered, I can see no reason for fearing that Moscow will perceive any interests of its own in luring or forcing the members of the near-abroad to resume anything like their former state of subservience to Russia, or that the existing abnormalities of the relationship of these countries to the Russian center will not find their eventual solution in ways that should not give rise to great anxieties on the part of Western nations. The only eventuality that might basically change this state of affairs would be a close military association of any of these new countries with another major power or group of powers. But this is a form of sensitivity that others, and particularly the United States with its Monroe Doctrine tradition, should not find unnatural.

So much for some of the individual situations and problems of the near-abroad. Beyond the shaping of a new Russian relationship to the countries of that area lie the prospects for a similar new relationship to what could be called the "less than near" European abroad, and particularly to Russia's Eastern European neighbors and to the various forms of multilateral European organization, of which the European Union and NATO are only the most prominent examples.

Plainly, there will eventually have to be many new forms of interaction in economic and financial matters between Russia and the rest of Europe; and some of these may require attention in the near future. But the most pressing immediate requirement, even in the economic field, is for the modernization of the Russian economy itself: the establishment of the necessary firm controls over crime (including economic crime) and inflation and the establishment and enforcement of new facilities and institutions for private enterprise. Only when these changes have been brought about will it be possible to define in more permanent form the ways in which the Russian economy might interact with the remainder of Europe. Meanwhile, the achievement of these internal reforms should be seen as the highest priority for the preoccupations and the policies of the Russian government.

But this, to all appearances, is not the way that things are now developing. The airwaves and the print media have been full, in recent months and weeks, of speculations and communications about the relations of Russia and the other Eastern European countries to the remainder of Europe in the military field, and particularly the question of how far, if at all, membership of NATO should be expanded into the Eastern and Central European regions. The communications already exchanged between the interested governments on these questions, and the attentions the whole matter has recently been given in the international media, have been of such voluminousness and intricacy as far to exceed the limits of any attention that could be given to them within the framework of this article.

I would like to say, however, that I find this entire discussion of the military interrelationships between Russia and her Eastern European neighbors, and of all of them with NATO, to be unreal, unnecessary, and in highest degree deplorable. Even if this were still a world in which peacetime military structures were viewed as the most important components of a country's position in international life, years would have to pass before a proper concept of the place of the new Russia in such a world community could be arrived at. In the meantime, there is a veritable host of questions more deserving of official Russian and general-European attention than the ones to which this recent discussion has been devoted.

But beyond that, there is the far greater question of the role military forces might be expected to play, generally, in the emergent realities of international life. It is not Russia alone for whom the great military conflicts of this brutal passing century have been something close to a final disaster. It is not Russia alone that has reason to ask itself whether it could hope to remain a center of civilized life if new orgies of military destruction should be added to those in which Europe has already indulged within the memory of many of us alive today. Surely, it is everywhere apparent that the destructive potential of modern weapons, and not only the weapons of mass destruction, is of such appalling dimensions that every resort to them by members of the developed world, or even by those less developed nations that are encouraged to import them, can only have suicidal significance. If the minds of governmental leaders and of people at large cannot be open to the consciousness of these realities, there is no hope for any of us anywhere.

It is true, and this has been the subject of much comment in the Western media, that voices have recently been heard from various quarters of the Russian political spectrum calling for what looks like a return to earlier Communist patterns or for militantly anti-Western nationalistic policies, or both. But these have remained, for the most part, minority voices. They have shown no promise of dominating the political spectrum. They come from the older, not the younger, elements of the population. There is no serious unity among them. Most serious are perhaps those of embittered professional military figures. But there is, fortunately, no established tradition of Caesarism of Russia. Nor could the armed forces provide a suitable administrative framework for the governing of the country, even if the road to that sort of responsibility were open to them. There is also, to be sure, much disillusionment, skepticism, and sometimes even bitterness in popular attitudes toward the present regime. But rarely do these attitudes include any yearnings for a return to the patterns of the past, and least of all to the sort of Communism exemplified by Brezhnev and his predecessors. And while the present leadership has indeed revealed a disturbing tendency to blunt these disquieting chauvinistic voices by echoing small portions of their messages, there is no reason to view them as immediate dangers. Stronger threats to those now in power would seem to be the separatist movements, calling for greater independence by the various provinces at the expense of the powers of the central government.

It is also true that the arrangements of international life in Eastern and Central Europe with which the Second World War ended embrace a large number of artificialities and absurdities. Examples might be the present Russian position in East Prussia, cut off as this once-German province is from Russia by the intervening Lithuania, or some of the borders within which the new Ukrainian state was established, or the lines of transportation and communication across Chinese Manchuria to the Russian maritime provinces along the Pacific. Others could be named.

But it is the unavoidable duty of all of us to learn to live peaceably with such artificialities and absurdities. Any effort to remove them by force of arms would not only risk the development of far wider armed conflicts, but would probably serve only to replace the present ones by others that would not necessarily be much more acceptable. The Balkan crisis should have been a lesson to us all of the necessity of peaceful acceptance of the fact that the contemporary concept of the nation-state as the seat of residence solely for a single nationality, excluding all that does not fit into the nation-state category, is simply impossible as a rational organization of international life. We are all going to have to learn to live in the intimate proximity of groups of human beings who do not share our own sense of national identity. And if we cannot make this accommodation peacefully and with good humor, relying on patience and tolerance to soften the rough edges of seemingly odd and confused geographic arrangements, we are nowhere at all in our efforts to find a hopeful future of international life.

These reflections are not meant to convey the view that even in places where these principles are accepted there is no place at all for military forces. Such forces, as the Finns and the Swiss and others have taught us, can serve purposes other than those of constituting threats, challenges, or admonitions to other countries. These reflections do mean, however, that military preparations must no longer be allowed to stand in the forefront of the interactions among modern powers. If the realization of all this can be given its due in the designing of the relationships between Eastern Europe and the other parts of the continent, we will, if only for the first time, be on a truly hopeful path into the future.

Let time be taken, then, before we attempt to give final definition to the military interrelations of the countries of Central and Eastern Europe among themselves and with the remainder of Europe. The future of Russia is (like that of most other great modern countries) wholly unpredictable. Yes, as noted above, there are present in Russian society forces that reflect some of the most unpleasant past examples of Russian despotism and nationalism. Were these forces to succeed in achieving a commanding position in the political life of that country, and were they to have at their disposal armed forces even approximately as powerful as those of the Soviet Union of recent memory, there might be reason for serious uneasiness about the behavior of Russia in international life. But the first of these hypotheses is most unlikely to materialize, whereas the second is predicated on a situation that could not be realized, even theoretically, for many years into the future.

That Russia will ever achieve "democracy," in the sense of political, social, and economic institutions similar to our own, is not to be expected. And even if Russian forms of self-government should differ significantly from our own, it is not to be postulated that this would be entirely a bad thing. Our own models, as most of us would agree, are not all that perfect. And there will continue to be ups and downs in our relationship with Russia, as there are today.

But nothing now evident, and nothing in the realm of probability, justifies a view of that country that equates it with some of the worst examples of imperialistic despotism of earlier years of this century and justifies the assumption that only an elaborate defensive alliance, embracing the major powers of Western Europe as well as the United States, could terrify the Russians into a pattern of behavior compatible with the minimum of peace in the modern age.

There are, I fear, a great many whose concept of international relations was formed under the dominating shadows of Hitler and Stalin—shadows that at one time served for them as justification for the systematic externalization of evil and for no small measure of collective self-admiration. For these people, the end of the Cold War and the disappearance of the Soviet Union created a vacuum that they now call upon their imagination to fill.

It is going to take time for the new Russia to come to terms with itself. Until it does so, it will be hard for us to make fundamental decisions about how we are to come to terms with it.

Very well. But let us, in the meantime, not confuse ourselves, and let us not unnecessarily complicate our problem, by creating a Russia of our own imagination to take the place of the one that did, alas, once exist, but fortunately is no more.

Index